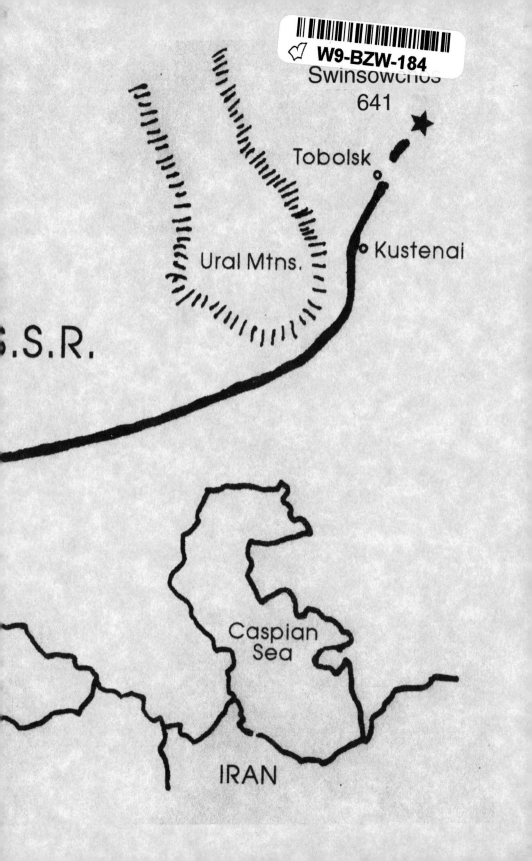

W9-BZW-184

Swinsowcnos
641

Tobolsk

Kustenai

Ural Mtns.

S.S.R.

Caspian
Sea

IRAN

EXILED
TO SIBERIA

"Only by those who reverence it can life be mastered."
Commentary, W. H. Auden

EXILED
TO SIBERIA
A POLISH CHILD'S WWII JOURNEY

KLAUS HERGT
FOREWORD BY TADEUSZ PIOTROWSKI

Crescent
Lake
Publishing
Cheboygan, Michigan

Copyright © 2000 by Klaus Hergt
Foreword © 2000 by Tadeusz Piotrowski

All rights reserved. No part of this book may be reproduced or transmitted in any form or by any means, electronic or mechanical, including photocopying, recording, or by any information storage and retrieval system, without permission in writing from the publisher.

Published by CRESCENT LAKE PUBLISHING
404 North Ball
Cheboygan, Michigan 49721
Tel. & Fax: 231-627-9748
e-mail: creslkpub@straits area.com

Publisher's Cataloging-in-Publication Data
Hergt, Klaus
Exiled to siberia: a polish child's journey during the second world war / Klaus Hergt; with a foreword by Tadeusz Piotrowski. —Cheboygan, Mich.: Crescent Lake Publishing, 2000.

p.   ill.   cm.
ISBN 0-9700432-0-1

Includes bibliographical references and index.

1. Birecki, Henryk. 2. World War, 1939–1945—Poland—Biography. 3. World War, 1939–1945—Refugees—Biography. I. Title.

D809 .P6 H47   2000   00-0914118
940.531/61/092   dc—21   CIP

Cover design by Dana Gibson

PROJECT COORDINATION BY BookPublishing.com

04 03 02 01 00 ～ 5 4 3 2 1

Printed in the United States of America

To the memory of my parents and especially my grandmother Katarzyna Demkow whose love and guidance carried me through the most troubling time of my life.

To my dear wife, Mary Lou, for her loving devotion to my father, Florian, during the last years of his life.

And also in deep gratitude to the members of the Polish National Alliance of North American and the many other Americans who brought me to this country.

Henryk (Hank) J. Birecki

Contents

Contents

Maps:

Acknowledgments

With love, I bestow my heartfelt "Thank you" to my dear wife, Sabra, not only for the many times she responded to my "Please take your red pencil and read this over" but also for putting up with my isolation at the computer.

I am deeply grateful for the editorial and historical reviews by Greta Anderson of Iowa City, Iowa; Joan Otto of Cheboygan, Michigan; and Professor Tadeusz Piotrowski of Manchester, New Hampshire.

I also thank Anita Paschwa-Kozicka for her support of my project and her permission to use the photographs of SS *Zdanov* and USS *Hermitage*.

To my daughter, Deanna, I can express my appreciation for her moving concept of the chapter illustration best by using Hank's words: "That's the way it was."

My most profound thanks, however, go to Hank Birecki for sharing with me his undoubtedly deeply disturbing and painful memories and thereby helping me gain additional insights into and find a perspective on the events surrounding my own youth.

Foreword

by Tadeusz Piotrowski

⌒

To the dismay of the West, the August 23, 1939, Soviet-German Pact of Non-Aggression allied the Communist Soviet Union with the Nazi Third Reich. In that pact a secret protocol was also drawn up for the reorganization of Central Europe. That September, in violation of their own treaties with Poland, both Germany and the Soviet Union invaded and partitioned the Second Polish Republic. Thus began the Second World War.

According to Stalin, the joint aim of the Soviet Union and Germany was "to restore peace and order in Poland, which had been destroyed by the disintegration of the Polish State, and to help the Polish people establish new conditions for its political life."[1] Needless to say, that "disintegration of the Polish State" had been brought about by the very powers which now promised to restore "peace and order."

This foreword is adapted from Professor Tadeusz Piotrowski's presentation "Deportation, 'Amnesty,' and the Polish Diaspora," at the University of Toronto on April 27, 2000. Included herein with his kind permission.

On September 28, 1939, the German-Soviet Boundary and Friendship Treaty announced the new borders of the "respective national interests" of Germany and the Soviet Union in "the former Polish State and promised to "assure the people living there a peaceful life in keeping with their national character."[2] Instead of assuring "peace and order" in the "former Polish State," however, both allies subjected the populace of Poland to a reign of terror the likes of which had seldom been seen before in the annals of human history. Their mutual aim was to completely suppress the political and socio-cultural life of the Polish people forever.[3]

One of the monstrous measures carried out by the Soviet government was the massive deportation of Polish citizens from the Soviet zone, or the so-called Soviet sphere of influence, to the barren wastes of Siberia and Arkhangelsk—the Gulag Archipelago—where, as we know from Aleksandr Solzhenitsyn's masterful epic, millions of Soviet citizens were dumped after the Bolshevik Revolution.

Similar deportations of Polish citizens occurred under the tsars in 1832, 1864, and 1906. Another earlier and less-known two-volume work on the topic is George Kennan's *Siberia and the Exile System*, penned in 1891. Although this pioneering work does not deal specifically with Polish exiles, the author states that "First and last, about 100,000 Poles have been banished".[4] Official Russian records indicate that between 1863 and 1866 alone, 18,623 Poles were deported to Siberia.[5]

During the Stalinist Great Purge of 1936-38, Poles accounted for about 40 percent of the victims of the Soviet war on national minorities.[6]

In the nineteenth and twentieth centuries, therefore, the threat of deportation was all too real to the Poles. Jan Plater-Gajewski's family history was shared by many of them: His great-grandfather spent seven years, his grandfather eleven, his father five, and he himself seventeen years in that barren wasteland of Siberia.[7]

Some of the sources dealing with the four major waves of deportations from Eastern Poland in 1939-41 include the Soviet NKVD index and instructions relating to "Anti-Soviet Elements." This document identifies the various categories of people deemed subversive to the

Soviet Union and its interests. These categories include "all citizens of foreign countries," "repatriates," "Polish refugees," land and shop owners, and the clergy to name but a few. But there are many more categories and they are all-embracing.

We have Ivan Serov's "Basic Instructions on Deportations Order No. 001223," dated October 11, 1939, [see the Appendix]. These instructions detail the procedures for carrying out the deportation of the "anti-Soviet elements" in the above-mentioned NKVD index.

We also have the Katyn document signed by Stalin and his Politburo members, a document that orders the summary execution (or in the words of the document itself, "the supreme penalty: shooting") of some 25,700 Polish citizens, mostly ethnic Poles, many of them civilians.[8]

In addition, the Polish Government Collection, the Wladyslaw Anders Collection, and the Poland, Ambasada (USSR) Collection at the Hoover Institution on War Revolution and Peace at Stanford, California, contain over 20,000 accounts and transcripts of interviews conducted with Polish citizens deported to the Soviet Union between 1939 and 1941. All this information was gathered shortly after the "amnesty" while it was still fresh in the minds of the victims. Among the most moving of these accounts are the ones written by children in the Polish camp-schools of the British-controlled Middle East where they were sent. 120 of these essays have been published in the English language by Irena Grudzinska-Gross and Jan Tomasz Gross in a 1981 book entitled *War Through Children's Eyes*.

The General Sikorski Historical Institute Archives in London is another source of invaluable information.

Finally, a number of important publications, many of them memoirs, have come out in both Polish and English that deal with the deportations [see the bibliography]. Two of these works deserve a special mention: *The Dark Side of the Moon*, a work published anonymously in 1946 with a preface by T. S. Eliot; and *The Black Book of Communism*, which came out in English in 1999.

The four previously-mentioned major deportations of Polish citizens from the Soviet zone took place on February 8-10, April 13-15, and the final days of June and the beginning of July in 1940, and from

May 21 and into June in 1941. (Daniel Bockowski, however, argues that in addition there was a fairly large deportation in October 1939 as well.)[9]

How many people were deported? No one really knows and chances are that no one will ever know the full scale of that Soviet ethnic-cleansing campaign. Here are some earlier estimates of well-known historians: Jan Tomasz Gross—1.2 million; Norman Davies—1.5 million; Zbigniew S. Siemaszko—1.646 million; and Wladyslaw Pobog-Malinowski—1.7 million.

One promising approach to this question of numbers is provided by Polish railway employees who, after all, had firsthand knowledge of the preparations being made for the deportations and who operated the trains bound for the interior of the Soviet Union. According to their reckoning, the occupation authorities utilized from 120 to 150 trains, each train carrying an average of 2,000 persons. Using this information and relying on additional information provided by the deportees, Bohdan Podoski—himself a victim of NKVD arrest and exile—estimates that 110 trains were used in the first deportation, 160 in the second, 120 in the third, and 120 in the deportation of June of 1941.

Moreover, he estimates that about ten percent of the deportees and prisoners were marched or transported by trucks into the Soviet Union just before the German invasion. Thus, according to Podoski, 220,000 persons were deported in February, 320,000 in April, 240,000 in June 1940, and 265,000 in June of the following year. That last deportation consisted of 170,000 exiles and 95,000 prisoners. In addition, there were approximately 647,000 POWs, Polish Red Army draftees, and concentration-camp victims in the Soviet Union as of June 1941. Podoski's grand total, therefore, of all Polish citizens deported to the Soviet Union in 1939–41 stands at 1,692,000.[10]

The most recent, and the most conservative, Polish count based on Soviet documents was published in 1997 by the Main Commission in Warsaw.[11] Jozef Lewandowski summarizes the current findings of Russian historians as follows: "Altogether 314,000–325,000 persons were deported.... As of August 1, 1941, there were 381,000 Polish prisoners and deportees in the Soviet Union. Of these, 335,000 were deportees and their families."[12]

If to Lewandowski's figures we add the various other deportations, smaller in scale, resulting in the displacement of some 50,000 civilians, 22,500 prisoners of war, and the 80,000–90,000 people arrested for political reasons and detained in the prisons of Eastern Poland, about half of whom were eventually deported to Soviet forced-labor camps, we will arrive at 400,000 to 500,000 as the grand total of those deported using the Soviet documents as our point of departure.

By including voluntary workers, those who fled in June/July 1941, army draftees, and other such categories, Daniel Bockowski arrives at approximately 750,000 to 780,000 as the total number of Polish citizens who found themselves in the Soviet Union as a result of the Soviet occupation of Eastern Poland.[13]

In the Soviet Union, the destination of the exiled Polish citizens was the northern and central regions of the Soviet Union—the area between the Arctic Circle in the North and the Mongolian border in the south—in Siberia, Kazakhstan, and Arkhangelsk. Some ended up in penal- or forced-labor camps, others were dumped into remote settlements, and still others wound up in kolkhozes (collective farms). Their fate was the same wherever they were sent: slave labor in exchange for the barest necessities of life. As a result, hundreds of thousands died of cold, hunger, and disease.

Such was the lot of the deportees until the invasion of the Soviet Union by Germany in June 1941. The Polish-Soviet agreement of July 30, 1941 provided for the release of all Poles from exile, prisons, and labor camps (the "amnesty"), as well as for the formation of a Polish army on Soviet soil under General Wladyslaw Anders.

Elated by this turn of events the far-flung Polish deportees began to make their way southward, to where Anders' army was forming, in the hope of liberation. These journeys, often several weeks long, brought new suffering and many people died from hunger, cold, heat, disease, and exhaustion on that trip to freedom. For many, the help provided by the Polish Army, the United States, and Great Britain was too little and too late. In the Samarkand district alone, in a two-and-a-half-month period in 1942, out of 27,000, 1,632 Polish citizens perished from typhus and malnutrition.[14]

Nevertheless, during the two great evacuation operations in March-April and August-September 1942, about 115,000 people (including some 40,000 civilians) left the Soviet Union. The soldiers of Anders' army went on to fight in many battles, including the one at Monte Cassino; the civilians, because they could not be repatriated, were forced to remain in foreign lands for the remainder of the war.

After leaving the Soviet Union the first stop of the Polish exiles was Iran, where they found temporary quarters in large transit camps in Pahlevi, Teheran, and Ahvaz. There were even several camps for the thousands of orphaned Polish children at Isfahan. The relief assistance afforded by Polish, British, American, and Iranian authorities soon improved their living conditions and brought the devastating contagious diseases under control.

Because of the hostility of the Soviet troops occupying northern Iran and because of the threat of the German armies which had already reached the Caucasus, the liberated refugees had to move on. Some found asylum in India in transit camps around Karachi; for example in the Country Club Camp, Haji Pilgrims Camp, and the Malir Camp. But more stable settlements also emerged such as those in Balachadi and Valivade. In Valivade, near Kolhapur, south of Dekan, there were 5,000 Poles, and they had their own self-government. They even succeeded in establishing four elementary schools, a high school, a junior college, and a trade school. In all, 15 Polish schools were attended by some 2,300 Polish children in India. Moreover, several Polish periodicals were published, Polish amateur theaters were founded, and Polish business enterprises flourished.

Africa provided another safe harbor for the Poles. In mid-1944, East Africa hosted over 13,000 Polish citizens. They settled in transit and permanent camps in the British colonies of Uganda, Kenya, and Tanganyika. In Uganda, the camps were located in Mosindi and Koya on Lake Victoria. In Kenya, they were located in Rongai and Makindu. In Tanganyika, the largest settlement was Tengeru and smaller camps were located in Kondoa, Ifunda, Morogoro, and Kidugala.

South Africa, South Rhodesia, and North Rhodesia also became the home of Poles. The largest of these settlements were: in the Union of South Africa—Oudtshoorn; in North Rhodesia—Abercorn, Bwana Mkubwa, Livingstone, Lusaka; in South Rhodesia—Digglefold, Marandellas, and Rusape. There, with British assistance, schools, churches, hospitals, civic centers, and manufacturing and service cooperatives were founded and Polish culture prospered. African radio stations ran programs in the Polish language and there was even a Polish press. In South Africa alone there were 18 Polish schools with about 1,800 students in attendance.

A large Polish settlement was also founded in Mexico. Although provisions were made to resettle several thousand Poles in that country, only two transports arrived in the summer and fall of 1943 with a total of approximately 1,500 refugees. Their home became a deserted hacienda in Santa Rosa, near León. The settlement was financed by American institutions, including the National Catholic Welfare Conference and the Polish American Council.

Finally, a few hundred Polish children arrived in New Zealand on November 1, 1944. They were housed in a camp located in Pahiatua.

All the camps and settlements established in Iran, India, Africa, Mexico, and New Zealand were meant to be temporary quarters for the Polish refugees until the end of the war and the expected liberation of their country. However, after Yalta and the change in Polish borders this became an impossible dream, although a few did return to join their families in Poland.

What became of the rest? Those who wound up in New Zealand and the Union of South Africa remained where they were brought. The Polish refugees in India and Africa moved to Great Britain and its dominions, Canada and Australia, from where some of them later emigrated to the United States. And a few years ago, in 1996 in Chicago, the Poles of Santa Rosa celebrated the 50th anniversary of their arrival in the United States.

Thus ended the saga of the deportees from Eastern Poland who managed to get out of the Soviet Union under the provisions of the "amnesty" of 1941. But what happened to the rest of the hundreds of thousands who did not leave with Anders' army? To be sure, many of them were repatriated to the "recovered territories" of western Poland during the massive population exchanges following the Second World War. As for what happened to those who never got out, God only knows. Some, no doubt, are still there.

Professor Tadeusz Piotrowski, author of
Vengeance of the Swallows, Poland's Holocaust
and *Genocide and Rescue in Wolyn*
University of New Hampshire,
February 10, 2000

Notes

1. Schulenburg Dispatch, September 10, as cited in William Shirer, *The Rise and Fall of the Third Reich* (Greenwich CT: Fawcett, 1960), 832.

2. Cited in Shirer, 835. In keeping with the terms of the German-Soviet Boundary and Friendship Treaty, the Soviet government also pledged to actively support and *did* actively support the German war effort against Poland and the West. See Zbigniew S. Siemaszko, "The Mass Deportations of the Polish Population to the USSR, 1940-1941," in Keith Sword, ed., *The Soviet Takeover of the Polish Eastern Provinces, 1939-1941* (New York: St. Martin's Press, 1991), 234, n. 9; Aleksander Bregman, *Najlepszy sojusznik Hitlera: Studium o wspolpracy niemiecko-sowieckiej 1939-1941*, 3d ed. (London: Orbis, 1967), see his "Wspolpraca wojskowa i gospodarcza", Chapter 9, 94-108; Documentary Survey by Vice-Admiral Ossman, *Trials of War Criminals Before the Nuremberg Military Tribunals*, vol. 34 (Washington, DC: U.S. Government Printing Office, 1951-52), 674; and Edward E. Ericson, *Feeding the German Eagle: Soviet Economic Aid to Nazi Germany, 1933-1941* (Westport, CT: Praeger, 1999).

3. Some of these measures have been documented in Tadeusz Piotrowski, *Poland's Holocaust: Ethnic Strife, Collaboration with Occupying Forces and Genocide in the Second Republic, 1918-1947* (Jefferson, NC: McFarland, 1998), Chapters 1 and 2.

4. George Kennan, *Siberia and the Exile System*, (London: James R. Osgood, McIlvaine & Co., 1891; New York: Praeger Publishers, 1970), vol. 1, 82.

5. Kennan, vol. 2, 280, n. 1, basing himself on Maximof (who had access to the official records), *Siberia and Penal Servitude* (St. Petersburg, 1871), vol 3, 80-81.

6. Jozef Lewandowski, "Rosjanie o Europie Wschodniej i Polsce," *Zeszyty Historyczne*, no. 126 (1998): 180-82. See also Mikolaj Iwanow, *Pierwszy narod ukarany: Polacy w Zwiazku Radzieckim 1921-1939* (Warszawa: Panstwowe Wydawnictwo Naukowe, 1991), 324-78; Stanislaw Morozow, "Deportacje polskiej ludnosci cywilnej z radzieckich terenow zachodnich w glab ZSRR w latach 1935-1936," *Pamiec i sprawiedliwosc: Biuletyn Glownej Komisji Badania Zbrodni przeciwko Narodowi Polskiemu Instytut Pamieci Narodowej* 40 (1997-98): 267-81; and Andrzej Paczkowski, "Poland, the 'Enemy Nation,' in Stephene Courtois, et al., *The Black Book of Communism: Crimes, Terror, Repression,* trans. by Jonathan Murphy and Mark Kramer (Cambridge, MA: Harvard University Press, 1999), 366-67.

7. Keith Sword, *Deportation and Exile: Poles in the Soviet Union, 1939-48.* (London: St. Martin's Press, 1994), viii-ix, 17-18.

8. These three documents appear in the Appendix of Piotrowski.

9. Daniel Bockowski, Czas nadziei: Obywatele Rzeczypospolitej Polskiej w ZSRR i opieka nad nimi placowek polskich w latach 1940-1943 (Warszawa: Wydawnictwo Neriton i Wydawnictwo IH PAN, 1999), 59-66.

10. See Elzbieta Wrobel and Janusz Wrobel, Rozproszeni po swiecie: Obozy i osiedla uchodzcow polskich ze Zwiazku Sowieckiego 1942-1950 (Chicago: n.p., 1992), 12-13.

11. Wojciech Materski, "Martyrologia obywateli polskich na wschodzie po 17 wrzesnia 1939 r.," in Janina Mikoda, ed., Zbrodnicza ewakuacja wiezien i arresztow NKWD na Kresach Wschodnich II Rzeczypospolitej w czerwcu-lipcu 1941 roku: Materialy z sesji naukowej w 55. rocznice ewakuacji wiezniow NKWD w glab ZSRR (Lodz, 10 czerwca 1996 r.) (Warszawa: Glowna Komisja Badania Zbrodni przeciwko Narodowi Polskiemu i Okregowa Komisja Badania Zbrodni przeciwko Narodowi Polskiemu w Lodzi, 1997), 8-9.

12. Lewandowski, 182-83.

13. Bockowski, 92, 377.

14. See the May 25, 1942, report of a deputy delegate in Samarkand, cited in Wrobel and Wrobel, 52. What follows is based on Wrobel and Wrobel.

1.

Setting the Stage

Hank, a ten-year-old boy from Poland, experiences the terrors of war and of Stalin's work camps. Torn from an untroubled childhood, he suffers the personal and physical deprivations of deportation to forced labor in Siberia. After years of life in camps he reaches America on the brink of manhood and finds security, freedom, and personal fulfillment.

I have been asked, and I have asked myself, "Why write about this, not only now—more than 50 years later—but why at all?" Thousands of testimonies to these experiences have been deposited in archives around the world, and a number of books have been written which reveal how children had been "robbed of all that had given them security" and how "within hours their easy existence gave way to a life of terror" (Bruno Bettelheim, 1981). But the helplessness and innocence of children do not only appeal to our instinct to nurture and to protect; these attributes also symbolize all that is opposed to oppression,

1

terror, and war. The fate of children under those conditions deserves our never-ending attention.

Tadeusz Piotrowski, who at an early age experienced a fate similar to Hank's, writes in his book *Vengeance of the Swallows* that his family history is also a history shared by so many people scattered throughout the world, and he expresses the hope that "it will stand as a testament to those who shared [these] experiences during the Second World War." He answers the question "why such a book" even more directly: "Write, for when a person dies, a whole library is lost." Above all, he wanted his children to know.

In the foreseeable future the voices of the survivors of this time will be stilled, but later generations should have a record of what befell their parents and grandparents, and how they coped with it all. The strengths and weaknesses of our ancestors, their struggles, and their triumphs are part of our make-up and of our collective destiny.

The story of Hank's life is not the story of one isolated child. It exemplifies the fate of over 200,000 Polish children during the Second World War: a time when over two million ethnic Poles perished, ground between the otherwise violently opposed ideologies and imperial ambitions of Nazi Germany and communist Soviet Union.

Beyond this historical setting, Hank's story reflects the fate of all those torn from their homes and families because they belonged to the "wrong" race, religion, or ethnic group. What happened to this boy from Poland during the Second World War is a sobering commentary on the fate of people caught under any totalitarian system or between any warring factions and opposed ideologies throughout the world. What he experienced more than 50 years ago will always remain relevant. A change in names and locations makes it the news of today. It is still timely, too, as the ideologies and symbols of that period which victimized Hank are being resurrected and imitated among the radical fringe of contemporary society. His saga is one more piece of evidence that will help to silence those revisionist historians who attempt to rewrite history by denying that such events actually happened.

I have also asked myself whether writing Hank's story is an attempt on my part to come to terms with the political influences on my own childhood. Certainly, though only in part.

I was born in Germany. When Hitler came to power I was five years old. I therefore grew up under the Nazi regime and could not help being affected by its ideology. What was committed in the name of Germany during the Second World War is based in part, I believe, on the then-prevailing attitude toward its history: the exultation in national supremacy, in military achievements, and in hero-worship—an attitude which had characterized the mass of the German people since the Napoleonic wars.

The universal suffering of people who are "different," who belong to the "others" because of their religious or ethnic roots, has not only moved me deeply but also has confirmed my belief that the fate of individuals is an essential part of the history of their time.

To talk of one—or a million—as a statistic is to take a *quantitative* view of history. Numbers of victims reflect the power of the perpetrators, not the depth of the individual ordeals. To feel the *quality* of any period of time one needs to empathize with those that have lived through it, to imagine oneself in the place of a particular person, to try to take part in his or her anguish and pain, his or her steadfastness, and his or her—however rare—triumph. Herein lies the significance of individual histories: They help us understand a specific period and make it alive for us.

Abel Herzberg stressed this individualized approach when he said that not six million Jews were killed, but that one Jew was killed, then another, and another, until we arrive at the six million. So too, must the stories of the survivors such as Hank be documented one by one in the hope that some day they will belong to the recorded past—and to the past only. The fate of children like him will thereby not be obliterated by time, but thus will become a continuous reminder to us all of the "sanctity of man," of man's essential inviolability, and of the need to end "man's inhumanity to man."

A concept of history in which the nameless are forgotten or survive only as a cipher in a statistic, where only the movers—a Hitler, a Stalin, a Tamerlane "the Great"—are assured their place, but not their victims, is one "that leads to the destruction of the soul instead of broadening its powers" (Elie Wiesel, 1961).

The historical events bearing on Hank's childhood are unique in history and form the background against which his fate must be interpreted. They were dominated by both Hitler and Stalin whose policies toward Poland were based on firmly entrenched ideologies and on centuries old imperialistic ambitions. Their policies are the more contemptible as they did not result from an outburst of nationalistic frenzy, but were rather carried out with unprecedented calculation and systematically imposed on non-combatants, including children. The perpetrators of these policies came from societies that embraced Western culture and civilization—not to mention Christianity.

Civilized societies abided by the notion that in case of a future war children at least should be spared. In her foreword to Withold Majewski's *Polish Children Suffer* Helena Sikorska, widow of the Polish Commander-in-Chief and government-in-exile President General Wladyslaw Sikorski, wrote in 1943, that it was assumed that "the defenselessness and childish weakness in itself would protect the child from being intentionally wronged, and from injustice on the part of the adult." This humanistic ideal was part and parcel of the culture of the Western World. In the United States the events which are at the core of Hank's story had been withheld from the general public during the war and, when finally revealed, therefore often met with utter disbelief and accusations of "Polish propaganda."

Unfortunately the ideals of civilization had greatly eroded since the First World War and were torn to shreds in Europe in 1939. Coldly efficient bureaucracies with their rapid communications, refined technology, and deadly weaponry became ready tools of mass destruction and resurrected the specter of "ethnic cleansing" in the 20th century: the systematic deportation and liquidation of entire indigenous populations. Helena Sikorska concluded: "Nothing distinguishes our century from the most cruel, barbaric periods."

Her words, though spoken in relation to the German actions in Poland, equally apply to one of the Western Allies: the Soviet Union which spread terror across all of Eastern Europe.

The uprooting and destruction of entire populations, though most egregious in the case of the Jews of Europe by Nazi Germany, engulfed all the peoples of Eastern Europe, and eventually large segments of the German population as well. After the Second World War these policies were perpetuated by Stalin in Poland and the Baltic countries. The scope of these events, in their depth, breadth, and length, seemed at first unimaginable to the civilized mind. Though the effects of Stalin's policies on Poland and its people had been recorded since 1940 and movingly portrayed as early as 1946 in *The Dark Side of the Moon*, only now—due to the heightened awareness of the Jewish Holocaust and deeper insights into Soviet policies—have they led to a broader comprehension of those times. The extermination of the Polish people as an ethnic group by Stalin and Hitler was second in scope only to the annihilation of the Jews.

The actions of the Soviets in occupied Poland and elsewhere were as reprehensible as those of the Nazis: *Qualitatively*, if one considers the extent and the depth of human suffering, as well as *quantitatively*, their victims numbered into the millions. Since ethnic cleansing and genocide were the direct consequences of their actions in Poland and the Baltic countries, should not the term "holocaust" embrace these victims as well?

In his recent book, *Poland's Holocaust*, Tadeusz Piotrowski defines "holocaust" as "an event in historical time involving an officially sanctioned policy of genocide," genocide being the "systematic destruction, in whole or in part, of indigenous populations *as such*." He concludes that the term "holocaust" should therefore apply to "the victims of both [the Stalin and the Hitler] regimes and their collaborators." Hank's story is a contribution to our understanding of the history of these tragic times from the perspective of one of those victims.

The summary deportations of civilians who were presumed to be a threat to the Soviet system are a partial but, in sheer numbers alone, significant aspect of the holocaust in Poland. They affected over a million Polish citizens, the vast majority of whom were ethnic Poles.

A ten-year-old girl from Latvia gave graphic expression to these events in a series of drawings now on display in the Museum of Occupation in Riga, Latvia. Their simple lines show the process of deportation in moving detail: the round up, the long train of freight cars, the transport in open trucks packed full of people, and the field labor at the end of their road.

The history of these crucial years shows that national-socialist Germany and communist Soviet Russia, despite their ideological enmity, had been united in their greed for Polish territory and the subjugation of the Polish people. Their approach, rationalized by their respective ideologies and almost identical in its execution, was but an intensified continuation of policies begun long ago by their aristocratic predecessors, the Prussian kings and the tsars.

Writing in 1911, Joseph Conrad, who at the age of six witnessed his parents' exile to Siberia under the tsar, spoke of the Poles as "that nationality not so much alive as surviving, which persists in thinking, breathing, speaking, hoping, and suffering in its grave, railed in by a million bayonets and triple sealed with the seals of three [German, Austro-Hungarian, Tsarist] empires." (Conrad's *Prince Roman* is a story based on the 1831 Polish insurrection against the Russian tsar.)

Nazi Germany and the Soviet Union carried out the destruction of the Polish people along the same paths: by forced assimilation through kidnapping young children to be educated as their own, by deportation, by using the population—including children—for slave labor, by mass executions, and by intentional starvation. Whether they were sent to Germany or the Soviet Union the lot of the Poles was the same: no heat, inadequate clothing, and back-breaking labor, be it in the German *Baudiensts* (compulsory labor service), as *Ostarbeiters* (forced laborers from the eastern countries), or in the Soviet work camps. Even their daily rations were the same: a few slices of bread and a bowl of thin cabbage soup. The photographs of starved Polish children after their release from the Soviet Union, stored at the Hoover Archives, and those published in Lucjan Krolikowski's book, *Stolen Childhood*, could have been taken straight from the annals of Buchenwald or any other Nazi concentration camp. For the individual concerned, starving to death in a Soviet work camp in Arkhangelsk was no different from dying of exhaustion in the stone quarry of Buchenwald. A death warrant was a death warrant whether stamped with Hammer and Sickle or the Swastika.

There was a difference, however, between the Nazis and the Soviets, a difference not of methods or procedures—these were surprisingly similar—nor in the end results—these also did not differ—

but in the underlying philosophy and intent. Almost paranoid in their thinking, the Soviets aimed to remove any, even imagined, threat to their socialist revolution not only from among the newly occupied territories but also from among their own citizens. The Nazis, on the other hand, eliminated people because of their perceived racial or ethnic inferiority.

This value judgment regarding "inferior" races and cultures unfortunately was not new. It had its roots in the period of enlightenment in the Western World (Dinesh D'Sonza). In Germany, however, romanticism imbued this thinking with a mystical aura of "Volk" and "Volk-ish destiny" by emphasizing the subjective and the visionary, and by its preoccupation with hero-worship and German national and cultural superiority (George L. Mosse). These ideas entered the Nazi ideology as an integral part and justified to them the extermination of perceived inferior racial and cultural groups.

The Soviet ideology also incorporated a differential value system: the "exploited" versus their "exploiters," the "workers" versus the "capitalists," the "proletariat" versus the "bourgeoisie." The Soviets considered the "bourgeois capitalist exploiters" a threat to their system and therefore to be liquidated. It was a question of a "social prophylaxis" (Aleksandr Solzhenitsyn). To remove "threatening elements," be it by prolonged imprisonment or even by execution, was considered a necessary step to finally achieve the "workers' paradise." Their value system, however, was based on class, on one's social position—or so they maintained. It supposedly had neither national, nor racial, nor cultural borders. To a degree, it even permitted some graduation: some of the "exploiters" could be "reeducated." Should their "anti-Soviet" activities not warrant execution, they were sent to one of the work camps in the Gulag.

In the Soviet ideology, as in that of the Nazis, physical labor was surrounded by an almost mystic quality of spiritual purification and regeneration. In its actual implementation, however, this ideal was cynically perverted, as the victims of the Soviet euphemism "correctional labor" and those of the Nazi slogan *Arbeit macht Frei* (labor makes free, the sign displayed in bold letters across the gates of German concentration camps) can readily attest.

Soviet thinking was furthermore imbued with centuries-old enmity toward the Poles and Imperial Russia's claim on the eastern Polish territories. This claim had originated with Tsar Peter the Great and had persisted through the rule of Nicholas II, the last tsar. Though repudiated by Lenin and his government, the Imperial Russian claim on Eastern Poland was readily revived by Stalin after his ascent to power.

These are the significant historical and ideological currents underlying the Soviet invasion of Eastern Poland in 1939 and the subsequent displacement of the Polish population in this area. They form the background to Hank Birecki's story, and are essential for interpreting the latter within the framework of the former.

But the story of Hank, the ten-year-old boy from Poland, has a wider human dimension. It is more than another anecdotal story about suffering and deprivation, more than a recounting of historical facts; nor are its implications limited to a specific population during the Second World War.

Hank's life as a child in rural prewar Poland helped to build his self-reliance and his inner-strength and to develop his resourcefulness and his faith—character traits allowing him to grow into manhood while preserving his dignity and humanity in the face of adversity. His courage to defy his oppressors, culminating in acts of open rebellion, is an integral part of his personality.

His story and those of others in similar circumstances present a portrait of a people who, despite their losses, preserved their dignity, their faith, and their courage—attributes they never hesitated to display wherever and whenever they could. Referring to the Soviets, one person—Hank's teacher in Mexico who had traveled the same road as Hank—said: "We were all defiant." Elie Wiesel, himself a victim of the Nazis during the Second World War and as one dedicated to preserving the memory and the significance of these times, wrote: "Other people's suffering attracts me only to the extent that it allows man to become conscious of his strength and of his weakness, in a climate that favors rebellion."

Hank's resourcefulness, his sense of responsibility, and even his defiance are mirrored in many children of his age: the hunted Jewish boy who gloried in "twisting Hitler's nose" by recklessly attending

German events in occupied Warsaw and who finally made his mark as a courier in the Warsaw uprising; the child who squeezed through narrow passageways in order to supply the Warsaw ghetto inmates with food; the boy from a Brazilian shantytown who from early on had to help sustain his family; the pioneer boy who took charge of his sisters after both parents died on the wagon trek to the west; the young Sioux on his first warpath at age eleven; the ten-year-old child-cowboy; or the child of the East European peasant who had to be self-sufficient by the age of ten.

I profoundly admire these children's capability to act responsibly against all odds and to take charge of their own lives and the lives of those close to them. I admire them even more when, in spite of all, they are able to shed their burdens and still delight in being children at play. These traits are to me the true bulwarks of freedom and fuel the embers that radiate our humanity.

Hank's story is based on the events of his life as he related them to me. In interpreting his thoughts and emotions I relied on his own memories. The reader, as I often did, may at times wish for Hank to have elaborated more on one or another of his experiences, but alas, memory does not treat all events or encounters alike. It imprints them the deeper when stirred by emotions, and it replays the more remote in often only snapshot-like recalls.

I have taken the liberty to include some of my personal thoughts and experiences as they apply to the narrative hoping to give Hank's story an additional perspective.

The bibliography lists mostly English-language autobiographies and historical works directly related to Hank's story. I have, in addition, included references marginally related to this subject, but ones which allow insights into the personalities of children, refugees, and immigrants, as well as pertinent cultural and historical currents and facts.

2.

Hank and I

One day in the summer of 1995, Hank planned to stop by on his way into town: he wanted to pick up some books he had lent me. When he phoned before coming, I told him I also had a surprise for him, as well as a small jug of Dutch salted herring, a treat I knew he would enjoy.

That morning the mailman had left an oblong package on my porch. It contained three maps of former southeastern Poland, the country of Hank's childhood. The larger map highlighted the region around Lwow; the other two were of smaller scale. One of them detailed Krasne, a village about 20 miles east of Lwow and Hank's birthplace; the other focused on Sassow, some 30 miles farther east and off to the north. There Hank's father's family had worked the land as independent Polish farmers for generations, and there Hank's father Florian was born, one of several children.

Lately Hank and I had talked at length about his home and his childhood. I had tried to form a mental picture of the topography of

Map of Krasne, Busk, Kutkorz, Zuratyn

Hank's birthplace and its surroundings when I accidentally found detailed Austrian maps of this part of Poland (former Eastern Galicia; now Western Ukraine). The maps dated back to the Austrian occupation of this area prior to the end of the First World War in 1918. The major cities therefore carried German names, such as Lemberg for the Polish city of Lwow (Lviv, after its incorporation into the Ukrainian SSR during the Second World War). The lesser towns and villages had kept their Polish names under the Austrians.

The smaller maps clearly showed every creek and country road as well as the layout of every town and village with their streets and market squares. Black dots marked the individual houses. Though additional buildings had been erected from the time the maps were printed to Hank's childhood, a period of about 50 years, the essential arrangement of the communities had not changed, nor had any new construction significantly affected the location of houses as they were recorded on the map.

I cleared the living room table and spread the maps when Hank arrived. We sharpened a match stick to use as a pointer. Hank studied the maps with a magnifying glass. He showed me the village of Zuratyn, the birthplace of his mother, about two and a half miles north of Krasne and pointed to a fork in the road: "On this corner was kind of a grocery store and something like a temporary jail. The windows were all barred. See this bare spot, north of these houses? It must be the cemetery where my grandfather is buried." He then moved the match stick a few millimeters to a small black square, "Here is where my grandparents lived. Their land went all the way down to the river, here." I followed the pointer as Hank traced a large bend in the Peltero, a tributary of the Bug River which it entered a few kilometers downstream near the town of Busk.

"That black square could be the house of the carpenter who made the furniture for my parents," he said and moved the match stick to a spot near another bend in the river. "Close to this bend was the swinging footbridge I told you about," and, "We went swimming here." He showed me where the Gotogorka River, which flowed past Krasne and soon joined the Peltero, was crossed by the railroad. "And here, at this wide part of the Gotogarka was the dam and the gristmill. Somewhere should be the woods my grandfather left to me when he died. It could be in this patch of trees." He pointed to a stretch of woods west of Zuratyn and extending north almost to the town of Busk, "It says 'Na. Grabinie.' I'm sure grandfather owned some of the woods and had a field next to it. Now I finally understand what my grandmother meant when she said that grandfather went 'to Grabinie.' My father also used those words. We got our firewood from there."

Hank was pressed for time. We ran off several copies of those areas on the maps which related to his childhood and his family and repackaged them into the container. He took them with him when he left. Hank's joy of recognition and the excitement with which he perused the maps had touched me deeply. We stood together on the driveway as he was leaving.

"I thank you so much," he said. I felt his arms around me, saw his blue eyes shine, and heard a tremor in his voice. "This brings back so many memories," he said with a smile.

"I hope they are good ones," I replied.

"Oh yes, for the most part they are," he said.

I helped him stow his packages into his car and waved to him as he drove off.

The first time I had heard Hank mention, ever so briefly, his childhood and the events which brought him to this country, I sensed an air of evasiveness. I got the impression that talking about his past was too painful for him. My concern not to inflame any old wounds was so strong that for most of the nearly 20 years I knew Hank and his wife, Mary Lou, I consciously refrained from asking him about his early life in prewar Poland and his deportation to Siberia.

Only much later, after we were well into our talks about his experiences, did I find out the true reason for Hank's hesitation to speak about this time. I also discovered that an unrelated event had finally allowed him to make peace with this part of his past.

From the very beginning, however, his time in Siberia had aroused my interest, and it was not from idle curiosity. I profoundly admired anyone who had been exiled there, particularly at such a young age, and who had survived. My personal conception of that forbidding country had been formed when, as a boy, I read a number of books from the First World War about German prisoners of war in Siberia, often existing under conditions not much better than those later reported of Stalin's camps. This "fear of Siberia" drove me to do my utmost to avoid becoming a prisoner of war of the Soviets at the end of the Second World War.

Eventually, in the spring of 1995, I overcame my reluctance to delve into Hank's painful past. At that time he was well into his recovery from a coronary bypass operation, though the pain from his incision still limited him physically. "I want to write your story," I told him.

"I realize," I said, "that many of the things that happened to you during the war left you with sad and bitter memories. You have not said much on your own. Do you think we can talk about it?" I assured him that should he feel uncomfortable or should I evoke too painful a memory, we would stop right there and not mention the subject any more.

"No," he said, he would be happy to talk about his childhood, the deportation of his family, and the death of his mother in Siberia, and to tell me how he and his sister passed through a temporary gap in what then already could be called an "Iron Curtain," and how both of them trekked almost three quarters of the world to a temporary refuge in Mexico and finally found a new life in the security of the United States of America.

After I had shown Hank the maps, his positive reaction removed any remaining anxiety on my part, and I felt satisfied that probing into his past would not disturb the peace he had made with it earlier. I was finally confident that my need to question him, at times repeatedly, not only about events but also about his thoughts and feelings related to his stay in Soviet Russia, would not reawaken any long-suppressed painful memories.

Although the actions of Germany were the proximate cause of Hank's trials, for years he directed his bitterness toward the Soviets. He hated them, but he always emphasized that he despised the communists, not the Russian people as such, for their destruction of his home and his family. This feeling had stayed with him for more than 25 years after the end of the war, until one evening, occasioned by a completely unrelated event—and one of those that suddenly throws our lives onto a different track—Hank experienced a release from the pain and gained a new perspective on those years of his childhood.

Hank described that event as follows: "Mary Lou and I were driving home one evening in early spring. It was getting dark, and the road was slick with ice. The car in front of us went into a spin and ended up broadside in the middle of the road. I tried to brake and felt my car slide. I could not evade the other car. We braced ourselves for the impact, but our cars stopped inches away from each other. We felt shaken. For a moment everything went blank. But ever since that night I found myself looking at that grim time of my childhood without any feeling of bitterness or hatred. I even forgave those who had a hand in my mother's death."

"I had another reason why I did not want to talk about that time," Hank told me later when I questioned him about his initial evasiveness. "Many people did not believe me!"

"I had just come to this country," he explained. "I was seventeen then. Several of us had come from the orphanage in Mexico to Chicago and were invited to a Polish-American party. They asked us to go on a stage and tell about our homes, what happened to us, and how we came to this country. I told them how I grew up in Krasne, how we barely survived in Siberia, and what my grandmother had said about my mother's body being all cut up when she went to bury her. When I came down from the stage, I overheard one lady say that she thought I didn't know what I was talking about, that it could not have been that bad. From then on, I just kept quiet."

As his story unfolded I came to know more about this critical period of his life: the complete uprooting of an adolescent boy and his long and dangerous journey to adulthood. I came to admire his resilient spirit and realized how the love and example of his elders, together with his deep religious convictions, had given him a firm foundation and prepared him to endure and grow as a human being in the face of adversity until finally he was able to find that inner peace which follows acceptance.

I first met Hank in 1975 when I was in practice as a general surgeon in a small town in northern Michigan. Since both he and I came from the "old country," many of our interests coincided. We both gardened, talked about fruit trees, and exchanged flowers and bulbs. Hank was particularly helpful with my home projects, not only by freely dispensing advice but also by loaning me books and giving me ready access to any of his tools. Both of us were intrigued by the usefulness of many plants and often talked about edibles from the wild.

"Dandelions are not weeds," Hank once said. "You can batter the blossoms and deep-fry them. They also make good wine. The leaves make excellent salad, and you can brown and grind the root for 'Ersatz' coffee."

"Isn't the sap poisonous?" I asked.

Hank did not think so. One of his relatives had put some dandelion sap on his warts. "His warts went away," Hank said with a chuckle. "Even the sap must be good for something."

It took me some time to fully appreciate the significance of Hank's, and also Mary Lou's, interest in nature's gifts. Even as a child in Poland Hank and his family had used them extensively; during his time in Siberia, they became a matter of survival. Mary Lou, too, had grown up in a family where hunting, fishing, and the pursuit of edibles from the wild had been an integral part of their lifestyle. While in this respect Hank and Mary Lou were the active participants, I simply remained an interested observer.

After Hank retired from his work as an aircraft mechanic, he and Mary Lou went to live among the maple- and aspen-clad rolling hills of the northern part of the lower peninsula of Michigan. The great bridge, which spans the Mackinac Straits and marks the junction between Lake Michigan to the west and Lake Huron to the east, is not far, nor are the historic fort of Michillimackinac and the tourist attractions of Mackinac Island.

Their home stands at the end of a road, in front of an old apple orchard, and next to the homestead of Mary Lou's parents. Where the road ends young maple trees grow thickly, and beyond the apple orchard the land trails off into the thicket of a cedar swamp. Deer are regular visitors, and the proximity of the woods provides cover to a host of birds. These feathered friends throng the bird feeders in winter; in summer, they flutter and chirp among the branches in the cool mornings and the long evening hours of this country north of the 45th degree latitude. Between their home, the garden, and the woods stand several sheds for Hank's garden implements, his wood-crafting sets, and his machine tools—ready witnesses to the wide range of interests and the expertise of their owner.

The center of the yard is dominated by a house trailer. I first stepped inside its cramped space on a cold day, and my bulky jacket forced me to squeeze past showcases filled with belt buckles, chains, and pendants cut and polished from minerals and semi-precious stones. A narrow corridor between boxes of uncut stones led to a workshop full of lapidary tools: a diamond saw, drills, polishing wheels, and tumblers. This was Hank's main work area where he plied his craft. He had been well prepared for this line of work by his training as a silversmith in the Polish orphanage in Mexico and later by his years of tending to sensitive and delicate machinery as an aircraft mechanic. It both suited his creativity and aptly matched his inclination. "I always liked to work with my hands," he said. Mary Lou had introduced him to this medium. "I was a rock hound when I was younger," she said.

I readily empathized with Hank's comment. As a surgeon I also "worked with my hands." It was another sign of our kinship, as was our mutual enjoyment of liberal helpings of homemade sauerkraut, Polish sausage, and pierogi served at lunch time "dinner"—for Hank, still the main meal of the day; and for me, a reminder of my "Old World" youth.

Moreover, I shared his interest in rocks and minerals, an interest that I owe to another friend of long ago with whom I began to analyze field stones from among the nearby glacial deposits. We even obtained maps and instructions from the Canadian Bureau of Mining where to prospect for gold in the wilds of northern Ontario. When we got there, however, our interest in prospecting dissipated rather quickly. We had come to the end of a gravel road and climbed an isolated rock for a better view of the country we were to traverse. The desolate landscape and the dense cloud of mosquitoes swirling around us dissuaded us quite convincingly from any further pursuit of riches yet buried in the ground. We gladly, and quite quickly, decided to return to our respective occupations. But the intense preparations for that adventure allowed me to imagine the deep purple of polished amethyst when holding a raw crystal and together with Hank glory in the fine dendrite inclusions in a slab of moss agate. Yet, as with the foods from the wild, the doctor remained the interested observer while the artist applied his hands to the material.

Years ago, during one of my earliest visits, Hank showed me a coffee mill made from an artillery shell casing. We were sitting and talking when Hank suddenly got up and retrieved a coffee mill from among his books on a shelf. "This was made from a 50 millimeter artillery shell casing, probably from the First World War," was his only explanation at the time. I was impressed with its workmanship, especially the gears for fine and coarse grind and by the tight fit of its bottom cap. It reminded me of a Turkish coffee mill my mother had, a gift from someone. I remembered its ornate engravings and how difficult it was to grind the coffee. To do so I always had to squeeze the mill tightly between my knees. Now, years later, as we began to delve into Hank's past, I finally learned about the history and the deep personal significance of Hank's home-made coffee mill.

Old shells and ammunition, even unexploded ones, were buried in the fields around Hank's childhood home, a violently contested area of Poland during the First World War known as Eastern Galicia. The place of origin of the coffee mill reminded me of a painting I had seen as a boy. It was called "Winter in Galicia," and its mood of desolation had etched it permanently into my memory. The painting portrayed a field gun, a group of soldiers, and some horses standing forlorn and wind-blown in drifting snow surrounded by a bleak snow-covered landscape. Like the painting, the coffee mill embodied a piece of history of that region and had a profound relationship to a significant period in Hank's life.

After the First World War it was quite common for a farmer to plow up pieces of old military equipment and ammunition. In this way the well-preserved artillery shell casing had found its way into the hands of one of Hank's uncles, a railroad mechanic, who turned it into a coffee mill and presented it as a gift to Hank's parents for their wedding. Eventually Hank became its owner. Together with a couple of photographs of his parents that he had managed to preserve, this coffee

Coffee mill made from a 50-millimeter artillery shell casing,
probably from World War I.

mill was the only tangible link to his childhood. It also had been vital
to his survival in Siberia.

Galicia once encompassed the entire area of southern Poland and
the western part of the Ukraine. Its eastern part, also known as
Malopolska Wschodnia, had a very turbulent history. In 1349, when
the Polish king annexed Galicia to Poland, Roman Catholicism and
the Polish language and institutions were introduced and the Polish
gentry became the ruling class. After the first partition of Poland
(1772), as well as after the second (1793) and third (1795), Galicia
came under the rule of the Austrian Hapsburg monarchy until 1918.
Poland did regain its independence briefly after the first partition. Its
constitution, the first in Europe and second in the world after
America's, was written on May 3, 1791.

Eastern Galicia bore the brunt of the fighting in the First World
War. In 1914 the Russian army conquered it; the Austrians recaptured
it in 1915. After that it was Russia's turn again, this time with its
newly-organized Red Army (the Polish-Soviet war of 1920-21). The
fighting over Lwow was particularly fierce and exhausting. The
regional capital during the Austrian rule, this ancient city was also an
economic, cultural, and educational center and was close to the passes
through the Carpathian Mountains. The turmoil of war had spread to

Krasne and its surroundings. The advent of the railroads had made Krasne an important railroad junction with one line continuing east into Russia, the other going south into Romania. When Hank was growing up many of the people in Krasne earned their livelihood directly or indirectly from its extensive railroad installations.

This turbulent history influenced the political and social climate of the region around Hank's birthplace well into the 20th century. It gave rise to the political upheavals and ethnic strife so common in Europe despite the progress of civilization and enlightenment.

By the end of the 19th century the Polish influence in Eastern Galicia had become well-established and had resulted in the formation of a Polish aristocracy. The landowners were mostly Poles; the peasants were predominantly of Ukrainian descent.

Although serfdom had been abolished in the wake of the unsuccessful revolutions of 1848-49, many of the Ukrainian former serfs remained in the employ of the Polish landowners. The large Jewish community consisted mostly of middle-class shopkeepers and managers. This social stratification served to heighten the national and religious differences. The subsequent political unrest was aggravated further when, after the First World War, this area was acquired by Poland and the Polish government began to Polonize it by a land-reform policy that encouraged colonization by Polish military veterans.

The Polish people were traditionally anti-German, but also anti-Russian and, since the rise of communism, anti-Bolshevik. In addition, due to the large Ukrainian population in this area, Polish-Ukrainian relations had always been strained. The more radically minded Ukrainians were strongly opposed to the Polish rule and yearned for national independence and the reunification of all Ukrainian lands. To achieve these objectives they formed the illegal Ukrainian Military Organization (UVO) in 1920 which in 1929 became the military arm of the Organization of Ukrainian Nationalists (OUN). Both organizations engaged in acts of terror against the Polish government and people. Poland, in turn, established a concentration camp near Lwow where many of them wound up along with the communists. Meanwhile, Polish administrators continued to discriminate against

Ukrainians in employment and other areas treating them often as second-class citizens.

As I delved deeper into Hank's upbringing and his childhood, the circumstances and details of his deportation to Siberia, and his subsequent journey to America, I became aware not only of the many similarities but also of the essential differences in our formative years and our early teens.

We both grew up among concerned and loving parents and relatives who provided for our physical and psychological well-being. We both soon asserted ourselves and readily gained independence. For both of us the last few years before the war were years of innocence in the comfort of close family relationships, full of the joy of discovery, and of visits to friends and relatives. We were without any apprehension for the future. The differences in lifestyle occasioned by the differences in the income levels of our parents and families were purely external, as was the fact that Hank had been raised in the country whereas I grew up in the city.

My father was a sought-after pediatrician in a German provincial capital, and my relatives were independent business people. We went for Sunday drives and vacationed every year for two weeks at the seashore. Our social life centered on the immediate family, our close relatives, and my parents' few friends. It was the life of a well-to-do bourgeoisie with all its social trappings: afternoon teas for my mother's lady friends in the garden, Sunday excursions for coffee and cake with my grandparents, or an evening of beer and *Braetle*—charcoal-roasted pork loin—for the men.

Hank's family came from a farming background, and although as a policeman in a small community his father was a person of respect and authority, their economic independence and security demanded that gardening and small-scale farming fill their spare time. The family, with its small circle of friends, and their extended family were close knit, particularly on Hank's mother's side. All participated in the social life of the village which revolved around the religious holidays and the harvest and its festivals. In the basic aspects of life and in the enjoyment of family and friends there were no essential differences between Hank's family and mine.

Although our paths diverged radically with the onset of our teens, we still shared some common attitudes. For example, we both took responsibility for ourselves early: Hank, the older of two children, not only had to look after himself at the age of thirteen but also after his sister; I, being a little more than two years older, assumed responsibility for myself with the onset of the war and the induction of my father into the German Navy. Before the war ended, I was also accepted to its medical officer's curriculum.

Well aware of the shadows on the political horizon, our parents wanted to protect us from the upheavals of the world of our youth. During Hank's childhood political subjects were not mentioned in front of the children. In my family, including my extended family, political events, be it for or against the prevailing politics, were likewise never discussed.

As a child, Hank therefore remained blissfully unaware of the political currents of the day. Due to my parents' silence, I, in contrast, was exposed to the glitter of the fools gold of Nazi propaganda. Painted in glorious colors and proclaimed in official language, it did not stimulate any critical thought in a boy my age, though at times certain inconsistencies in the various pronouncements made me wonder. My doubts, however, never went beyond raising questions, the real answers to which I never pursued. After the war, in answer to my remonstrations, my father replied: "We saw no sense in bringing you up against the Nazi regime. After all, it looked at that time that you may have to spend your life under it." At the same time he told me why, ever since I had turned fourteen in 1940, he had been so insistent that I study medicine: "You were our only child. In case we would lose the war or you were taken prisoner your chances to survive would have been best in the medical corps." My father took pride in being a very practical man.

Around the age of ten, an age when children become conscious of a world beyond their families, a world where by choice, by circumstance, or by compulsion they begin to participate in the events of the day, our lives, Hank's and mine, took a completely different track. From that age on Hank first had to live under the constant threat to his survival in the Soviet system, and later, he had to cope not only with the loss of his childhood home but also of his family. I, on the contrary, enjoyed a certain freedom purchased by my own and my parents' acceptance of the political realities of Hitler's National-Socialism which by then, however, had already lost its "socialism." By the time I was ten years old in 1936, my friends and I were exposed to nothing but a blatant and increasingly violent nationalism and militarism.

Hank and I also traveled on different paths spiritually. From early on Hank had a deep and unwavering religious faith which has stayed with him throughout his life, a feeling that I have been unable to experience. My parents never expressed any religious sentiments; my extended family participated only minimally in religious practices. Hank's father, a son of Polish farmers, came from a Roman Catholic family and was a man of strong religious convictions. Hank's mother, though she converted to Roman Catholicism at the time of her marriage, had been brought up in the Greek Orthodox faith by her family, and her religious convictions were as strong as those of her parents. The firmness of Hank's belief was not only a source of strength for him, particularly during the time of his deportation, it also shaped his attitude toward other people from childhood onward. This attitude was reinforced by the living example of his parents and by his experiences in Siberia. It expressed itself in a strong sense of justice in which bigotry and intolerance played no part.

Over the centuries the southeastern part of Poland, the home of Hank's extended family, had been the scene of bitter religious confrontations. (The Polish population there was almost exclusively Roman Catholic, while most of the Ukrainians followed the Greek Catholic or Uniate faith.) In time however, and despite local frictions and sporadic clashes, an uneasy modus vivendi had been established in this area, that is until the Soviets and later the Nazis rekindled the old hatreds and initiated their policies of ethnic cleansing on a large scale.

Despite the many rigid attitudes and prejudices of this period people still intermarried, and the marital union of Hank's parents, like that of so many others, served as a living example of a possible ethnic, religious, and social commingling. His parents lived on the border of two different and at times opposing societies. Hank witnessed his parents straddle this precarious boundary, and they in turn fostered that spirit of tolerance in him by word and deed. It manifested itself, for example, in the selection of Hank's playmates and in their dealings and relationships with people of different faiths or ethnic backgrounds. This non-judgmental attitude and the love his parents bore for their children were an essential part of Hank's seemingly blissful childhood.

From early on Hank also became aware of the disadvantages of this "life at the border." It affected his father's career (he never received his well-deserved promotion) and it blighted the relationship with his father's parents who rejected their son's "Ukrainian" family. Consequently Hank knew little about his paternal grandparents.

During my own childhood the official racial hatred preached by the Nazis had fortunately never been reinforced at home nor in school. This, just as the silence concerning the politics of the time, was due to acts of omission by my parents and teachers and not, as in Hank's case, by a conscious effort to teach respect and tolerance for the individual regardless of his or her ethnic or cultural origin.

The increasingly vicious official position in Germany toward the Jewish and other ethnic groups was never supported in the circle of my family and relatives: on my father's side because of his liberal inclinations and his parents' many former business acquaintances; on my mother's side because of past business relationships and a long-standing contact with the art world. I have a nebulous recollection from early childhood of a personal friendship between my parents and a Jewish banking family who suddenly left town. Nevertheless, my parents and relatives, at least outwardly, seemed to accommodate themselves to the official Nazi line and kept silent.

Even in school, a place where our nationalist and militarist heritage was actively promoted and where anti-Semitism and similar prejudicial attitudes were supposed to be stressed in the curriculum, our teachers —with one notable exception—avoided these subjects. Our biology teacher, for instance, who should have been at the forefront of racial teaching, limited his comments to the so-called distinguishing physical characteristics of races by contrasting the "blue-eyed, slender, tall Nordic" type with the "dark-haired, shorter, brown-eyed Mediterranean" type—a type which became more and more acceptable as Germany's involvement with Fascist Italy deepened. He never commented, however, on any of their alleged personality and character differences. The teacher who was the exception manifested such blatant anti-Semitism that he became our laughingstock, and we intentionally tried to provoke him on this topic at every turn. At times he got so carried away by the subject that he would forget to check our assignments and home work.

After the war, when the atrocities committed by my countrymen in the name of national supremacy and racial superiority became known, I was filled with an overwhelming urge to dissociate myself from the country of my birth and its people, including my relatives. I had to struggle with the "collective guilt of the German people." I felt betrayed as I came to realize that my youthful idealism had been abused. Doris Lessing once said most aptly that people's political complacency brought Hitler to power, while the thoughts and actions of the socially active and concerned put Stalin in his position. And so I blamed my parents and their generation for their lack of vision, their lack of foresight, and their complacency. For years I tried to deny my roots.

Only after I realized that *any* totalitarian system or radical creed can breed terror, inhumanity, and cruelty, have I been able to reconcile myself to my German heritage. The history of the world since the Second World War is filled with examples of genocide and willful extermination. We know only too well that even in our American society elements exist that would not shrink from using terror to achieve their aims. We still carry the burden of segregation. Have we forgotten that eugenics and the false ideals of "racial purity" and of the "supremacy of the Nordic race"—commonly attributed to Hitler—had been actively espoused in the United States and England by leading scientists and legislators for decades before Hitler came to power; and that in this country thousands were sterilized in the name of those "ideals"?

Though Hank was spared this inner turmoil that plagued me for years, he, despite the Allied victory, had to cope with the permanent loss of his home and his family, and he and his sister were faced with carving out new lives for themselves 5,000 miles from their native soil in an unknown and, at times, strange country.

Is it an irony of fate or is it, rather, an affirmation of the true spirit of the American way of life that Hank and I were able to establish a close relationship in this country, having grown up in Europe under two antagonistic regimes, a scant 600 miles from each other, but at that time worlds apart?

For both of us the Second World War started on a sunny day at about the same time, but while Hank heard the screaming of falling bombs and cowered before their explosions, I was sitting with my mother at breakfast listening to Hitler's harangue about "Poland's sudden and unprovoked attack on Germany." I remember his words: "As of 4:45 in the morning we are shooting back." I also remember that the announcer described Hitler as wearing a *new* uniform of plain, unadorned field gray, and that I could not reconcile this with a "sudden and unprovoked attack by Poland" because it seemed to me that it would usually take a week or so to make a new uniform. I was unaware then, that early in 1939 Hitler had already signed the directive for "Operation White," the war on Poland.

The war on Poland had been Germany's response to its failed attempts to induce the Polish government to engage in a joint action against the Soviet Union. Germany had tried to do this from as early as 1935—Hitler had consolidated his power by then—until the beginning of 1939. The Polish government, however, had consistently refused to cooperate with these German plans and to break the Polish-Soviet Non-Aggression Pact of 1932 which had been extended in 1934 until December of 1945.

3.

A Boy's Eden

⌐

H ank's world in Krasne was a child's Eden—literally a land of milk and honey: honey from his uncle's bees; milk from their own cow. His Eden had everything a growing boy needed including adequate shelter and freedom from want. Though not rich in material things, he was secure in the love and affection of his family and grounded in an accepted and established religion. He had the opportunity to develop, to eagerly pursue experiences, and to test himself under the watchful but tolerant eyes of his parents. His love of new challenges made him explore, try different things. He was eager to "do things on his own," and he cherished his success all the more when it justified the trust his parents had put in him.

Hank was born Henryk Birecki on March 8, 1929 in Krasne, *powiat Zloczow, wojewodztwo Tarnopolskie* (Zloczow county, Tarnopol province) in southeastern Poland. Later, at his confirmation, he adopted the middle name Joseph. When Hank was five years old his sister Romana was born.

Krasne, a village, had two butcher shops, two bakeries, and a grocery store which was always filled with the smell of kerosene and herring. A fenced-in lumberyard occupied a large space next to the tracks near the railroad station. Hank often stood by its entrance and watched the steam engine drive a gang of saws and turn the logs into lumber. He was captivated by the chugging of the engine in rhythm with the whine of the saws going up and down through the big logs, by the rushing drive belts, and by the big, spinning flywheel. Across the road from the lumberyard was the village hall where assemblies, dances, and plays were held. Hank received his religious instructions there, and ever since he was small he went there with his parents to a party on Christmas Eve. This hall also served as an armory for the Polish National Guard.

The Catholic church where Hank and his parents attended religious services was not far from the railroad station. It stood in an old cemetery, and an ancient chapel was further back among the graves. The chapel was locked, but through the windows Hank had seen gravestones on its floor and along the walls. "They are old family graves," his father explained to him. The village Orthodox church was just a few blocks away.

In the center of the village was an open grassy area with a shallow pond. The police station looked out on it. Nearby was the tavern. There were no market days in Krasne; the nearest market town was Busk, about five miles away. There, every weekday was market day, and his parents went to Busk for such needs as clothing or hardware. Except for the police station and the railroad installations the village had no electricity; in the evenings people lit their homes with kerosene lamps.

In winter, when the pond froze, Hank and the other children skated or slid on the ice. Early one spring, when the ice was breaking up and had already split into several large floes, Hank tried to get across by jumping from floe to floe. Unfortunately he slipped and fell in. His father, who was watching him from the police station and saw him fall into the icy water, helped him out and quickly brought him to the station. Hank trembled, as much from the cold as from fear of the expected scolding or worse, but his father was not angry. He stripped

Hank of his wet clothes and wrapped him in a blanket. "You learned something today, didn't you?" he admonished his son.

A small river, the Gotogorka, flowed through the village. A grist-mill stood on its bank upstream from the railroad bridge. The mill dam channeled the flow of water toward the water-driven wheel and formed the millpond. People fished there.

Krasne had become important because of the railroad. One of Hank's uncles, the husband of his mother's sister, worked there in the switching tower. His house stood just across the road from the large switching yard, only a few blocks' walk from Hank's home. The road, his uncle's yard, and those of others nearby were covered with slag which lay in heaps along the tracks. Hank liked to stop at his uncle's house; his aunt always had a treat for him. His favorite was a soft chocolate cream covered with lemon sauce. After visiting his aunt Hank often continued on across the many tracks to the switching tower to visit his uncle at work.

Hank liked to look out from the switching tower high above the tracks and watch the trains come and go: passenger trains to and from Lwow, long freight trains on their way east toward Tarnopol and Kiev, and those heading south into Romania. A big blackboard on the wall above rows of levers indicated where the trains were coming from, their time of arrival, and which track they would be using. The levers controlled the switches.

"These levers connect to long cables," Hank's uncle had once explained to him and pointed through the window. "See the boards next to the tracks? The cables run underneath them. If I pull on a lever, the cable moves the switch."

Sometimes his uncle threw several switches in succession and a locomotive went back and forth pushing freight cars from one siding onto another. At other times an engine might chug over the turntable tracks coming from the big round house, piles of coal and the water tower nearby. Sometimes Hank could see the switch move as his uncle pulled its lever. The mechanism fascinated him, and he admired his uncle for knowing just which lever to pull.

Whenever Hank saw one of the big locomotives roll past the switching tower, belching smoke and steam hissing from the piston casings, he dreamt of someday riding on a train all the way to Gdansk on the Baltic sea as his uncle and aunt had done. But Hank did go by train to Lwow to shop with his mother and to Zloczow, about thirty miles east of Krasne, to visit an aunt, his father's sister. To be on a train was exciting, was to lose all sense of time. Hank loved train travel.

On one of his visits to Lwow with his mother, he saw a toy tank in a department store. A wind-up mechanism made it run, and a friction wheel threw sparks as it rolled along. Hank was more intrigued, however, by its mechanism than by the idea of the military power it portrayed. That he should become a witness to this power never entered his mind at that time. Yet it was to become reality only a few years later and only a few blocks from his own home. Unfortunately the toy was too expensive. Hearing about his disappointment one of his uncles made him a toy tank from a spool of thread, two matches, and a rubber band. As the rubber band unwound, the little spool moved forward and scampered over the obstacles placed in its way just as well as any store-bought toy tank.

Hank went on his longest train ride when the whole family visited distant friends. In Krasne his family had formed a close bond of friendship with the family of the police chief, who had been transferred to a town on a lake. Hank and their son Joseph, who was Hank's age, also got along very well. Next to Duszko, a neighbor's son, Hank considered Joseph a trusted friend. On this visit the families went for walks along the lake and on picnics. Hank and Joseph roamed the broken walls and towers of an old castle and paddled in kayaks around the lake. Hank also took his sister, then about four years old, for a kayak ride. He enjoyed paddling about the lake with her, but he felt especially pleased that his father trusted him with her. As they roamed the walls of the ancient ruin, as they floated in the kayaks among the cattails in the lake, both boys were blissfully unaware that only a few years hence and under circumstances then unthinkable they were to have a brief and sad reunion.

The railroad, its installations, and the station house with its surroundings formed the background for some of Hank's early recollections. These memories helped to ease the pain of later years during the war and deportation when the railroad also became the focal point of his experiences. For Hank the station house and its environs became both the symbol of his national pride and of Poland's later defeat.

To get to the station house Hank had to pass his uncle's home and take the road parallel to the tracks then cross them on a bridge. The station house had a waiting room and a restaurant. At a kiosk one could buy newspapers and books. Some of the books, however, could be borrowed for a fee, and his father generously permitted him to take out any number of them. Every so often his father went to the kiosk to settle Hank's account.

In front of the station house was a ramp with a long hitching rail for horses. Many people still came by horse-drawn wagon or carriage and usually several fiacres were lined up as taxis waiting for passengers. Only a few cars were yet on the roads and, unused to their presence, many horses were often spooked by a passing car. Once, when a tethered horse shied and tried to jump up onto the ramp, its traces became entangled in the hitching rail. The horse suddenly collapsed and lay snorting. In vain it tried to get on its feet; it had broken its forelegs. Hank was just walking toward the station with his mother when he saw a policeman bend over the fallen horse, pull out his revolver, and shoot the struggling animal. Hank started to cry, but his mother explained that the horse's legs would never heal and that to shoot it was the kindest way to end its suffering quickly.

On the ramp stood a hand pump for drinking water. Hank was still quite small when he happened to see a man step up to the pump, start the flow of water, and then proceed to take out his dentures. Hank was aghast. He had never seen anyone take their teeth out of their mouth, and he awaited anxiously the big gush of blood he was sure to follow. To Hank's surprise, the man rinsed off his dentures, pushed them back into his mouth, and walked off.

Across the road from the station was a small park. It had a pond with a bridge leading to an island in the center on which stood a bandstand. Every year on May 3, the Polish Constitution Day, people joined in a parade which began in the village, passed the station ramp, and ended on the island. There, someone gave a speech, others recited poetry, and the army band from nearby Busk gave a concert. Hank was too young to join in the parade even after he became a Cub Scout, but he always stood in the crowd and watched.

On May 12, 1935, Marshal Jozef Pilsudski, beloved by many as the hero of Polish independence, died. On this official day of mourning, post stamps with his picture surrounded by a black border were issued and special Masses were celebrated. Plans were made for a monument in his memory to be built with soil from all parts of Poland. Hank saw wagons full of soil being driven toward the station from the villages around Krasne and loaded on a special train.

Hank's home, located a little north of the village, fronted the road between Krasne and Busk. Several years earlier his father had bought an unfinished house and had it transported to this site. Between the road and the house ran a narrow-gauge rail track that began at a large estate near Busk. In the fall, iron-wheeled, horse-drawn carts brought produce from the estate, mainly sugar beets, along the tracks to the railroad station. Next to the tracks was a three-foot-deep ditch. Often sugar beets fell off the overloaded wagons and landed in the ditch or on the road. Hank helped to salvage them as fodder for their cow. A fence of whitewashed boards with a large gate for wagons and a small one for people separated the front garden and the house from the road. Planks, partly covered with sod, crossed the ditch in front of the gates.

Hank's mother had two garden plots. She grew her flowers and early vegetables in front, between the house and the fence. A larger garden for potatoes, corn, and cucumbers was behind the house on the other side of the yard. Both his mother and father tended the gardens, and Hank helped pick the produce. They grew most of their vegetables and stored in the root cellar what they could not can or use fresh. Once a year, in late fall, Hank's father hired someone to plow the garden.

Hank's favorite vegetables were fresh, ripe cucumbers. He loved to eat them right out of the patch. When he was old enough, his mother would give him a knife, salt, and pepper, and he sat down in the ankle-deep patch and ate as many as he wished. A few of the smaller cucumbers were placed into a bottle while they were still on the vine. They continued to grow, and when they filled the bottle they were broken off their vines. A small amount of alcohol was put into the bottle, lit, and the bottle was quickly corked and sealed with paraffin. The bottled cucumbers stayed fresh until Christmas when they were served as a special treat. But nothing was wasted. Before she served the bottled cucumbers, Hank's mother encircled the bottles at the base of their necks with a heavy string soaked in kerosene, set it on fire, and after it had burned off, poured cold water over the bottles. The bottles cracked at the hot spot, and she saved their wide bases as jars for jellies and jams.

Raspberries grew on the side of the house; gooseberry and currant bushes stood adjacent to the driveway. Hank always helped pick the berries.

Even when Hank was still too small to help, he liked to watch his father and the other grown-ups at their work, be it in field, garden, or house. He was allowed to look on when his father made whitewash, but had to keep his distance from the caustic lime. In the first year his father dug a pit in the clayey ground and filled it with burned lime. He covered the lime with soil and left it undisturbed until the following year. By that time it had turned into a thick pasty material which could be either dissolved in water and used as whitewash or left undiluted to plaster the wooden lath which spanned the frame of the house.

Hank looked at trees, particularly fruit trees, from the perspective peculiar to children: how well they were suited for climbing. In the center of their garden stood a pear tree which Hank liked to climb. Two cherry trees stood near the house, but their trunks were too weak to be serious contenders. Hank's favorite cherry tree grew in the nearby yard of his uncle among his apple and pear trees; its cherries were particularly sweet. Though it had a tall and branchless trunk, Hank's cousin had taught him how to climb it. "Make a loop out of your belt, stretch it across the trunk, and put your feet into it on each side. Then lean back and, while you hold the trunk tight with your arms, push against the belt as hard as you can," he told Hank.

Hank followed his instructions. He cradled the trunk in his arms and pulled himself up. He then brought up his feet in the loops of the belt and, pushing the belt hard against the trunk, moved his arms higher. This worked well on the way up, and the cherries tasted delicious. On the way down, however, his belt slipped, and he slid down the trunk skinning his legs rather badly. Though he was not discouraged from climbing after the cherries again, their taste stayed linked to the smarting of his legs.

Quite a bit older, his cousin was always willing to show Hank something new. He studied bridge-building at the technical university in Lwow, and Hank was impressed by the big drawing board in his room. Earlier, while still in high school, he let Hank play with his toys or watch as he built his model airplanes in the big, unused attic of their barn. He had a younger sister, also older than Hank, and both taught Hank how to read before he started school.

If one faced Hank's home from the road, the drive leading to the yard was on its left; both the drive and the yard were covered with grass and slag. A field beyond the drive was part of the property. It stretched for about half a mile from the road, and a small stream ran through it.

The well was just across the drive from the house, its opening reinforced by a cement culvert which extended about three feet above the ground and just as far down through the topsoil. Deeper, no lining was needed since the solid clay beneath the topsoil gave sufficient support. After Hank had become strong enough to carry a full pail, his mother often asked him to fetch the water. He drew the water with a bucket hanging by a rope from a crank above the well and filled the pail from it.

Bath day was every two weeks. A wooden tub was pulled out, big enough to hold a chair, and filled with water. At one time, when Hank was sick with a fever and aches and the local doctor seemed to be unable to help him, Hank's father called on a folk healer from another village. She lived some distance away and was an older lady who never revealed the herbal secrets of her trade. She made Hank sit in the tub and hung a blanket over him. Then she asked his mother to put a hot brick into the bottom of the tub, sprinkled herbs around it, and had her pour warm water over the brick. Hank soon felt better after this homemade steam bath.

The house was rectangular without a basement. A wooden floor covered the joists. His parent's bedroom and an unfinished room faced the road. The entrance to the house, the kitchen, and two more rooms looked toward the yard. The short entrance hall led straight into the kitchen, and the chimney and the summer oven formed part of the wall of the adjoining bedroom.

The kitchen was not only the place for cooking and baking but also where they ate and carried out the other activities of the day. It had an oak dining table and several chairs. A brick stove and range with a metal top were built against the chimney which gave off enough heat to also warm the bedroom even in winter. On extremely cold nights Hank's mother would wrap a hot brick in a towel and put it under their bedcovers before going to bed. Although a fireplace was in the bedroom, it was hardly ever used.

The oven in the kitchen was large enough for Hank's mother to bake a dozen pie-sized loaves of bread at one time. She let the dough rise in woven straw baskets which she then turned over onto a short-handled peel. She removed the basket and used the peel to place the dough directly on the brick lining of the stove. Before she baked bread she would build a wood fire in the stove. When the bricks were hot enough, she swept the embers aside leaving only a thin layer of ash on the bricks to prevent the dough from sticking. A smaller bake oven for cakes and cookies was built into the chimney above the stove.

A doorway connected the kitchen with the bedroom where Hank slept with his parents in a wide bed. After his sister was born, Hank had to give up his spot in his parents' bed, and every evening a bed was made up for him in the kitchen. Like Hank, his sister was born at home. When the time came for the delivery, he was sent to stay at his uncle's house and told he would soon have a little brother or sister.

The family slept on a layer of straw covered with a linen sheet. Goose down filled the covers and pillows. The bed frame was off the floor, high enough for Hank to crawl underneath. Once, when Hank was still small, he slept late, got tangled in the bed sheets, and slid under the bed where he tried to hide. His mother played along and pretended she could not find him, then feigned surprise when he finally crawled out.

At the foot of the bed stood a table and against one wall a large wardrobe, both of solid oak like the bed. The furniture had been a wedding gift from Hank's mother's parents who had the carpenter in Zuratyn build it from lumber cut from their own trees. When her parents had married, they planted a grove of young oak trees behind their house. At the time of Hank's parents' wedding the trees had grown large enough to provide the lumber not only for the furniture in the bedroom but also for the dining table and the chairs in the kitchen.

On the other side of the hall, opposite the kitchen, was a storage room with another room behind it. It had an extra bed where Hank's grandparents slept when they came to visit. From there, a pull-down ladder gave access to the large attic. On rainy days Hank often climbed into the attic and, surrounded by the smell of the smoked sausages and hams hanging from the rafters, sat among the boxes and sacks of wheat and flour and listened to the rain drum on the metal roof. He enjoyed the snugness and peacefulness of his seclusion, and the steady sound of the falling rain gave it an added aura of solitude and timelessness. He looked at pictures in old magazines, and later, after he learned how to read, he took a book with him. Although Hank liked to play with other children and enjoyed their company, he also cherished the time when he could be just by himself. To be able to find pleasure in solitude was the beginning of Hank's sense of independence, a trait which was to deepen and contribute to his resourcefulness.

Hank's father worked on the unfinished front room only as time and money permitted. For the time being he let Hank keep some of his animals in it. Animals had been a part of Hank's life ever since he was small. His maternal grandfather knew of Hank's love of animals. Wild canaries fluttered in large numbers in the fields, and he caught some of them for Hank with snares he had made from horsehair. Hank kept them in the unfinished room for a day or two in a wicker cage his cousin had built for him and gave them water and grain. But he soon felt sorry for the little birds and let them go. For a time he also kept a hedgehog there. His grandfather had picked it up in the wild, and it proved to be a very good mouser.

Hank's parents, too, encouraged his love for animals. He learned early to treat them well and that they were a responsibility. "You feed the animals before you eat" was a rule he lived by. His first animal was a puppy. Hank was still small when his father bought it for him, and his mother often carried it in her apron pocket from where its little head peeked out at Hank. They grew up together. Hank called it "Migran," a name without any meaning; he just liked the sound of it. It followed him to school and waited for him until school was out. It also made friends with their cat. Both slept curled up together, and when the dog went outside the cat ran after it or mewed until the dog came back in. Once, when a neighbor's dog strayed into the yard, the little dog attacked it, and the cat jumped on its back. Together they chased the other dog away. The cat, a big tom with white fur, had Persian blood, and quite a few white kittens with long hair roamed about the neighborhood.

Besides the hedgehog and the wild canaries, his grandfather also once brought him a pet crow. Hank never caged it. He fed it grain, and it just stayed around. When Hank slept late and the window was open, the crow would fly in and peck at his face until he woke up and fed it.

Hank was five years old when his parents acquired a German Shepherd as a family guard dog. They called it Rex. Both the shepherd and the little dog followed Hank everywhere. Once Hank went swimming and pretended to be in trouble by splashing around and shouting as if he needed help. The Shepherd jumped in, grabbed him by his shorts and pulled him out; it did not let Hank back into the water again. From that time on Hank had to leave the dog in the house every time he wanted to go swimming. Just before the war someone poisoned Rex. Hank's father found the tainted bait.

At one time his parents gave Hank a year-old lamb. It was a ram, and as it grew older it started to butt him. When Hank teased it by trying to snort and to bleat, it became quite excited and aggressive. After it chased Hank on top of the fence and did not let him come down, its role as a playmate ended. Hank never found out what his father did with it.

His grandfather had told him how foxes hunt hedgehogs: "Hedgehogs curl up when they think they are in danger, so the fox rolls them into water. The hedgehog must uncurl to swim, and this gives the fox a chance to get at its soft underbelly."

His grandfather's favorite fox story, however, was how a fox gets rid of fleas: "The fox takes a stick in its mouth and jumps into the water. Then all the fleas gather on the stick, and when the fox lets the stick go they float away with it."

Hank loved his grandfather's stories and all the tricks he taught him. One of them was how to get an egg into a bottle. "First you soak the egg in vinegar," he told Hank. "That softens its shell. Then you put some alcohol into the bottle and light it. As quick as you can, you set the softened egg on top of the bottle. The alcohol will use up the air, and this draws the egg down into the bottle. Once the egg is at the bottom it takes on its usual shape."

Hank's father had planted a walnut tree between the driveway and the house. He told Hank: "If you want to grow seedlings from walnuts, you must first bury a flat rock or an old platter about a foot deep in the ground. When the walnuts sprout and the seedlings begin to grow, the rocks or platters stop the taproot from going too far down. In this way you won't disturb their roots when you transplant the seedlings. Walnut seedlings a foot high often have a tap root twice as long."

Behind the house and beyond the yard stood the barn and the chicken coop. Feeding the chickens was one of Hank's earliest tasks, although at first the basket with chicken feed was almost as large as he. Later, his mother let him also gather the eggs. When his parents had the German Shepherd, they put its house near the chicken coup. Hank's mother soon noticed that she found fewer eggs than usual. She discovered the reason for this when she saw Rex herd a chicken into the dog house to have it lay its eggs there. Evidently the dog had become fond of raw eggs.

Hank's parents also kept a cow that his mother milked twice a day. She put the day's milking on the stoop of the root cellar until the cream gathered on top. From this she churned her own butter. She let the skimmed milk sour, and when the whey separated she used it to make her own cottage cheese. Although she tried several times to show Hank how to milk, he was never able to milk the cow dry.

Hay for the winter was stored in the loft of the barn. Besides fodder for the cow, it was also a favorite place for Hank and his friends to jump and roll about and play hide-and-seek.

Hank, age four, feeding chickens.

The outhouse stood next to the barn behind the garden. To avoid the mud during rainy weather, Hank's father laid a row of planks across the garden to make a firm path to it.

In summer, a boy pastured the Birecki cow and four or five other people's cows in the village common, along the roadsides, and along railroad embankments. He was about twice Hank's age and belonged to one of the poorer families in the village. People paid him a few *groszy* (pennies) a day for his time. Hank was then about five years old. He brought the boy food and often tagged along. The boy showed Hank bird nests in the shrubs and bushes and taught him how to carve a whistle. Hank was impressed by what the boy knew and soon looked on him as a close friend. One day they found a large yellow flower growing along the railroad tracks. It did not look like a wildflower and they had no idea how it got there. The boy dug it up and brought it to Hank's mother who planted it in her front yard. It bloomed there every summer for several years.

Like her older sister who devoted her garden entirely to flowers, Hank's mother also enjoyed her flower garden. Flowers had been her love ever since she was a young girl. The owners of the estate where

Hank's mother, Filipina Demkow

she had worked knew of this and always remembered to bring her some special seeds from their travels, even after she was married. Like her singing—Hank's mother often sang while she worked—her love of flowers expressed a joyful nature that filled the house with beauty and grace and became for Hank another happy childhood memory.

Hank's mother, the younger of two sisters, was born Filipina Demkow and grew up in Zuratyn, a village a few miles north of Krasne. She was 21 years old when Hank was born. Tall and solidly built, she wore her brown hair in a single braid down her back. A picture from her railroad pass shows a young woman with a serious expression, her dark hair combed smoothly back from a high forehead.

Be it by example or with a few well placed words, Hank's parents surrounded him with an atmosphere of trust and guidance, which included respect for others and a deep compassion for the less fortunate. Hank's mother always had an open hand for the poor, the crippled, and the retarded, and they usually thanked her with the words: "I'll give you a prayer in return."

Since the boy who pastured the cows came from a poor family and his clothes were ragged, many of Hank's schoolmates ignored him; some even made fun of him. This upset Hank very much, and he told his mother about it. She made him see that it was wrong to look down upon those less favored by life. "Some don't realize they are people like us," she said.

Like so many children, however, Hank also had begun to mimic the thoughtlessness of some of his peers. When he once remarked how laughable a mentally handicapped person had behaved, his mother said firmly, "It's wrong to tease or to play pranks on these people. They always are 'Mr.' or 'Mrs.' to you." He never forgot her words.

New neighbors moved in next door when Hank was still in kindergarten. The father was a tinsmith and a sheet-metal worker, and the family belonged to the Seventh-Day Adventist church. Because of their different religion some people in the village shunned them and did not allow their children to play with the children of this family. Hank noticed this, but he also saw that they were readily welcomed in his own home. Soon they visited back and forth, played hide-and-seek in the barn, played ball, and swung on the swing Hank's father had built in the yard, a sturdy board suspended with ropes from a set of tripods. Their son Duszko, the same age as Hank, soon became his closest friend. They continued to play together and to explore the fields and meadows about the village until Hank's deportation.

As with many other things, Hank learned to swim by watching and imitating. The favorite swimming hole for the boys of the village was a widened part of the Gotogorka river where it flowed underneath the railroad bridge. While the other boys swam, Hank floated among them. He had improvised a float from his father's swimming trunks. Since they were far too big for him, he tied the legs shut with string. In the water, the trunks ballooned and helped him stay afloat. One day, however, when one of the strings snagged on a branch and pulled free, his trunks deflated and he lost his support. He tried the swimming motions he had seen the older boys do so many times before and was able to keep his head above water. Soon he was swimming. In the evening, when his father came home, Hank proudly told him: "I can swim." His father pretended to be unimpressed and only said, "Show me." Without any further comment he sat Hank on the frame of his bicycle and rode with him to the river. There they dismounted, and still without any further words, his father grabbed Hank with one hand by the seat of his pants and with the other by the collar and threw him into the water. Nevertheless, he stood on the bank and watched Hank's every move with concern. Satisfied that Hank could hold himself well above water, he motioned to him to swim to the bank and helped him climb out. They both stood for a while side by side; then his father stripped to his underclothes and they jumped in together.

After they swam for a while they rode home, still dripping wet. At home his father said: "All right, from now on you can go swimming by yourself."

As he grew older Hank helped out at home whenever the need arose. For example, he would clean the chimneys of the kerosene lamps or fetch the potatoes and carrots that lay buried in a pile of sand in one corner of the root cellar.

The root cellar was next to the barn. It was large and had a steel-reinforced cement ceiling. His father built it during the last years before the war. It had two doors with a stoop between them. If Hank's father had any thoughts about the storm clouds on the political horizon when he made the root cellar that sturdy, he never said so; nor did he talk in front of the children about what he heard on the little crystal radio he listened to every evening. Hank remained unaware of any of the fears for the future that pervaded the lives of many adults during those years. Liberal in their attitude toward others and intent on Hank's education, his parents also tried to be protective of his childhood. They kept from him those aspects of life which they could not influence, particularly the political issues and events of the day.

Hank's father turned the field next to the driveway into an orchard in preparation for his retirement. One of Hank's mother's cousins—Hank called him uncle—from Zuratyn who made his living raising fruit and honey, helped him with this. First, Hank's father planted the rootstocks he had obtained from the local forester. After they had taken root and grown sufficiently, they were ready for grafting. This was done during the cool days of early spring. The men cut off the tops of the rootstocks and applied the grafts. The grafts—apples, apricots, cherries, and pears—were special varieties this uncle had bought in Romania. Hank watched him shape and place the grafts using a very sharp knife. Then his father covered the junctions with a thick layer of clay. "Pit to seed and seed to pit," the uncle told Hank. After the grafts had taken, Hank's father replanted the young trees in even rows about thirty feet apart, enough space to plow in between. The trees grew well. The first crop of cherries ripened in the last summer before the war, and Hank was able to savor the first fruits from the young orchard.

Before Hank's father planted the orchard, the field had been sown with grain, usually wheat. Harvest time, much like the holidays, brought the community together. The neighbors helped each other going from field to field. Those whose field was being harvested played host and provided all the food for their guests. The men cut oats and barley with scythes; the women cut the wheat with sickles. Hank was told to stay out of the way of the scythes since he was yet small and could easily have gotten hurt. For the people of Hank's childhood, wheat represented more than just grain, flour, and bread. "Wheat is sacred," his mother said. "It is a gift from God. You should never let bread baked from wheat touch the ground." If someone dropped a slice of wheat bread, it was dusted off and eaten. It was never thrown away.

The cut grain was put into sheaves and the sheaves were stacked. The first sheaf was bent in the shape of a "U" and put down with the grain up. Several layers of sheaves, five to each layer, were piled around this one in a radial fashion also with the grain up. The stalks of the top sheaf were spread across the tops of the others to keep out the rain. Most people threshed their grain by machine during the winter. Hank's grandfather threshed his by hand with a flail: a wooden pole with a shorter flat piece of wood fastened to its end by a leather strap. His threshing floor was the hard and smooth clay floor in his barn. It was not easy to get the end of the flail to fall flat on the grain stalks, and Hank found it difficult to do. He admired the skill with which his grandfather handled this tool getting its end to fall just right time after time.

Once the work was done, harvest time became party time. The women served the food while people sang, chatted, or joked with each other. The potato harvest provided another such occasion. They dug the potatoes and heaped the dead stalks into piles to be burned. Hank and the other children helped gather the dried stalks and bring them to the fires. Potatoes were put into the hot embers until a thick black crust formed around them. If a potato was too hot to handle, Hank would juggle it from hand to hand until it cooled. He ate it dipped in sour milk or with salt and pepper.

Hank's parents did not keep a pig; there were not enough leftovers to feed one, and a pig could as easily be bought at the market. In the fall, Hank's family and relatives usually slaughtered a pig together. Much of the meat was turned into sausages and smoked. It was the simplest way to preserve it. When the sausages and hams were ready for smoking, a pit was dug in the yard. It was filled with cherry or apple wood which was then set on fire, and the pit with the burning wood was covered with sod. An upward-slanting covered trench, some ten to twenty feet in length, conducted the smoke to a barrel placed over its far opening. The sausages and hams hung from rods inside the top of the barrel and took two to three days to cure.

Hardly anyone kept rabbits since hundreds of them hopped about the fields around the village. Every fall people got together for a rabbit drive. They walked across the fields in rows about five feet apart, stirred up the rabbits from their burrows, and clubbed them to death when they emerged. The hunt usually yielded so many rabbits that they filled a farm wagon to capacity and hung down the sides. Whoever took part in the hunt received his share and divided it among his family, friends, and neighbors. Hank was still too young and could only trail along behind the others, but his older cousin was one of the hunters. Some boys hunted rabbits also in winter. They poked a stick into the rabbit hole, then clubbed the rabbit as it came out. Hank's mother used the rabbit meat mainly for meat loaf.

For breakfast Hank's family ate homebaked bread with their own homemade butter and jam. For bread Hank's mother used wheat; her mother, mainly rye flour. Hank and his sister drank milk, sometimes flavored with chocolate. The adults drank "coffee"—either real coffee mixed with chicory, or a mixture of roasted and ground wheat or barley with chicory. Chicory came in a stick in a red wrapper. One broke off a piece and dissolved it in the coffee or in the boiled grain mixture. To drink real coffee by itself was expensive, hence reserved for special occasions. On those occasions Hank's mother made coffee either from freshly-ground roasted beans that she bought or from green coffee beans which she roasted at home. Her coffee mill, the wedding gift from a brother-in-law, always stood within easy reach on a shelf above the stove. She ground her coffee beans or the grain mixture while the water was heating up.

Hank's father, Florian, then in his thirties, had dark hair and was of slender, but muscular build. He was a policeman in the village, having previously served in the military police of the Polish army. An early photograph shows him in his military police uniform with wrapped leggings and high-laced boots. The picture conveys a determined presence, yet it also reveals a deep kindness emanating from his eyes. He always sported a mustache, though as he became older, he trimmed it shorter.

His bearing and his uniform gave Florian an aura of authority, but it was his kindness and personal warmth that determined his interaction with people. He had a deep

Hank's father, Florian, wearing his Polish Military Police uniform, 1923.

Hank's father, Florian's, railroad pass photo.

sense of justice and compassion and thus easily established rapport and trust among the poor, the children, and the minorities. He was a representative of the Polish government and a person of dignity, but one who was well-liked and respected rather than feared. Children in particular responded to his personality as well as to the ready supply of candy in his pockets. To give but one example: When a burglary occurred at the workshop of a local silversmith and a quantity of silver wire was stolen, some children saw the thief hide it in his well and quickly informed Hank's father. His family ties also

45

eased his rapport with the Ukrainian people. This may explain the warning he received later on of his pending arrest by the Soviets.

Hank's parents were married on February 19, 1928. His father's family had resolutely refused to acknowledge their son's marriage because his bride was after all not only Ukrainian but also Greek Orthodox. This attitude unfortunately also affected Hank and his sister and prevented a close relationship between them and their father's family. One of his father's sisters was an exception. A kind and lively person, and regarded by some family members as their "black sheep," she lived in the county seat of Zloczow. After she married, she moved to Czechoslovakia. Her husband was a mechanic, the one who made the coffee mill as a wedding gift for Hank's parents. On one of her visits Hank was impressed by the ease with which his father switched from the Polish language to Czech. At other times he had heard his father speak Slovakian and Russian and talk to one of the Jewish people in Yiddish. He marveled at the many languages his father knew.

Hank's father rose early and left for work soon after daybreak. From his bed Hank often watched him through the open bedroom door eating his breakfast. He was dressed, but the coat of his dark-blue police uniform was still unbuttoned. Hank never saw his father in civilian clothes. He always wore his uniform on festive occasions, but even for work in the yard or the field he would wear his old uniform pants. At breakfast he sometimes slowly ate his bread or sipped his coffee looking out through the kitchen window, seemingly lost in thought.

"Are you worried your horse is going to run away, Florian?" Hank's mother would tease him. Even though a saddle hung in the barn, Hank had never seen his father on horseback.

After breakfast his father would button his coat with the high collar and sling the strap of his first-aid kit across his chest one way and his rifle the other. He would buckle his belt with the pistol on the side and put on his four-cornered cap with the emblem of the white Polish eagle and then pedal off on his bike toward the police station. It seemed almost impossible to Hank how much his father could carry and still ride his bicycle.

In winter his father either walked or, if the snow was too deep, skied to work. Even in the depth of winter the roads were usually not plowed. Only snow drifts which blocked a road were pushed aside with an angle plow. If necessary, people used sleighs to get around.

Hank learned to ride his father's bicycle by himself when he was six years old. Since the bicycle was too big for him and he could not reach the pedals from the seat, he stuck one foot through the frame and pedaled it from the side. At first he pushed himself along the fence standing on the pedals. After his father showed him how to steer Hank rode the bicycle around the yard even before he knew how to stop. As soon as he had mastered riding the bicycle, he took his sister along having her sit on the frame. Once, when she accidentally stuck her foot into the spokes, Hank lost control of the bicycle and both fell into the ditch by the road. His sister suffered a nasty cut just below her chin, and a small scar remained there. Hank scraped his legs. Hank's father treated their injuries with iodine and bandages from his first-aid kit. Hank was afraid he would be punished because his sister got hurt, but his parents only said: "Accidents will happen." They were not angry, nor did they forbid Hank to take his sister for bicycle rides again.

Their main meal of the day was at noon. Hank's mother usually served dumplings or potatoes together with boiled meat and gravy. If his father could not come home, she put his food into the warming oven until evening. Sometimes he ate his noon meal at the tavern across the street from the police station. On occasions he also bowled there.

After Hank started school he occasionally met his father at the tavern for their midday meal. At times other policemen joined them, and Hank listened to their talk as he nibbled some of the paprika-flavored bacon which was served free at the tables. One day his father's colleagues told them about a peddler who had purchased an old cavalry horse to pull his wagon. He was cruel to the poor beast; he beat it and made it pull to exhaustion. It happened in nearby Busk during a parade that a Polish cavalry troop rode past. At the sound of the bugle the horse perked up its ears; it galloped after them and joined their formation, wagon and all. The soldiers gave the peddler money for his horse and used it in the band to pull a large drum on wheels. At another time Hank's father mentioned a big explosion in a field. "Some boys must have collected a lot of old ammunition.

(Unexploded ammunition from the First World War could often be found in the fields.) They must have piled it into a trench and started a fire underneath it," he said. "It made quite a noise. I saw several boys run away." Hank kept quiet. He did not tell his father until many years later that he had been one of them.

The evening meal at Hank's home was usually light: soup and bread or sandwiches. Hank was always glad to see his father come home. At times his father arrived very late, and on some days not at all, particularly if his duties took him to one of the outlying villages which were part of his beat. Hank missed him when he was not home and worried about him if he was absent for a longer period of time.

Once, all policemen of the village were called away for an entire week. They were given extra ammunition and sent to one of the larger towns where a Ukrainian demonstration was to take place.

The Ukrainians accounted for nearly 60 percent of the population in some districts, and nationalist feelings were intense among many of them. They demonstrated often for greater recognition and an independent Ukraine. Even in Krasne Hank saw marchers with their blue and yellow flags, the Ukrainian national colors. When Hank's father came home from this special assignment, he said that many of the demonstrators had been arrested, including Hank's mother's cousin who had helped set up the orchard. He was very active in the Ukrainian movement. Hank's father said: "I was able to let him go." Though Hank did not understand the complex political background of the situation, he was aware that his father had been called away for a longer time than usual, farther, and for something quite serious.

After the First World War the promise of Western Ukrainian independence had brought about in Eastern Galicia, including the region of Lwow and Krasne, a hopeful but short-lived spring. This strong sentiment for an independent Ukraine persisted among the Ukrainians of Eastern Poland. (All of eastern Ukraine had become part of the Soviet Union.)

In 1920 General Pilsudski allied with Symon Petliura invaded the Soviet Union to establish an independent Ukraine east of the Zbrucz River (the 1920/1921 Polish-Soviet war). The price of that alliance was that the land west of the Zbrucz River was to be considered part of Poland. This territory, called Eastern Poland during the interwar years and thought of as Polish for centuries, had always been coveted by the tsars and much of it had been under Russian rule from the time of the partitions of Poland in the late 18th century until the Bolshevik revolution.

Only under Lenin, after the founding of the communist state, had these claims on Polish territory been repudiated, though they still continued to smolder among the Soviet military leaders. Lenin had looked upon tsarist Russia as the "hangman of Polish Freedom" and, addressing Poland, wanted to "wipe out the accursed past in which every Russian was looked upon as an oppressor."

In 1919, the Western Allies of the First World War formed a commission to bring about an armistice between the Soviet Union and Poland and to determine Poland's borders. The commission established the "Curzon line," named after the British foreign secretary Lord Curzon, one of the Allied commissioners, as the "minimum temporary" eastern border of Poland. This line ran from the Lithuanian border southward through Grodno, then along the Bug River to Sokoly, the old Austrian-Russian frontier prior to the First World War, and from there swung west of Lwow toward the Carpathian mountains. It left Eastern Galicia, and thus Lwow and Krasne, in the territory later claimed by the Soviets.

In the 1921 Treaty of Riga which ended the Polish-Soviet war, Poland's border with Russia was settled further east, keeping the disputed territory as a part of Poland. The final settlement came in 1923 when the Allied Council of Ambassadors recognized Poland's sovereign rights over this territory and the United States seconded that decision. Since this region had significant non-Polish minorities, the Polish government began to Polonize it with Polish settlers and a Polish administration. The many colonists and the at times heavy-handed Polish policies caused much resentment among the minority populations.

The Curzon line remained important. It not only became one of the symbols of Soviet imperialism—the Soviet Union always insisted on approximately this line as the proper Soviet-Polish border, be it in the German-Soviet treaty of 1939 or at both the Allied conferences, in

Poland's borders before World War II, Curzon line, Soviet advance.

November of 1943 at Teheran and in February of 1945 at Yalta. In both cases the Soviets got their way—but it also exemplified the high-handedness with which first the imperial European powers and later the Western democracies disposed of Polish territory. Neither at its creation by an act of the British foreign office, nor in its final acceptance at Yalta did the Polish government and people have any voice in the matter. At Yalta, Poland was compensated for its loss in the east with a large section of land in the west, also historically Polish but long since under German control.

In keeping with Lenin's attitude toward Poland, his Soviet government considered the Curzon line as being "too far west." Lenin, however, died in 1924. With Stalin's ascent to power Russia's imperialistic ambitions were revived.

After the Soviets invaded Poland on September 17, 1939, their advance halted at the demarcation line previously negotiated with Germany. This line approximated the Curzon line, and the Soviets incorporated the occupied territory east of this line into the Soviet Union. Thus the territory between the Curzon line on the west and the Zburcz River on the east was under Polish control only between the First and Second World Wars. Since the breakup of the Soviet Union this territory has been divided between Belarus (the northern part) and Ukraine (the southern part), except for a small northern section with the city of Wilno which went to Lithuania.

Between 1939 and 1945 this territory was "ethnically cleansed" of native Poles by the policies of the Soviet Union, Nazi Germany, and the Ukrainian nationalists. The Soviets deported all Poles, who had even the most tenuous ties to the former Polish government or its institutions, to penal and labor camps in the Soviet Union. They included also those Poles in their deportation scheme who had fled east before the advancing German troops and were therefore not native to this territory. After the war, in 1945, the Soviets insured the permanency of their claim by expelling all remaining ethnic Poles from the area.

These conflicting territorial claims as well as the nationalist ambitions and frustration of the various regimes and ethnic groups are but examples of the continuous strife which characterized the history of this region, and much of Europe as well, until the very present. They were among the roots of the two wars which engulfed the entire world and caused the death of approximately 50 million people in the Second World War alone. This historical period also has the dubious distinction of elevating ethnic cleansing to yet unprecedented levels.

The quiet authority of his father and the example of his mother had instilled a distinct sense of propriety in Hank. This, in turn, facilitated his self-expression and independence early in life. Hank's parents had little need to restrain his boyish exuberance by strong disciplinary measures. His mother had only to point her finger at him or to call him "Henryk" instead of "Heniu" to make him realize that he had overstepped his bounds. She dealt with more severe offenses, however rare, by slapping his ears with a wet dishrag. Hank's father never disciplined him.

But propriety or no, boys will be boys, and Hank was no exception. Because of his fascination with gunpowder and ammunition, Hank was once quite severely disciplined by his mother, though she had been upset more from worry than from anger.

Old, unexploded ammunition always attracted young boys, particularly curious ones like Hank, and rifle shells from the First World War were frequently plowed up in the fields. Hank liked to empty them of their powder. He did this by twisting and wiggling the projectile until it came off because someone had once warned him: "Don't ever use a tool on those shells!" Hank knew that many of the rifle shells would explode if hit with a hammer; one of his friends lost several fingers this way. Hank found that the shells contained three kinds of powder: oblong like pieces of pencil lead, small granules, and square flakes. All, however, burned in the same way. Once, when his mother had stepped out of the kitchen to feed the chickens, he took loose gunpowder and let it snake back and forth between the pots and pans on top of the cook stove. He expected the powder to burn like a fuse when lit: to catch fire at one end and then wend around. But the powder caught fire all at once just as his mother came back into the house. The wet dishrag about his ears was his deserved punishment.

Hank's ears felt the wet dish rag at another occasion. His grandfather had come for a visit and showed him how to catch sparrows. He soaked grain in vodka and spread it about the yard. The sparrows eagerly picked it and soon fell asleep. Hank and his grandfather gathered a bucket full of drunken sparrows and took it into the house. Needless to say, as the effect of the alcohol wore off, the house became filled with sparrows flapping about trying to find their way outside. Droppings splattered the furniture and the floor, and loose feathers blew about everywhere. Just then Hank's mother returned. Hank had never seen her berate her own father so angrily before. And that is how Hank got the wet dishrag again.

While Hank's grandfather was still alive, he and Hank spent much time together. He was not well and had not been able to work for several years. He died of cancer before Hank started school. During the last weeks of his life he was bedridden, and Hank's father often went to rub his back with alcohol to make him feel more comfortable. As long as he was able to, however, Hank's grandfather lavished his time and affection on Hank: he became Hank's "best buddy," and Hank, his favorite fishing companion.

When, on a summer's day, he came to visit, Hank could see him from afar walking along a grassy field path toward the house, the village of Zuratyn hazy in the distance behind him. His lean, sinewy figure was silhouetted against the blue sky, and the whiteness of his homespun linen stood out against the yellows and browns of the fields of ripening grain on either side of the path. A straw hat shaded his weathered face. He wore loose slacks and a blouse-like, collarless shirt gathered around the waist by a cord and reaching to his thighs. In his hands he carried a gift for his grandson: a wild canary he had snared, or a special loaf of bread baked for Hank by his grandmother. Seeing his grandfather come walking through the fields like this became for Hank one of his most cherished childhood memories of him.

His grandfather liked to take Hank down to the river at the end of his land to fish. He also kept his boat there. He had braided an eight-foot long fishing line for Hank from horse hair, tied it to a long pole, bent a straight pin for a hook, and used a cork as a float. Worms for bait were abundant in the rich soil, particularly near the compost pile. His square-ended boat could either be rowed or poled along. Since the Peltero river was quite polluted, they took the boat to the mouth of the Gotogorka, which ran clear. They fished among clumps of reeds and cattails or near creek inlets for crappies and bullheads. Sometimes Hank helped to pull up the trap nets his grandfather had set. They looked like a long funnel and stretched over a series of wooden rings. In the boat the rings folded flat like an accordion. To set the trap nets one pulled the rings apart and staked the net between poles with its opening against the current. Hank's grandmother cleaned their catch and usually boiled it into fish stew. When his grandfather caught a pike she baked it or made fish patties.

On holidays, especially Christmas, Hank's grandmother prepared "pike in aspic." She boiled and deboned the fish, placed it on a platter, poured the stock over it and let it gel. She then served it cold with boiled potatoes on the side. During Lent the family often ate marinated herring, or his grandmother made cabbage rolls using buckwheat in place of rice. They ate her buckwheat cakes with honey or sweetened with sugar; sometimes they topped them with finely chopped bacon and sour milk.

At times Hank and his grandfather went to catch crayfish. Large, five to six inch crayfish had their holes just below the waterline of a tributary where a steep bank of yellow clay fell sharply into the river. These holes were large enough to admit the hand of an adult.

"Stick your hand into the hole, wait for the crayfish to pinch your finger, and then pull your hand out with the crayfish hanging on," his grandfather instructed him—no small feat for a young boy! At home Hank's mother boiled and peeled the crayfish and served them in a horseradish sauce.

When Hank's grandfather died, the family butchered a pig and the neighbors baked and cooked for the wake. It was a big wake lasting two days, and the funeral was held in his grandparents' barn. Afterwards, led by the priest, they walked in procession behind the casket to the cemetery. Hank wore dark clothes and could not hold back his tears. Hank remained sad after the funeral, for his grandfather had been his "best buddy," the one who always called him "Heniu."

Hardly anyone among Hank's relatives and acquaintances celebrated anniversaries or birthdays. Name days, the feast days of people's patron saints, were very important however; weddings and funerals were always festive events. After some funerals the wake lasted for days with much eating and drinking. Men and women, young and old, mingled freely on these occasions and celebrated or mourned as the case may be.

Nevertheless, Hank's parents made little even of name days. In Hank's family such days usually passed without any special comment. Hank's sixth name day was an exception, perhaps because it also meant the beginning of school. It was celebrated in a big way. His godfather gave him a wristwatch, but also some vodka to drink. After the predictable results, Hank's mother was very angry with the godfather and sent Hank outside. Miffed by this turn of events, Hank stacked firewood against the door on the outside so that everybody had to climb out through a window. This time Hank's punishment was more than the usual wet dishrag about the ears, his mother spanked him and told him to stay in the yard. When he tried to play on the swing, he promptly fell off.

Whenever his parents and their friends visited, they often drank tea and served cakes and pastries. Hank's mother's specialty was a rich pastry made of several layers of dough with butter in-between, then fried and sprinkled with powdered sugar. Hank drank tea sweetened with "Eve's apples,"—crab apples preserved in syrup. On such visits Hank and his sister knew to be quiet at the table or when adults spoke, though at other times they received ready and patient answers to all their questions. His mother rarely went visiting by herself.

Hank was six or seven years old when he, his sister, and their mother suffered an influenza-like lingering illness. Because they coughed so much, Hank's father took them to a pine forest near Sassow not far from where his parents lived. He thought the fresh air and the aroma of pines would be of help.

They went by train as far as Zloczow, where a horse-drawn wagon met them for the remainder of their trip. (Hank's father's parents had arranged for it.) In the forest they camped on blankets under a tarpaulin. There was no undergrowth, only a thick layer of needles covered the ground, and the air was filled with the smell of pines. It was early summer, the sun shone brightly, the weather was balmy, birds sang, and there were no mosquitoes. Hank played with his sister

Hank's First Communion class. Hank is standing in the back row, fifth boy from the left.

among the trees, and the family had picnics eating the food his mother had brought along in a basket. After a few days they returned home feeling restored.

Hank's family was very devout. In the evening they all kneeled and prayed together. If his father could not be home, his mother led the prayer. Every Sunday they went to Mass, Hank in his Sunday clothes: a dark blue sailor suit with shorts. At the age of six Hank made his First Communion. His communion picture shows him in a white suit among the other children gathered around their priest, a Capuchin monk in a large hooded robe and sandals. It was a happy occasion for Hank and his proud parents.

Once Hank's family went on a pilgrimage to a shrine at Malinte, north of Zuratyn. It was a long walk and they had to stay overnight. His mother explained to him that a pilgrimage was a way of thanking God for everything He had done for them and that walking was part of expressing this. "If you ride in a buggy it is not a pilgrimage," she said. While in Siberia Hank vowed that he would make this pilgrimage to Malinte again should he ever be able to return home. Though

Church parades and pilgrimages were common activities for the entire villlage.

Hank's decision not to return to his Soviet-occupied home land made it impossible to fulfill his vow at Malinte, Hank was to give thanks for his delivery from Siberia by a pilgrimage to another shrine years later and more than five thousand miles away.

On visits to her parents in Zuratyn, Hank and his mother often attended services at the Orthodox chapel. After Hank's grandfather died they also went to Mass there every Memorial Day and afterwards joined the solemn procession to the cemetery where they visited his grave. In keeping with the custom of placing lighted candles on the graves of departed relatives, Hank placed one on his grandfather's grave. Hank was familiar with that cemetery since it was not far from his grandparents house. At one corner stood weathered gravestones, so old that their inscriptions were already difficult to read. Wind and rain had taken their toll over the years. Hank also walked in the processions on All Saint's Day in Krasne.

At school, a visiting priest gave instructions in religion once a week in the village hall. All school children marched in formation the two blocks from school to the hall and, as the religious instructions ended the school day, they were dismissed from there. Once Hank had been reprimanded and was made to stay after school in the auditorium of the hall. On leaving, the priest inadvertently forgot about him and locked the door. When Hank failed to come home as expected, his parents searched for him a long time and it took many inquiries before finding him.

The children of the Jewish community were excused from the religious instructions although they attended the same public school as Hank as they did not have a school of their own. The Jewish community consisted of a cluster of about fifty or sixty houses, each with its own garden, and was located not far from Hank's uncle's house near the railroad tracks. The people were quite poor; most of them worked as laborers on the railroad. Krasne had only a few shops and businesses.

Hank noticed that the Jewish children were at times ridiculed or abused by the others and tended to withdraw. He played with some of them and they visited each other's homes. His closest and steadfast companion, however, was Duszko, the neighbor's son.

Christmas, New Year's, and Easter were the main holidays. Hank always looked forward to Christmas. His mother had been baking for days in advance: breads, cakes, *placki*, and cookies, *babki*. The Christmas tree stood in the kitchen. It was trimmed with candles and a few glass ornaments, but mainly with homemade decorations. During the weeks before Christmas, Hank and the other children made chains and other ornaments from colored paper, eggs shells, or straw at home, in school, or at their Cub Scout meetings. He made his favorite ornament from strips of colored paper, which he folded back and forth many times, pierced their center, and then unfolded them over a straw.

On Christmas Eve Hank's family fasted until supper, the Wigilia. In the center of the table lay the thin Christmas wafer, the Oplatek, on a small bed of hay. Before they ate, his parents broke the wafer and all shared in it. After supper the family went to the village hall where Santa Claus (Saint Nicholas in Poland) sat on the stage surrounded by children's presents. The parents had marked each one with their child's name and left them at the hall earlier. The children stood in line and anxiously waited for their name to be called. Some adults, too, stood in line for their gifts; they liked to exchange them this way, and while they waited their turn, they shared their Christmas wishes with friends and neighbors and enjoyed this time together. Hank participated in this every Christmas, including the last one before the war. He was almost ten years old by then and had voiced his doubts about Santa Claus as a real person already a year or so earlier. His parents, however, warned him: "You better believe in him, or you might not get any presents." Hank therefore wisely kept his own counsel.

By the time all gifts had been passed out it was usually time for midnight Mass. After Mass Hank's family sat around the Christmas tree at home, lit the candles, and sang Christmas songs. Hank and his sister also lit sparklers. On Christmas Eve carolers went from door to door. After their performance they were invited to share in the food or were given money. During the Christmas season Hank's mother often sang carols before and after meals. Hank's favorite was "Silent Night."

On Christmas Day Hank's family again went to Mass and then back home for their Christmas dinner. The table was heaped with hams, sausages, fish, cookies, and pastry. Among the food were also some of the fresh cucumbers which had been grown in a bottle. The food was left out on the table for the rest of the day. Only Hank's immediate family got together for Christmas because travel was usually too difficult at that time of year.

On New Year's Day morning the carolers came again to wish everyone a "Happy New Year." They threw wheat across the steps and throughout the house to bring good luck in the coming year.

Easter was the time for the extended family to get together. By that time the country had started to green, and travel was easier. After an early Mass they gathered at Hank's parents' home since it could accommodate the largest number of people. Every Holy Saturday Hank's mother took a large basket filled with food—ham, eggs and a loaf of their special spiral-twisted bread to church to be blessed. Although they had no Easter egg hunts, the children and adults colored eggs and decorated some with wax-drawn designs. No one in the family, however, had the skill or the patience to decorate their Easter eggs in the elaborate style for which the Ukrainian people are so famous. Commercial fireworks were not common when Hank grew up, but one Easter his uncle who worked on the railroad brought him some carbide as a special treat. He showed Hank how the gas formed when he put the carbide into water and let its pressure pop corks out of bottles and blow tops off cans.

Many other festivals were celebrated throughout the year. In spring the older girls made wreaths of straw, put their names on them, and set a lighted candle in the center. Then they let the wreaths float down the river. Hank watched the wreaths drift slowly downstream and looked forward to the time when he would be among the boys trying to catch one of them to take back to the girl whose name it bore. This was one of the more clever ways for boys and girls to meet each other.

On another festival, held in early summer, Hank took part in sack races, played on homemade teeter-totters (a plank laid across a barrel) and rode on a merry-go-round made from a large wagon wheel. When he saw the older boys clamber up a greased pole and try to retrieve the prize, a ham tied to the top, he again anxiously wished that he were their age and could join them.

After the wheat harvest a big festival was celebrated on the soccer field outside the village. Girls danced in folk costumes with wreaths of straw and cornflowers in their hair. As Hank watched them, he never dreamt that a little more than a decade later and halfway around the earth, he would receive a certificate as an instructor in Polish folk dance.

People also observed the "framing-in," the moment when the rafters for the roof of a house being built had been placed and the house was ready to be closed in. To celebrate this occasion the work-men fastened a small tree and a bouquet of flowers to the gable, and the owner gave them a party with food and drink.

Zuratyn, Hank's mother's home village, was a small hamlet of about two or three hundred houses which clustered around the large estate of a Polish landowner. Almost everyone in the village had worked on the estate at some time or other, including Hank's grand-parents and his mother. When she had been a child she had played with the landowner's children; later, she worked for them in the household. From childhood on she had earned their affection and respect, and they remained in touch with her until the war. During her work on the estate Hank's mother also had been taught some social graces, including the knack of arranging parties. She applied her knowledge to local celebrations and family events and readily assumed charge of the preparations. Hank's father was proud of her taste and skill; especially after the praise she received for her hall decorations at a policemen's ball.

When Hank wanted to visit his grandparents in Zuratyn, he followed a field path his mother had shown him. He knew it well enough to go by himself even before he had started school. "I am going to grandmother's," he would call to his mother and be off. Taking a path on the upland, he made his way down a steep twenty- to thirty-foot clay bank to the flood plain of the river where low-lying pastures and meadows stretched for more than a mile.

A planked bridge spanned the three- to four-yard width of the winding Gotogorka River flowing through them. Though a shallow ford existed further downstream, Hank preferred to go across the bridge. At the far side of the plain another wooden bridge led across the Peltero River and directly unto the opposite upland. This bridge was for foot traffic only and rose from the meadow to about sixteen feet above the river.

Hank loved to feel its long boards swing and sway in rhythm with his steps. The bridge brought him close to the house of his mother's cousin, the bee keeper who had helped Hank's father plant the orchard. When Hank stopped for a visit, there was always a freshly baked slice of bread smothered with homemade butter and honey for him. Neither Hank or his parents, nor this man and his wife could have ever imagined at that time that their close and cordial relationship would break under the stress of the Soviet rule.

Walking among the fields and meadows, searching the brush for bird's nests, and smelling the grass and the wildflowers was Hank's favorite pastime. After he had started school, he and his friends often spent their free days roaming the countryside. In the fields, the remnants of abandoned trenches and bunkers from the First World War, now overgrown with brush and brambles, made exciting play areas. If Hank was to be gone for a longer time he took a bottle of water along, and his mother gave him a supply of potatoes to bake and some matches with which to start a fire. Peat for a fire was easy to find in one of the boggy areas.

On one of their excursions he and a friend stumbled upon a pile of blankets, some empty tin cans, a pair of field glasses, a camera, and a train schedule in an old trench. They felt scared and sensed that something was wrong. They ran to Hank's father at the police station and told him about their discovery. His father and several other policemen had the boys show them the place, and Hank overheard them say: "It must have been a spy. He surely left in a hurry."

Hank was seven or eight years old when he caused his parents serious concern. His mother had gone to visit her sister, just a few blocks away, but he thought that his mother seemed to be gone an unusually long time. "Had she gone to Zuratyn to see his grandmother?" he wondered. He decided to go there and take his little sister along. Since she was only two or three years old at that time, he half-walked, half-carried her the entire way. When his mother came home she found the children gone; they were nowhere in the neighborhood. She was worried but hoped they had gone to her mother's. And so, she sent Hank's father to look for them. It was already evening when Hank saw his father bicycling toward his grandmother's house. He did not scold Hank for taking his little sister so far and not letting anyone know; rather, he put Hank on the handlebar, his sister on his back, and pedaled home.

Opposite Hank's mother's cousin's house in Zuratyn was the carpenter shop. The carpenter had made the furniture that Hank's grandparents gave his parents as their wedding gift. When Hank was five years old his grandfather had the carpenter also make a sled and a toy wagon for Hank from the leftover wood. The wagon had spoked wheels, and Hank liked to tie it behind some passing farmer's wagon to have himself pulled along. Alas, bouncing over ruts and hillocks soon broke the spokes. In winter Hank pulled his sled or he laid down on it and pushed himself forward with his hands. Hank always tried to imitate the older boys. Once, when he saw them jump the drop-off toward the river on their skis, he tried to do it on his sled. The sled, however, was not sturdy enough for this rough usage and quickly fell apart.

In Zuratyn it was but a short walk along the dirt road from his uncle's house and the carpenter's shop to his grandparents. Wooden sidewalks connected all houses in the village, since the deep mud in spring often made the road impassable. His grandparents' house stood behind a wooden fence and a row of trees. In the fall, mushrooms grew in the rich compost of the fallen leaves. Hank liked to pick mushrooms, there or in the woods, while on school outings or on walks with his grandmother.

Hank's grandparents' house was built from a wooden frame; clay mixed with straw filled the spaces between the studs. It was an old house. One entered through a porch with an overhanging roof supported by two upright beams. The beams were studded with shell fragments and shrapnel from the First World War, and Hank often pried marble-sized pieces from their pitted surfaces with his pocketknife. The pocketknife had been a gift from his grandfather who once had bartered something for it. The practice of bartering was common among the people of Hank's childhood. Money changed hands infrequently, except in the stores, but there also his grandmother often obtained goods for a supply of eggs or home-grown produce.

On entering his grandparents' house one first encountered the grindstone on which his grandmother milled her flour. It was round; its hollowed-out center accommodated a smaller round stone which fitted rather snugly. A long stick was fastened to the ceiling and inserted off-center into the inner stone. When one pushed on the stick, the inner stone turned inside the outer one milling the grain in the narrow space between them.

The entrance way opened into the kitchen where a big clay oven took up most of the space. This great oven reached to the ceiling. It had a cooking area in front, and a bake oven on the side. Above the bake oven was a ledge, about seven feet long and wide enough for two people to lay side by side. His grandparents slept there in the winter.

On baking days his grandmother often crafted a small, special loaf for Hank and decorated it with a swirl or similar design. His grandfather brought it with him when he came to visit. To decorate baked goods with swirls and spirals, especially the big wedding cakes so characteristic of that region, was a common practice in Hank's home land.

Hank's grandmother wove her own linen; her large loom occupied most of the only other room of the house. She grew flax on a long strip of land next to her garden. After gathering the flax, she would save some of its seeds for next year's crop and press oil from the remainder. She soaked and beat the stalks, then separated the fibers and spun them into thread from which she wove the finished cloth. She wove the linen for the bedding and for her husband's clothes. When one of Hank's cousins went away to college, he wore a white suit made from her linen. In spring and summer Hank's grandmother spread the newly woven linen on a flat, grassy area behind the house between the shed and the barn. She wet it down and let the sun bleach it until it was snow-white. As for herself, she usually wore a house dress sewn from store-bought material. During the winter evenings she often worked her loom by the light of a kerosene lamp, and Hank could hear her throw the shuttle back and forth while the frame of the loom squeaked and rattled in rhythm with the motion of her feet.

Hank's grandmother was a tall, muscular woman, strong and energetic. Even in her sixties she still could carry a sack of wheat across her shoulders. Her solid appearance and her thinking betrayed her peasant stock. Direct and concerned with the task at hand, she nevertheless was aware of the events in the world around her and had her own opinions. Her practical wisdom and her deep religious convictions would some day play a major role in Hank's and his sister's survival. Being Ukrainian, she was well aware of the fierce nationalism endemic among her people and of their anti-Polish sentiments. She also knew of the political activism in which her own relatives and friends engaged, but she dismissed these radical attitudes and activities as "crazy stuff," done by "crazy people," and remained aloof from the political strife of the day.

Spinning and weaving filled many of the long evenings of fall and winter and was often an occasion for a gathering of friends and neighbors, for singing, for gossip, and for telling spooky tales. Some worked on quilts while others plucked goose down for pillows and bed covers as they drank tea and served cookies. On those evenings Hank either sat and listened or he played with the other children.

The well and a root cellar lay beyond the grassy area where his grandmother bleached her linen. The walls of the well, from which she hauled water in a bucket raised and lowered by a winch, were clay. To one side of the bleaching lawn was the barn; to the other, a row of sheds for animals and farm implements. The traces and the horse harness still hung in one of the sheds, but both the horse and the wagon were gone; they had been sold when Hank's grandfather became too ill to farm. From the sheds, the land sloped toward the river and became marshy. It was used as a hayfield.

A stork's nest perched on the roof of the barn. When Hank's grandfather built the barn, he placed an old wagon wheel on the roof for the stork to build its nest. "A nesting stork brings good luck," he said, repeating a common saying. Did it arise out of the belief that storks pick burning embers off a roof to protect their nest and thereby also protect the building? No wonder people also said that it brought bad luck to destroy a stork's nest.

"When you work on the roof, you better not get too close to the stork," Hank's grandfather had warned him. "Its beak is long and sharp."

One fall, when Hank was in the second grade, he saw a stork that seemed to be sick and could not fly. He wanted to take it home, but it pecked at him and did not let him come close. His father told him to leave it alone. Soon more than twenty-five other storks gathered around it clapping their beaks and craning their necks back and forth. After a while, they killed the sick stork. Hank was very upset, but he also understood that he could not interfere. His father explained to him the meaning of a mercy killing, that the stork was too sick to fly and would have starved to death in the winter. "It was a funeral song the other storks sang before they killed it," he told Hank.

Once, when Hank was whittling with his pocket knife, a splinter flew into one of his eyes and his mother had to take him to the doctor in Busk. Hank still has a scar on his eye as a permanent reminder of this. When he was six or seven years old, he went to Busk by himself to see the dentist. By then he had learned the alphabet in

Hank (holding his dog) with his Cub Scout troop.

kindergarten, and his cousins had taught him how to read even before he started school. He set out by himself with a sandwich, some spending money, and a note with the name and address of the dentist in his pocket. The trip took him all day, and he was justifiably proud of having accomplished it on his own.

In grade school, besides reading, writing, and arithmetic, Hank learned about history and about plants and animals. The study of "nature" soon became his favorite subject. It began in the second grade. He learned all about wild fruits, roots, berries, as well as where to find different kinds of mushrooms and which ones were safe to eat. A book about nature was to become his most treasured possession, and one of the few items he took with him to Siberia.

His school teachers were all unmarried women and well-respected. They taught every subject except religion. His favorite teacher lived only a block away, and a visit to her was always good for some cookies. She also came to Hank's home as his parents had engaged her to give him lessons in German and French as soon as he started second grade. Hank's mother supervised his homework. At the age of seven he also joined the Cub Scouts. From his Cub Scout leader, a woman who liked to teach the children nature lore, he learned more about the woods, fields, and flowers on their walks through the country.

Gypsies came often into the area, but his parents warned him to stay away from them. They camped their wagons along the river where they cut willow branches to make wicker furniture for barter. "Lock the chicken coup," his mother would say. "The gypsies are coming."

In 1939, at the beginning of summer, Hank finished the third grade. Near the end of this summer, he was ten-and-a-half years old and looked forward to entering the fourth grade. He was anxious for school to start. Hank loved school. Though every day spent playing or helping around the house seemed to pass quickly, looking back he felt it had been a long summer. His days had been so full of activities. Earlier that summer he had tasted some of the first cherries from the new orchard; later he ate fresh cucumbers right out of the patch. Off and on he visited his grandmother in Zuratyn and on his way stopped on the foot bridge to make its boards sway. He caught crayfish and remembered the time his grandfather had shown him how. He roamed the fields and the meadows with his friend Duszko, and together they emptied old rifle shells of powder and watched it burn. At home he again tried his hand at milking, though without much success, picked berries, and brought in water from the well. Every so often his aunt treated him to his favorite chocolate, and his uncle gave him another piece of carbide.

Gradually Hank was also forming his own view of the world. Though still limited to his village and the surrounding towns, his contact with other children at school, scouting, or play made him outgrow the confines of home and family. His faith was firm; he had developed compassion and a strong sense of justice. As yet he was untouched by the worries, anxieties, and subterfuges of the adult world. But for the death of his grandfather, his "best buddy," his childhood so far had been quite untroubled.

4.

A Boy's Eden Lost

⌒

September 1, 1939, promised to be another beautiful late summer day. The sun rose and after the mist lifted, its rays soon dried the dew from the grass and the flowers. Later in the forenoon Hank slowly walked to his aunt's house for one of her treats, perhaps then to go on and visit his uncle, or perhaps just to wait for his cousins to come home.

Thumbs tucked into the corners of his pants pockets he strolled about his aunt's yard, anxiously awaiting her call to come into the house. Already the smell of boiling chocolate wafted through the open kitchen window. "I hope she puts lemon sauce on it," he thought as he watched some of the ducks nip and tear on the short grass of the yard. He kicked a piece of loose cinder that filled the low spots and watched it fly toward one of the chickens. Startled, it scurried away with outspread wings.

It was just after noon, and the warm air stood calm between the buildings. Hank walked toward the shade of a cherry tree. He looked at its tall, limbless trunk and remembered the sweetness of its cherries earlier that summer and how his legs smarted when he had lost his foothold and slid down its trunk. "I should have used a wider belt," he said to himself.

In a couple of hours his cousins were expected home. "First I'll go and visit uncle at the switching tower," he decided, "but not until I've had some chocolate." Maybe his uncle would give him another piece of carbide. He remembered how it sizzled after he put it into water and the bright flame and the acrid smell of the burning acetylene when he had struck a match to the fumes. Hank looked forward to climbing the switching tower with its large room and the rows of levers to set the switches, and to looking out over the tracks, the giant round house, and the huge piles of coal.

Hank was still walking toward the cherry tree when a distant droning filled the air. "Probably bumble bees; the warm sun brings them out," he thought. But the droning became louder and more distinct. Planes! Airplanes! Hank rushed out into the center of the yard. His eyes searched into the hazy, blue sky. He was just able to make out several planes flying in formation when the air was filled with a screaming, whistling sound. It rose to a crescendo and then ended abruptly in a series of loud explosions. The air shook, clouds of smoke rose from the direction of the railroad station, somewhere glass shattered. "Bombs! Uncle is at the station!" flashed through Hank's mind. His aunt came rushing out of the house: "Get into the root cellar! Hurry! The war has started!" she shouted to him.

"No! I must get home!" Hank turned and started to run across a nearby potato field toward his parents' house. Every time he heard the screaming whistle of the bombs he threw himself between one of the rows or into the nearest depression. He soon realized that he could run when he heard the explosions and that he had to take cover as soon as he heard the whistling of the falling bombs. Across the field he saw a girl in a red dress; she was running too. "Lie down!" he shouted to her. Only then did he recognize her. She was one his school friends, a girl from the Jewish community.

At home his mother was standing at the door of the root cellar. "Thank God you're home," she said and quickly pulled him inside.

Hank's ears were ringing, and it took several days for him to regain his hearing. The screaming whistle of the falling bombs was to stay with him and fill him with fright every time he recalled that sound.

On September 1, 1939, literally "out of the blue," a carefree and protected childhood came to an end and Hank, a ten-year-old boy, was propelled onto a road of sorrow and deprivation, and toward years of foreign exile.

5.

Dead Horses

⌐———

Germany invaded Poland on September 1, 1939. Intense propaganda about the alleged harassment and persecution of the German minority in Poland had filled the newspapers of Nazi Germany for several months before, just as it had during the time preceding the "Sudeten Crisis" between Germany and Czechoslovakia early in 1938. At that time the British Prime Minister Neville Chamberlain had announced that the Munich agreement had achieved "peace in our time." Less than six months later the Czech lands were incorporated into Hitler's "Reich."

The Polish government was unsuccessful in defusing the crisis with negotiations and extensive concessions. Most important, Poland was willing to grant Germany free access to its province of Ostpreussen through that part of Poland known as the "Polish Corridor," also called Pomorze or Pomerania, which separated the province of Ostpreussen from the main body of Germany. Pomerania was ancient Polish land, site of the first Slavic settlement and legendary birthplace of the white Polish eagle, the emblem of Poland. One of its myths held that of the three brothers Lech, Czech, and Rus, Lech was the founder of Poland. In the fourteenth century, Poznan (German: Posen), its major city, was the first capital of Poland. The region had come under German control with the last partition of Poland in the late eighteenth century, but was returned to Polish sovereignty by the Treaty of Versailles in 1919 at the conclusion of the First World War.

A few days prior to the German attack on Poland, a raid on a radio station near the town of Gliwice (German: Gleiwitz) in the German province of Silesia was staged by SS troops disguised as Polish soldiers. In his speech on the morning of September 1, Hitler used this staged raid to justify to the German people his declaration of war on Poland. Later records showed that this fake attack was being planned by Germany while Hitler pretended to negotiate for a peaceful resolution of the Polish question.

The words of Joseph Conrad in his story *Prince Roman*, set a century earlier, can equally be applied to 1939: "[A]n historic date, one of these fatal years when in the presence of the world's passive indignation and eloquent sympathies we [Poles] had once more to murmur '*Vae Victis*'" (Latin: Woe to the vanquished).

Hank's parents knew that the first air raid on this important railroad was only the beginning; eventually it was bombed on 39 separate occasions. They also realized that their house stood too close to the railroad not to be in danger. Though the root cellar was large and reinforced, they were reluctant to entrust their safety to it. A few bombs had strayed and fallen on the village. One buried itself deep into the soft earth barely 100 yards from their house. Its explosion threw a geyser of dirt into the air and left a deep crater which soon filled with water. All windows in the house were shattered, as were most in the village. Hank's father hurriedly covered the window openings with boards.

Hank, his mother, and sister joined the many who tried to put some distance between themselves and the imminent danger. Those who had friends or relatives in another village packed their essential belongings and valuables and moved as far away from Krasne as possible. Hank's mother decided to take her children to Zuratyn to stay with her mother, there to await the end of the attack. Hank's father had to remain on duty in the village. He attended to the wounded, helped clear debris, and patrolled the railroad installations.

They left early the next morning after Hank's mother finished milking and took the path through the fields and pastures to Zuratyn. At the bluff they saw many people from Krasne digging caves into the firm clay of the bank planning to spend the ensuing days in the protection of the earth and to return home only at night to get supplies and to tend to their livestock. One of the villagers, perhaps recalling his experiences from the First World War, dug a trench near his house in a zigzag pattern and covered it with heavy timbers and soil.

Staying at their grandmother's in Zuratyn soon became monotonous for Hank and his sister. They were not permitted to roam about; they had to stay either close to the house, or remain indoors. And the house was very small. All four of them slept in one room where Hank's grandmother had made up a double bed on top of a large chest under the window. Often they heard gunfire and explosions in the distance and saw planes bomb and strafe the railroad station. Whenever they heard the whine of the falling bombs, they hurried to the root cellar. Hank often thought about his uncle in the switching tower who had to remain at his post during all these attacks. Fortunately he was not hurt. Though his uncle continued to work at his station even after the arrival of the Red Army, Hank never had the chance to talk to him again. His wife, Hank's aunt, also chose to stay at home regardless of the danger. Hank was to see her only a few more times after the Russians came, and then only briefly.

Every evening Hank's mother made the long walk to their house in Krasne and returned late at night. She went for needed belongings, to milk the cow, to feed the chickens and gather the eggs, perhaps also to share a few minutes with her husband and to make him a warm meal. To find her way in the dark she carried a kerosene lantern.

Hank accompanied her a few times. The first time it was already dark when they climbed the bluff. Walking through the fields toward their house they came across a mass of dead horses. Two or three days before, a cavalry regiment was attacked aboard a train. The soldiers were able to open the wagon doors, but the attacking planes bombed

73

and strafed the horses as they tried to gallop away. Their bloated silhouettes rose eerily in the moonlight as Hank and his mother threaded
their way through the field, and their swollen carcasses lying haphaz-
ardly among the bomb craters filled the air with an almost unbearable
stench. The odor of decaying flesh, like the screeching and whistling
of the falling bombs, would stay in Hank's mind for years to come.
They returned to Zuratyn in the early light of day. During the next few
days, every time they went from Zuratyn to Krasne and back they had
to pass this scene. The dead horses were Hank's first encounter with
the sights and smells of war, the indiscriminate slaughter of innocent
creatures in the interest of power and dominion.

During this entire time Hank never saw any German soldiers. They
did not enter Lwow but stopped west of it, then turned north. Hank
and his parents found out the reason for this when within a few weeks
the first troops of the Red Army arrived.

6.

Under Hammer and Sickle

From the back of the house in Zuratyn they watched the Red Army arrive. Across the river from them columns of soldiers in earth-brown uniforms marched along the road from Krasne to Busk. Two days later Hank's mother took the children back home.

On August 23, 1939, much to the surprise of France and Britain and to the disbelief of many Germans as well, Hitler's government had concluded a non-aggression and economic assistance pact with the communist Soviet Union, until then its archenemy. A secret amendment to this treaty gave Germany a free hand in western Poland, and the Soviets agreed to attack Poland from the east. In return, Germany recognized the Soviet's exclusive interest in the eastern part of Poland and in the Baltic states of Lithuania, Latvia, and Estonia.

The German advance, therefore, halted west of Lwow to allow the Soviet forces to invade those areas of Eastern Poland which they had claimed. The Polish lands in question lay east of the Bug River and included the eastern parts of former Galicia, thus the regions of Lwow and Krasne. The western boundary of the Soviet occupation, therefore, conformed approximately to the Curzon line of 1919. On September 28, 1939, Germany and the Soviet Union issued a joint declaration that, having made a few modifications to the demarcation line, they considered this new frontier "final" and would "resist any interference...on the part of any other powers."

The Red Army invaded Poland on September 17, 1939, thereby violating the Polish-Soviet Non-Aggression Treaty of 1932 and several other bilateral and multilateral treaties as well. Shortly thereafter, on October 10, the Soviets occupied the Baltic States. They incorporated the invaded areas into the Soviet Union. After the German attack on the Soviet Union in June 1941, these territories came under German control, only to revert back to Soviet rule at the end of the Second World War.

The Soviet forces advanced quickly and, understandably, against minimal resistance. Their main thrust toward Krasne and Lwow came via Tarnopol. Soon after their arrival, they rounded up the remnants of the Polish army and took thousands of Polish soldiers as prisoners of war. In the wake of their advance, the political officers of the Red Army agitated among the anti-Polish Ukrainian, Belorussian, and Jewish population in an attempt to use these alienated local nationalists and communists as their tools in the Soviet takeover of Poland. They opened the prisons and allowed convicted criminals to arrest Polish officials and loot the homes of the well-to-do. The criminals had been "victims of the capitalist system," they argued.

To use the national ambitions of disaffected minorities for his purpose was part and parcel of Stalin's cynical ideology. In 1924, he wrote that "support should be given to national movements which weaken imperial power," but only temporarily, since "the 'rights of nations' must be subordinate to the proletarian revolution."

What had been tolerated and insidiously promoted under Stalin was brought to a full and terrifying fruition by the German-Ukrainian-Nationalist Alliance soon after the German conquest of this area in 1941. Bands of Ukrainian nationalists vented their fury on the local Polish civilian population. They singled out the remnants of the former Polish administration, the teachers, and the Polish colonists. (The colonists, or *osadniki*, were Polish veterans of war, who had been given land in that region in order to help Polonize it.) Soon their fury encompassed all "foreigners" irrespective of age, gender, or nationality. Even dissenting Ukrainians became their victims. Tadeusz Piotrowski in his book *Vengeance of the Swallows* told in detail about the unrestrained pillage and murder of these Polish settlers and other Polish citizens. His most recent book, *Genocide and Rescue in Wolyn*, tells the same story, but in the words of the survivors themselves. At least 100,000 ethnic Poles were brutally murdered in that region by bands of Ukrainian nationalists. Another 400,000 had to flee to escape annihilation.

True to its totalitarian form the Nazi regime used people, their dreams, and their ambitions to further its own ends; in that area of Poland, they continued what had begun under Stalin. They used local Ukrainian nationalists to attain their own aims, especially to round up the Jewish population and to assist in *their* takeover of Eastern Poland.

After the Red Army arrived, Hank and his family still heard sporadic shots and muffled explosions, but within a few days silence settled over the land. It was not a silence of restfulness, of dreams, and of peace; rather it was a silence grounded in insecurity and fear—at first fear of the unknown, but soon fear of the oppressor, fear for one's life and existence. In that great silence which fell over the country, people avoided eye contact. They walked with their eyes cast down, as if *not noticing* was synonymous with *not being noticed*. And when they spoke, they spoke in a low voice, as if fearing that their words would echo like shouts through the streets of the village. With that silence came a general drabness of appearance, of clothing, of houses and gardens, and of streets. A dusky-gray sameness began to pervade every aspect of life. To remain inconspicuous was the order of the day. People went after their duties mechanically. Laughter was not heard— there was no reason for it; and even the smiles addressed to their loved ones were filled with sadness.

Every day columns of Soviet soldiers marched up and down the roads, occasionally tanks rattled along, rows of trucks rumbled past, and infantry followed closely upon the heels of their horse-drawn supply wagons. Some soldiers rode bicycles. Was one of the bicycles his father's? Hank wondered. There was no news of him. He had simply vanished. The villagers had heard about arrests and executions, and Hank and his family were filled with constant worry. Their only hope was that someone had warned him in time, and that he had been able to escape and hide.

What news there was Hank's mother heard from the neighbors or on the street. Hank's father's crystal radio had been silenced, its antenna torn during one of the last German bombing raids on the railroad station. They also heard of lootings. The owners of the large estate near Zuratyn had left before the Soviets arrived. While some had called them deserters, others had joined them. They had taken as much of their valuables as possible on their way south to Romania and from there, hopefully, to France. Now Russian soldiers as well as some of the local people were returning from the estate with wagons piled high with furniture. Later, there would be hundreds upon hundreds of long trains filled with looted furnishings, machinery, and factory equipment going east.

Their house felt cold and desolate when they returned from Zuratyn. Apart from the absence of Hank's father, nothing was awry. The neighbors had milked the cow and fed the chickens. Their staples and their belongings were undisturbed. The boards on the windows let in just enough light to fill the cold rooms with a perpetual gloom. Fortunately, Hank's father had stacked plenty of firewood during the summer, and he also had bought coal. The cow had enough hay to get through the winter. But what would happen when all this was gone? Later that year Hank, like so many others, walked along the railroad tracks with a gunnysack over his arm picking up pieces of coal which may have fallen off the train or which had been thrown out on purpose by a well-meaning engineer.

Prompted by the needs of her family and of the animals, Hank's mother went about her duties regularly, perfunctorily, spiritlessly. The unknown fate of her husband gnawed at her, and her worry spilled over onto the children. Both missed their father terribly.

The rumors of arrests and executions proved to be true. Bands of anti-Polish auxiliaries or militias appeared, equipped and goaded by the political commissars of the Red Army. They combed the country and rounded up straggling soldiers and officers, suspected Polish civilians, and police personnel—their "oppressors." Some of the Christian collaborators would later, when goaded by the Germans, use these skills to round up the Jewish population in the same way. Many used the occasion to settle personal scores. Government agents, lawyers, policemen, members of the Polish army, and foresters had been among the first to be arrested. They embodied the authority of the Polish State, or, as in the case of the foresters, the power of the large estates. The foresters had been regarded as their most visible incarnation. It had been their duty to protect the wildlife from poachers and from any other outside intruders. Besides, their intimate knowledge of the vast forests would make them invaluable guides for any group wishing to attempt resistance. The Soviets did not take any chances. People were arrested everywhere not for what they had done, but for what they *might* do.

Passed from person to person in hushed tones, the news of these events traveled fast. Hank, too, became aware of them...and began to lose his innocence. Shred by shred the events of the war and of the Soviet occupation tore it from his heart: It began with the first exploding bombs and continued with the steam engine he saw in a bomb crater, tilted awkwardly, cab and rear wheels in the air, its torn boiler half buried in the ground. The smell of the dead horses lingered in his memory and mixed with the taste of cordite which hung about the smoldering wrecks of the Polish tanks at the railroad station—and more was to follow, much more.

In an attempt to transport a part of the state treasury to the safety of Romania, three Polish army tanks had tried to make a run through Krasne. Two were surrounded by Soviet tanks in front of the railroad station, the third further down the road. "Hey boy! Give it up!" The Russian soldiers shouted at the Polish commander who, in reply, tossed a hand grenade through the open hatch of a Soviet tank. The fighting was brief, all three Polish tanks were destroyed, and the intense heat of the burning tanks melted the gold and the silver onto the steel. Lime was poured down the hatches on the burned bodies of the crews, and the metal of the wrecks stayed hot to the touch for days.

Before long these events involved Hank personally by deepening his concern for his father's safety. In Sassow, less than one hour's train ride from Krasne, a large number of Polish officials had been herded into the city hall. Someone, Soviet soldiers or Ukrainian nationalists, tossed hand-grenades through the windows and opened machine-gun fire into the building. "The blood ran out the doors and along the gutter," Hank heard someone say. Had his father been among those murdered? Unknown to Hank at that time, one of the victims was a close friend of his parents, a sergeant formerly in charge of the police post in Krasne. Joseph, their son, was one of Hank's close playmates, and—in a happier time—the two of them had swum together and paddled about a lake in a kayak. They would meet again in the future, though briefly, only to be abruptly separated forever.

Though neither Hank nor anyone else in the family knew it at the time, Hank's father had been able to hide. As a former policeman he would have been among the first to be arrested. Had he been warned, perhaps by one of his Ukrainian relatives? Evidently he had managed to get away in time. Every so often bits of information from the neighbors indicated that he was still free: some official had inquired where he might be, or if anyone had seen him. This gave the family hope, and they all clung to it.

With time the great silence which descended over the land deepened around Hank's family and isolated them. After all, they were the family of a former policeman who was still at large. Even Hank's Ukrainian aunt, his mother's sister, and her children seemed to avoid them. Her husband continued his work on the railroad, regularly, and he too never made any attempt to communicate with Hank's family. Fall passed, winter came. They were alone.

In the depth of one winter's night someone scratched on the boards barring the bedroom window. Soon Hank's father stood in the kitchen. As happy as Hank was to see him, his fear for his father's safety got the best of him. "I wish you would go away," was all Hank could say. His father disappeared into the night as silently as he had come. It was the last Hank saw or heard of him for years.

Hank's grandmother came from Zuratyn, for a few day's visit at first, but then she decided to stay. She made her bed in the spare room. She was near sixty then, but the years had done little to lessen her physical strength and endurance. She felt Hank's mother, the younger of her two daughters, needed her more than her older daughter whose children were already grown and whose husband still had the railroad job. Hank and his sister were still small, their Polish father was gone and could never return home under the present circumstances. She herself knew the loneliness of life without a husband: hers had died a little over five years ago. As much as she admired her younger daughter's former gaiety, always singing at work, her touch with decorating and arranging parties, she could not help worrying about her ability to cope with all the practical demands of daily living under the Soviet occupation.

"Two can live as cheaply as one," she answered when her daughter inquired if she better not leave the house in Zuratyn unattended. "Besides," she added, "I don't want to stay there alone with all the Russians around. We'll see how things look in spring."

From then on, and for the rest of their days together, she kept her emotional resilience and fiercely supported those around her. She used her physical strength and her practical thinking to provide for their physical needs. Her unfailing religious devotion was a wellspring of spiritual support for them as well. With infinite tact she assisted her daughter with the care and guidance of the children. Only after her daughter died did she "take over." For Hank she eventually became "the adult the child can rely upon."

Anna Freud, in her studies in *Children and War*, reported that "children exposed to bombing, destruction, even injuries and death during the air raids look at such experiences as 'accidents'...as long as their mothers or a familiar substitute cares for them, and on whom they can rely on during these times." After his mother's death, Hank looked to his grandmother as that "familiar substitute."

To lose a beloved parent is always an overwhelming disaster for a child. For Hank and his sister that loss was compounded in Siberia by their uncertainty about their father's fate, by the loss of home and freedom, and by their daily struggle for survival. Hank's grandmother helped them cope. Her presence and care gave them a semblance of family continuity. Though his sister would remain withdrawn for years, his grandmother's emotional support made Hank capable at the age of barely 13 not only to stand on his own but also to assume the responsibility for the life and well-being of his sister.

As the weeks of the Soviet occupation stretched into months, Hank gradually felt more sure of himself and became accustomed to his changed surroundings. He again began to explore. In a destroyed railroad car, he found a damaged typewriter which he took home in order to take it apart to see how it worked. He found a broken cavalry lance which he hid in a pile of straw across the street to keep as a souvenir. One day in winter he upset everyone in the neighborhood when he came home pulling a sled loaded with unexploded cluster bombs. Red Army soldiers had simply stacked them in a pile, and Hank had helped himself liberally. In no uncertain terms people told him to put them back where he found them and to do so as speedily as he could.

But for Hank being able to roam did not mean a return to normal times, either for him or for the village. The schools and the churches in Krasne remained closed, and the Polish white eagle was removed or painted over. The Soviets had taken many Polish soldiers as prisoners of war and put them to work rebuilding the road to Busk with cobblestones to make it suitable for heavy equipment. Their emaciated bodies showed how undernourished they were. Hank's mother baked extra bread, and Hank crawled through the wild raspberry bushes along the road to hide it among the piles of paving stones brought from a quarry. When the prisoners began to haul the stones away, they found the bread. One day Hank took several loaves and squeezed through a hole in the fence of the prisoners' compound. A Russian guard saw him and shouted at him. Fortunately he did not pursue him.

For a few days Russian soldiers camped in the yard of Hank's home. The soldiers slept outside in their coats, on blankets, or on pieces of tarpaulin, and their officer slept in the kitchen. One morning, as the officer stood by the window looking out, without turning around he said to Hank's mother: "You better get away." She realized then that someday she, or all of them, would be taken away. But where could she, a mother with two children, go? She stayed awaiting the inevitable.

They had gotten through the fall and the beginning of winter. The house was warm, thanks to the foresight of Hank's father the previous summer. They still had eggs, the milk from the cow, and the vegetables in the root cellar. Christmas passed, celebrated only in their hearts, and they looked toward the New Year with fear and trepidation.

It was the beginning of February, 1940. Although still winter and very cold, little snow covered the ground, and spring seemed at least in sight. The pounding on the door rudely awoke them early one morning, between four and five o'clock. The Soviets barged in. They had a list. Hank's family was in the first wave to be taken.

7.

"You Have Half an Hour . . ."

After a few months the Soviets began a systematic deportation of the local, predominantly Polish, people who were families regarded as belonging to the "anti-Soviet elements." Called *spetspieresedlentsy*, "specially transferred settlers," they were deported under a secret administrative ruling.

Jan T. Gross in his book about the Soviet conquest of these eastern Polish lands writes that unlike the prisoners sentenced by a court, these families had not appeared before any sentencing tribunal nor were they informed of any administrative procedure against them. Rather, they were subject to a secret procedure and were neither given any reasons for their deportation nor were they put before a court. These *spetspieresedlentsy* were not in "need of correctional labor." Their selection can be summarized in one sentence: "Who is not with us, is against us."

The deportations proceeded along well-tested, previously-prepared guidelines and protocols (see appendix). Their chief organizer and administrator was General Ivan Serov, a "Deputy People's Commissar for Public Security." After the German retreat from the Soviet Union in 1943, General Serov supervised the deportations of Kazakhs, Uzbeks, and Chechens suspected of collaborating with the German troops. He was decorated, eventually became the head of the KGB, survived the Stalin regime, and died peacefully at his dacha. Two of his immediate subordinates were executed, however, after the Stalin era.

The deportations came in waves and included entire families. The first wave, on February 10, 1940, took the families of political leaders, policemen and border guards. In April 1940, those of former army personnel and government workers were seized. In June of the same year white collar workers, people not to the Soviets' liking, and those who had fled from western Poland in front of the German army and therefore were not native to the Soviet-occupied territory, were deported. A few Jewish businessmen and their families were given a reprieve which lasted until early 1941.

The intent and procedures of the deportations were always the same; in fact, they had changed but little since the days of the tsars. In his book *The Soviet Takeover of the Polish Eastern Provinces* Keith Sword writes that "there was a continuity between the exile policy under successive Tsarist regimes and those of the Stalinist period." Norman Davies wrote that "each generation of Poles dumped in the tundra or the steppe in 1832, 1864, 1906, 1940, and in 1945 encountered Poles of an earlier generation who had shared the same fate."

Anita Paschwa-Kozicka, a Polish orphan who, like Hank, had been deported as a child and, like he, came to the United States via Colonia Santa Rosa in Mexico, visited Tbilisi in the Soviet Union in 1989. She writes in her book *My Flight to Freedom*: "I found many Polish people living there. Those were the people who came from Siberia [at the time of the amnesty], but were stuck in Russia when Stalin closed the borders to Polish refugees after we had been sent to Iran."

Without exception the roundup came early in the morning with that ominous knock at the door and the command "*Otkroite!*" ("Open up!"). In front of the door stood armed Red Army soldiers and a civilian official with a list prepared by local collaborators. "You have half an hour to gather your things!" The official ordered. For most it was a good-by to their home forever.

Then came a cart, a sled, or a truck, and a quick transport to the nearest railroad siding. The deportees were loaded into freight cars with high, barred windows, and the doors were locked from the outside. With luck their sanitary facility was a bucket, but usually it was only a hole in the floor. Some were fortunate enough to have wooden bunks in their cars; the majority, however, had to sleep among their bundles on the filthy floor. Some were even more lucky; their car had a small stove for which they occasionally received a pittance of coal. But most could only bunch together and try to share their body heat with that of their fellow prisoners. Locked in, fifty to eighty people in each car, they waited sometimes for days until the train was fully assembled. They traveled for weeks to an unknown destination without relief from crowding, without a chance to wash or stretch their legs. Their daily nourishment was a piece of bread and a bowl of watery cabbage soup.

Relying on General Sikorski's files an anonymous author described the trains and the process of entrainment in *The Dark Side of the Moon* as follows:

The trains were very long, and seemed also extraordinarily high. The last was because they seldom stood along platforms, and the whole train was accordingly seen from the level of the ground. Later, some Polish trains were also employed, but the earliest were all typically long Russian trains brought in for the purpose; dark green in colour with doors coming together in the middle of box cars as they do in cars on the Underground [subway]. In each of these cars, very high up, just under the roof, were two tiny grated rectangles, the only windows and the only spaces by which air or light could enter once the doors were fast. This great length of the waiting trains, always coiling away somewhere and always partly lost to sight, was in itself terrifying to the imagination. Those about to be deported were brought to the stations heavily guarded: for the most part loaded unto armoured cars, but also, when these gave out, on sledges and on little country carts shaped like tumbrils, ordinarily used for the carting of dung.

The roofs of the cars were piled with fresh snow but the ground all about was trampled and fouled. The trains, after being loaded, often stood for days before leaving, and the tracks along which they stood would become piled with excrement and yellow and boggy from the urine running down off the floors. Against the background of white, the silhouettes of the NKVD soldiers were shaggy and outlandish....Each soldier carried a fixed bayonet at the end of his rifle. Immense crowds of people swayed backwards and forwards. The soldiers with their bayonets forced back all except those who were to leave on the trains....Families were broken up all the time, husbands and wives separated, children being pushed into one part of the train while their parents were pushed into another.

One in ten died on the way, first the old and the infirm, then the nursing babies. The dead were thrown off the cars when the train stopped; weather permitting, they were sometimes hastily dug into the ground. Their families were never given the chance to bury their loved ones.

Survivors' memoirs and thousands of reports in archives around the world testify to this systematic and planned destruction of the Polish population. The political and military leadership, other representatives of the Polish state, teachers, and many members of the clergy were immediately arrested when the Soviets arrived. The political officers accompanying the Red Army brought with them lists of names which had been prepared in advance.

Those arrested were tried and condemned to the vast Gulag Archipelago, unless they were executed by decree, simply gunned down in their cells, or died on death marches in front of the advancing German troops in 1941. Other victims were shot in the back of the head, like the Polish officers at Katyn, or were otherwise disposed off.

The mass of Polish soldiers taken as prisoners of war, like the deported families, were subjected to a planned starvation. While still at home, Hank had seen the emaciated Polish soldiers building roads. He and his mother had tried to help them as much as they could. Hank, his family, and thousands of others were soon to experience hunger themselves. The insufficient food supply for the deportees during their transport cannot be explained by poor organization. Their rations had been fixed well in advance like everything else: the equipment, the trains, and the personnel required. At their destination abysmal shelters and lack of adequate provisions greeted the deportees.

Jan T. Gross observed that "the substance of their experience was in their struggle for survival. To die of cold, excessive heat, hunger, thirst, lice infestation, foul air, dirt, or diarrhea takes time and makes people succumb in stages, while putting up a fight. Some suffered more, some less, depending on climate, and on what the raiding party allowed them to take from home. It, finally, added up to death for some, torment for a great many, and mere discomfort for a happy few. The deportees were tortured in earnest; they were truly wasted."

It was early in the morning of February 10, 1940, and still dark outside. Hank's mother answered the pounding on the door. Two Russian soldiers with fixed bayonets and an official-looking man in civilian clothes stood at the door. They pushed their way past her and ordered: "Get into the kitchen!" The official had a list compiled by local Soviet sympathizers. He read off their names: Hank's mother's, Hank's, and his sister's.

"Get together what you can carry. Be ready in half an hour," he commanded.

"You're not on the list. You can stay," he said to Hank's grandmother.

"I am going with them," she replied.

Hank's grandmother was not surprised. Ever since that morning when, standing in her kitchen, the Russian officer had told Hank's mother "You better get away," his grandmother knew what to expect. As a young woman during the reign of the last tsar, she had heard about transports and exile, about the knock on the door under the cover of darkness, and the long treks to somewhere in Siberia. White tsar or Red, it always was the same: crowding, toil, and hunger. Occasionally someone came back after years of exile. She firmly believed that God would protect her. Thanks to her practical sense and her ability to concentrate on the task at hand she always knew what to do in a time of crisis. Almost instinctively she knew how to act, not aggressively, not as a fighter, but ever resourceful she became acutely aware of the needs and opportunities offered by a given occasion and applied herself to the demands of the situation. In other words, she took charge.

The children were told to dress quickly and as warmly as possible. She told Hank's mother what to pack: clothes, bedding, and all the food they could carry. Hank's mother followed her instructions mechanically. She spread a bed sheet onto which they dumped everything. They left the pillows behind; clothing and kitchen utensils were more important.

His grandmother took the coffee mill. Though she did not expect to have any coffee to grind, she knew she would find use for it. They packed the bread they had just baked for the week ahead; they were out of meat already, and potatoes or canned goods were too heavy to carry. There was neither place nor time for nonessentials, but they took a few photographs. Hank brought his favorite book on nature and his wristwatch. His savings account book? No, there would be no need for it, though it still had 38 zloty in his account. His sister sat on a chair in the kitchen quietly crying. All this took place under the eyes of the Russian soldiers. They stood and watched; neither of the soldiers offered to help, but every so often one said: "Take what you need, but take only what you can carry."

Hank sneaked outside. The guards did not pay any attention. He wanted to say good-by to a girl next door, a schoolmate. One of seven children in the family she had a badly deformed back, and Hank always looked upon her with particular affection. As he had done so many times before, he crawled through a hole in the fence and past a few bushes to get to her house. But the house was dark, and nobody answered his knock. "I could run away and hide like dad," Hank thought, but he felt he could not leave his mother or sister. And so he returned home.

Half an hour is a short time in which to gather one's essentials and to bid farewell to one's home. Soon creaking wheels and clopping hooves approached their house, then suddenly stopped. A horse snorted. The soldiers told them to take their things and leave the house. Outside they heard subdued sobbing and lamenting. An infant was crying. In front of the house stood a horse-drawn wagon requisitioned from a farmer nearby. Two families were already on it. The soldiers helped Hank and his family mount the wagon and threw their bundles after them.

When the wagon started to roll Hank looked back at his house. Perhaps someday they could come back. He hoped the neighbors would milk the cow.

The ride to the railroad station was short. Their wagon rolled down a ramp, jolted and bumped across the tracks, and halted at the farthest siding. A long train of freight cars stood guarded by armed soldiers. Hank and his family were made to climb into one of the cars with their packs of clothes and bedding. A number of people had come before them. Most sat silently on their belongings, some stared at the floor, others sobbed. A few wailed and carried on for a while, but they soon fell silent too.

Hank and his family put their things into a free corner and sat down. His sister buried her face into the folds of her mother's coat. Nobody spoke. Those who came later had to make do with an open space in the center. Eventually 78 of them crowded together in the freight car with no room to spare. Except for two old men from Busk, all were women and children. One of the men was a machinist, the other, a tool and die maker. There were no bunks; there was no straw. Someone produced a hatchet and began to chop a hole in the floor. They needed a toilet. At first people turned their backs when someone had to use it, but as time went on a blank stare into the distance provided at least a semblance of privacy. This was only the first step in the continuing degradation of their lives.

When the freight car was filled with the designated number of people, the door was slammed shut and locked with an iron bar on the outside. This defined the rest of the day for the captives.

"Slamming the door shut and the clank of the bar falling into place were the most awful sounds—we all cried out," Hank vividly remembered.

Their frightening day had begun with the shouts and the sharp rap on the door before dawn. Now it had ended like this, even though daylight still filtered through the small, grated window—their only connection to the world outside.

They were prisoners. The affront and the injustice of it all grated on Hank. It made him furious. Later, when someone would ask him to pinpoint the time that he became conscious of his hatred for the Soviets, he would choose that precise moment.

For three days Hank's train sat on the siding waiting for its quota of prisoners to be met. For three days they received neither food nor water. They heard other people arrive and saw some of them through the small window; they heard other wagon doors being shut. Every so often another car would be added to the train and jolt them out of their daze.

At one time a woman's voice called from outside and a young woman in their car got up and passed her newborn infant through the barred window. The baby was small enough to fit through the space between two iron rods. Hank caught a glimpse of a woman running across the field with the baby in her arms. Then someone pulled him away and covered his eyes. He heard shouts, then a shot. Soon the baby was passed back through the bars to its mother. Hank does not recall how long it survived. His sister, then five years old, would be one of the youngest children in their group to leave Soviet Russia alive. And she was far from being the youngest child on that train.

Finally the train started to roll. Where to? Nobody told them. For how long? Nobody knew, and the guards would not answer any questions. Still numbed by the sudden change in their lives they sat or stood about. Denial was not possible, although some may have tried to console themselves by thinking that this might be a bad dream from which they would soon awaken. The swaying of the moving car, the rhythmic beat of the wheels, the sounds and the smells of its occupants, the impossibility of stretching one's cramped limbs without crowding one's neighbor, forced the reality of their situation into their consciousness at every turn. What was going to happen to them? Very few words passed between them.

His new surroundings terrified Hank. He felt lost. He missed his father. Where had he gone? Thinking about him filled Hank with apprehension and fear.

Soon death, too, came. It crept in with the moans of the sick and stayed with them through their final struggle for breath. Covering

Hank's eyes with their hands or their coats, his mother or grandmother tried to shield him as much as possible from the dead and the dying and from seeing the soldiers remove the corpses. Yet they could not close his ears to the sobs, the crying, and the prayers of the family of the deceased. Hank soon became aware that death and dying were to become his constant companions. This only deepened his worry about his father. His sister remained silent and kept hiding her face in her mother's or her grandmother's coat. His mother tried to maintain her composure, but the tears welling up in her eyes betrayed her sadness, a sadness Hank could not help but notice. Giving words to their despair, many said: "That's it—the end. We have no way out." Hank's grandmother stood apart. She was the exception. She was their rock. "Let us pray to get through this," she said.

They first ate what they had brought along. Not until they stopped in Kiev, after four days travel and some 250 miles to the east, were they given food: a weak soup containing a few cabbage leaves, a piece of potato here and there, and a little barley. They were also handed a small piece of coarse and heavy bread. The train had stopped on a siding. When the doors were opened they saw the cupolas of an Orthodox church. Many started to cry, others prayed. Someone began to sing a psalm and soon everyone joined in.

From then on, every morning and every evening the train stopped, the doors were unlocked, the watery soup with a little bread and drinking water were portioned out, and the guards removed the corpses of those who had died since the last stop. Hunger and death were constant, but worse still were the uncertainty and the worry about the future.

Cold, hungry, and nearly smothered by the smell of unwashed bodies, they rolled day after day, monotonously, through the flat lands of eastern Russia. At one time somebody said: "We have just crossed the Volga." Later they saw mountains. Still later the train passed through an endless expanse of forests. Few cared, numb to their surroundings, numb to time. Thanks to his grandmother's resilient spirit and his own growing sense of resistance, even adventure, in the depth of his soul Hank was convinced that God would take care of him and that someday he would get out of Russia—that he knew for certain. As this conviction deepened, his fear left him. "There is nothing to be afraid of any longer. They took away everything already. There's nothing else they can do to me," he said to himself.

Had they traveled two weeks? Or three? Was it the end of February, or already one of the first days of March? They had lost all track of time. One day, the train stopped and did not start up again: they had come to the end of the railroad. Deep snow still covered the ground. This was Siberia.

8.

"Your Mother Died This Morning . . ."

K ustenai, in the north of Kazakhstan (the Kazakh Soviet Socialist
Republic) was the railway terminal. It lay past the Ural mountains a
thousand miles northeast of Kiev. There the deportees were unloaded
from the train and packed onto open trucks, which then parceled out
their human cargo among the many camps throughout the region.

Everyone from Hank's freight car was sent to the same camp.
Huddled together against the wind and the cold, they rode north. As
much as they had longed to stretch, to breathe fresh air after the filthy
confines of their railroad car, they now eagerly crowded together to
lessen the fierce bite of the driving wind. Their destination—
Swinsowchos 641 (Swine Farm 641), *Tobolsk Rejon, Kustanai Oblast*—a
Russian village in the marshy forests of Siberia lay more than 400 miles
north, past Tobolsk, past the Demyanka River. It was still dark when
they left Kustenai; when they arrived, it was dark again. Their bleak
quarters were unheated wooden barracks surrounded by deep snow.

From 1939 to 1941, over one million people, two-thirds of them ethnic Poles, were dispersed in this way from the Soviet-occupied Polish territory throughout 56 provinces of the Soviet Union. Almost 3,000 Soviet camps sprawled from the Arctic ocean and Siberia to the plains of Kazakhstan, north to Arkhangelsk and east to Kamchatka. Whoever had the misfortune of winding up in these camps had to exist in barracks, in stables, or in sod houses with neither windows nor floors, devoid of any furniture and infested with vermin and insects.

Prisoners by all standards, they worked as forced laborers in forests, on Solchos (agricultural combines), and on railroads. Children over the age of 14 labored like adults; those from 12 to 14 years of age were given lighter duties. The usual workday was ten hours, but longer with lengthening daylight. During the short summer in the north, they worked from six in the morning until nine at night, and up to 18 hours during the harvest season. Daily attendance was taken at work. Being late for work meant a cut in rations. Any unauthorized absence was punished by withholding their food, at times even by imprisonment.

Their work was subject to quotas; so many cubic meters of timber had to be cut, so many kilos of potatoes picked, so many items produced in a given workday. If they did not fulfill their quota, their rations were cut or, worse, they would be accused of "sabotage" and threatened with arrest. Age did not matter, neither did their physical condition nor defective equipment. Soon a vicious cycle developed: weakened by hunger they were unable to fulfill their expected quotas, only to receive less food and so on until at the end they could work no more. It became the road to a slow death.

Lumbering is one of the physically most demanding jobs: a lumberjack burns 3,000 to 3,500 calories a day. How did the deportees adjust to this demand on their bodies? To supplement their meager diets to such levels was simply impossible under the circumstances.

Chicanery and corruption were also rife among their bosses and supervisors. They often deprived the deportees even of the little that should have been the fruit of their labors. The deportees had no recourse, no laws to protect them; they were "political prisoners" and therefore, under the Soviet system, deprived not only of their liberty but also of all their rights.

One deportee was denied payment because she had not "fulfilled her quota." It did not matter that she had not been told what was expected of her and that she was unfamiliar with that particular work assignment. Another young deportee narrowly escaped summary execution for "sabotage" because the engine of his tractor froze up after one of his Russian co-workers had surreptitiously drained its radiator. The deportees in an isolated camp in the forest near Arkhangelsk had to pile their entire potato harvest on the bank of a nearby river only to watch it freeze and rot while they were near starvation. These were not isolated occurrences. They are examples gleaned from the various memoirs of survivors representing but the tip of that abysmal iceberg.

If they needed to be excused from work on account of illness, they had to have a fever above 39 degrees Centigrade (102.2 Fahrenheit) or show some other cogent evidence of illness before an excuse would be written by a physician. Medical care for chronic heart, lung, or intestinal ailments was not available. Only those who might return to work received any kind of treatment.

The daily food allowance was 400 grams (14.1 oz.) of bread (in some camps a little more, often less) and half a liter of watery soup— less than 1,000 calories and never enough to fulfill the needs of the body, least of all under the demands of heavy physical labor. Children and those who could not work received smaller rations.

In some camps they were paid minimal wages with which they had to buy their food, provided any was available. One of the survivors from the steppes of Kazakhstan, for example, told that at the end of the harvest season he was paid 100 Rubles, supposedly enough to buy his food for the coming winter when no work would be available, but that all supplies had been sold out and that there was nothing left to buy.

Always hungry, people were forced to trade away what few belongings they had brought along. Extra clothing and bedding went first. Eventually their most precious possessions, a wedding ring, a gilt framed photo, had to be traded for food. To trade with the local population often meant walking for miles to the nearest settlement. When and where they could, they scoured the woods for berries and mushrooms to add some extra nourishment and to put up a supply for the long winter ahead.

Life was often reduced to bare subsistence. Any time or energy left at the end of a long work day had to be spent in the pursuit of that little extra food to survive another day, in finding an extra rag to put into their shoes, a stick of wood for the fire—not to keep warm, but just to avoid freezing to death in the snow storms of the steppes or the -50 degree Centigrade (-58 Fahrenheit) temperature of the Siberian winter.

Day after day starvation took its toll. The old, the infirm, and the small children were the first to die They were followed by the leading family members who often denied themselves their food so that their children would have more to eat. Ultimately between one-fifth and one-half of the Polish deportees died in Soviet Russia; more than one-third of them were children. From one small town in Poland which in 1940 had 7,000 Polish inhabitants, 2,000 died.

After the fall of France, a Polish government-in-exile had been set up in London with General Sikorski as its premier (replaced after his death by Stanislaw Micolajczyk). This government was well aware of the Soviet actions from the very beginning through its contacts via radio and couriers with the underground Polish Home Army. The premier informed the British government of the plight of his countrymen, but he also realized that the British were unable to offer any assistance. The defeat of Germany was a priority. Moreover, after the fall of France and until the entry of the United States into the war, Britain shouldered the lion's share of the burden. During this time thousands of Polish prisoners of war in Soviet hands perished from disease and starvation, or were summarily executed.

Swinsowchos 641, a Russian village of about 50 houses, some horse stables, and pigsties was the administrative center for the Polish camp housing Hank's family. Although winter wheat, potatoes, and a variety of small melons grew in the area, timber was the main product. It provided work for the villagers and the deportees alike.

Plenty of berries and mushrooms grew in the woods, and low bushes of wild cherries were abundant. Their fruits were small and very tart. The soil was rich; the country, flat. The hot summers and cold winters were bridged by short-lasting springs and autumns. The sudden advent of warm weather brought hordes of mosquitoes which

97

swarmed about everyone in thick, dark clouds, particularly in the woods; it was even worse after sundown.

When Hank's group arrived the snow was still too high to deliver them to their permanent quarters. Three wooden barracks, as bare inside as the desolate expanse of snow outside, became their temporary shelter. They had neither stoves for heat or cooking nor any furniture to sit on or rest against.

Beating their arms against their bodies to keep warm, they paced back and forth during the day carefully threading through the bundles and boxes of everyone's belongings on the floor. After they cleared the frosted windowpanes their eyes beheld a bleak, snow-covered land extending to the dark edge of the forest. Here and there they could see the rustic houses of the Russian settlement half-buried in the deep snow. With envy they looked on the smoke curling from their chimneys. Come nightfall they spread their bedding across the bare planks of the floor for a fitful and shivering sleep.

Every day a horse-drawn sleigh delivered their rations: the usual portion of coarse bread and a kettle of watery soup which by then was barely lukewarm. They had no toilet; a fresh snowfall would cover the stains left by their bodies' needs.

In this northern latitude the sun ascended rapidly and the days lengthened fast. This brought some relief. They could now spend more time outside and warm themselves in the sun. The Siberian nights, however, still chilled them to their bones. At last the snow began to melt.

After existing ("living" is too optimistic a word) several weeks in the barracks, they were moved into their designated home: a large, unused, former horse stable with the stalls still intact. They entered by its only door, heavy and large enough for a horse to pass through, and dragged themselves and their belongings to an open area at the opposite end where, in the past, harnesses and traces had been stored. There stood their only source of heat, an old stove, but after the unheated barracks it seemed a gift from heaven itself. They immediately crowded around it to absorb its precious warmth since it still was bitterly cold outside. Later they stuffed the cracks in the walls with straw to keep out the wind and scraped the ice from the inside of the building. As the weather warmed and they became more settled, they spread throughout the old stable.

Six stalls each, large enough for two horses, lined both sides of a central walkway between the door and the open area containing the stove. Their cement partitions reached to the ceiling. A small window high on the wall admitted some light, yet the stalls remained in perpetual semi-darkness. Every stall had a narrow chimney and a small stove of clay and bricks. Most of them had disintegrated due to years of disuse, but they were the only source of heat, place to cook, and at night illumination. They had neither candles nor oil lamps. Two or three families remained in the larger space by the old stove, while the others tried to find a stall of their own, a semblance of privacy. Those who did not find room in the stalls had to return to the wooden barracks.

Hank's family settled in one of the stalls and tried to adjust to their new surroundings. Tree stumps served as chairs. At night, they spread their bedding over a pad of straw and all four of them huddled closely under their down cover listening to the eerie howling of the wolves outside. As for the rats, Hank's grandmother chased them away with a stove poker.

Hank's grandmother repaired the small stove with clay and stones. The often damp and green, resinous wood soon blackened their pots and kettle. She therefore stacked branches and kindling into a corner to let them dry, and one of Hank's chores was to keep up her supply. Matches were at a premium as was everything else needed to start a fire. They salvaged every scrap of paper, even dry grass and moss. Hank's grandmother always tried to keep a few embers glowing in the ashes to provide a quick fire in the mornings and after work.

Their toilet was a large, unscreened pit with sloping sides behind the building. One night, nature called, Hank had to go but was afraid because wolves howled nearby. His grandmother, therefore, went with him, walking ahead with a broomstick to beat them off if need be.

They drew their water from a well that was more than two blocks away. Fetching water in a bucket was another one of Hank's daily chores and the task was not easy. How his grandmother had been able to get hold of that bucket Hank never found out. In winter a mound of ice surrounded the mouth of the well, and the hole across the top was barely large enough for the bucket to pass through.

They washed themselves from the bucket as best they could, first heating the water in their kettle. Seclusion was out of the question, particularly in winter when washing up was confined to the limited space of the stable. The piece of soap Hank's mother brought back from her overtime work was a rare luxury.

Occasionally Hank's grandmother was able to trade one thing or another with their Kirghiz neighbors for some tallow, which she then boiled with wood ash into soap for their laundry. To launder was next to impossible during the winter: they had no space, and the clothes would not dry. Even with washing, their outer garments never came thoroughly clean.

In their new life rats and roaches, body odors and stale air, soot and smoke complemented hunger and chilling cold in winter and sticky sweat in summer. Flies and mosquitoes became merely a nuisance. "After a while you got used to them," Hank said. "You didn't pay attention any longer."

When the others went to work, only the very old and children too young for either school or kindergarten, including Hank's sister, remained in camp. Those too old to work were assigned to supervise the young. Always hungry, always trying to survive one day at a time, no one had the energy to entertain or otherwise occupy the children. They received just enough supervision to keep them from getting hurt.

Ever since they had been brought there, Hank's sister hardly spoke. When her mother returned from her long hours of work, she clung to her silently, trying to hide her face in her mother's skirt, seeking protection from a world she did not understand. For years afterward she remained withdrawn and shy. Eventually her natural spontaneity reawakened, but that was not until she experienced the loving care of a family in the United States.

Hank's mother stayed active, but bereft of her former gaiety, and her eyes were filled with perpetual sadness. She hardly smiled any longer—not even when Hank brought her some wildflowers. Yet, until her final illness, she never slackened in her daily work and, despite a tiring day, she often helped the wife of the local NKVD commissar with her housework. This extra work supplemented their rations or provided her with a few kopecks for essentials: thread to repair their clothes, string to tie up their shoes, or matches to start the fire. Hank's grandmother on the other hand, thanks to her sturdy constitution, remained healthy throughout their ordeal.

She rose early, woke up the others, then started the fire. She did most of the cooking, serving hot drinks in the mornings—usually tea from herbs or wild strawberry leaves—and warm soup in the evenings. They ate from wooden bowls and wooden spoons gotten in trade from their Kirghiz neighbors. They scoured their utensils with soil and ashes, then rinsed them clear with hot water from their kettle. On the train they had used what was available: bowls, cups, or whatever was handy. Some of the prisoners had not had the foresight of Hank's grandmother and were forced to barter their few valuables for the most essential things. Hank's grandmother had even brought the kettle.

They traded for food what they could spare, at first any extra clothing, then whatever else they could do without. Back home in Krasne, Hank's father and an uncle had trapped wild mink for a coat for Hank's mother. She now felt lucky to be able to trade their thoughtful gift for a small sack of flour in the village.

A few times a parcel arrived from one of Hank's aunts. One parcel took so long to get there that the bacon in it had completely dried. Hank's grandmother cut it into small pieces and dispensed them sparingly into their soup for a long as they lasted. Some of the parcels also contained a few pieces of soap and linden-blossom tea.

In winter and in early spring Hank's grandmother volunteered to prepare seed potatoes. While she crouched in the damp root cellar cutting the sprouting potatoes she managed to secretly stash some away into bags tied to each of her legs beneath her bulky skirt. She took a great risk in doing this. Had she been found out, the least punishment would have been several months in prison.

During summer and fall they picked berries and mushrooms. With sacks from torn clothing they fought their way, often for hours, through undergrowth and brambles, through bogs and knee-deep water, taking care to mark their path so as not to lose the way back home. They gathered wild strawberries and made tea from the leaves. They dug a sweet-tasting, yellowish root which, dried and ground, took the place of sugar in their tea.

Hank thought back to his nature walks at school and as a Cub Scout. In the forests of Siberia he was proud of knowing which mushrooms were good to eat and which were poisonous, that one can grind this particular root into flour, and that these berries are sweet and those tart, and how to preserve them all by drying. Realizing that this knowledge contributed to his family's survival filled Hank with a deep satisfaction.

Every so often, while playing in the grain bin, Hank filled his pockets with wheat and brought it home. Thanks to her foresight, his grandmother had brought the coffee mill with her. Now she could grind the wheat and thicken their soups with it. Sporadic help also came from the Kirghiz families across the road: a little meat or Koumiss (similar to yogurt, but made from mare's milk).

Their camp was a little over two blocks from the Russian village. A dirt road, piled high with snow in the winter and deep mud after the rains, led to that settlement through a small stand of birches and poplars with dense undergrowth. The first building was a large wooden storage shed. Like all the buildings in the village, it stood on two-foot high piles to keep the entrance above the snow in winter. A tool shed, a large shed for agricultural machinery, and a huge grain bin stood nearby.

The storage shed served as the commissary and administrative center for the Polish deportees, for the Kirghiz, and for some Russian workers as well. There they received their food allotments and their work assignments. There they reported for work.

Early every morning, irrespective of weather and season, a designated member of each family trudged along the dirt road to the storage shed and lined up for the family's daily rations: a pie-shaped wedge of dark and heavy bread cut and weighed from a round loaf; sometimes "extras," such as a little salt, a piece of salted catfish, or flour; and on rare occasions some sugar or fatty bacon—it was never enough. Then their family name was checked off the list. Even the

Russian workers had to line up for their rations, but received a larger allotment.

The flour was full of chaff, and dumplings made from it shrank to the size of a thumbnail in boiling water. The fuzzy chaff irritated Hank's throat and nostrils, it made him cough and sneeze.

It was Hank's duty to go for the family's daily rations. He tried to get there early so that he could have a few minutes to eat before he had to report to work. By the time he returned his grandmother always had a cup of hot tea or thin soup for him. Often he had to wait for an hour or more for the shed to be unlocked, and there was always a rush to be among the first when the door opened.

Waiting outside was especially hard in winter. Torn from his sleep, Hank had to make his way through often waist-high snow in the cold and dark of early morning, then stand waiting as the chill penetrated his worn clothing. He did not dare to move around for fear of missing the rush to the opening door. All were cold, tired, and hungry, and their tempers were short; the strongest tried to get through the door first. Spring with its rains was not much better. The muddy road made every step a struggle. Hank's shoes leaked, and on many days he had to leave the camp with the work party before they had a chance to dry.

A steam whistle announced the beginning of their workday. Receiving their assignment the day before Hanks' family stayed together and worked as a unit. They were given a short break at midday to rest and to eat. Everyone carried their own bottle of water; Hank's grandmother carried and dispensed their food.

Cutting timber, particularly in winter, was the main work at *Swinsolchos 641*, of the Polish deportees, of the Kirghiz, and also of some Russians from the village. They trudged to their work site in the forest along the tracks left by the sleigh which carried the tools: large two-handed saws and axes. Like the others, Hank's mother and grandmother were shown a number of trees to fell and cut into sections; their quota for the day. Hank was given a hatchet with which to sever the branches and clear them out of the way. They worked silently. Every unnecessary word was a waste of energy and could break the rhythm of their tasks.

Hank's grandmother's physical strength pulled them through.

Seeing her swinging the ax stroke after stroke, Hank remembered her at home on the threshing floor, when she climbed the ladder to the top of the grain bin with a full sack of wheat across her shoulders. After Hank's mother died, his grandmother teamed up with one of the Kirghiz men.

In summer they worked in the fields from morning to night: They hoed rows of potatoes which never seemed to end; they forked load upon load of hay at haying season; they stacked sheaves during the wheat harvest and tossed them high upon the wagons. The fields were huge, the summer days were long and hot, and there was no shade. On their return to camp they lined up at the well waiting their turn to fill their bucket, then all three shared in it to wash off the sweat and the dust.

During the fall potato harvest they thrust heavy forks deep into the earth to lift the tubers, then hurriedly picked them up and dumped their full baskets into a passing wagon. Hank marveled at the ease with which his grandmother lifted the heavy baskets one after the other. When Hank was not picking the tubers, he was clearing the rows and heaping the dead stalks into a pile to be burned later. They dug pits in the ground in which to store the potatoes and covered them with branches, straw, and sod.

In the fields, too, they worked in silence; their work party an insignificant speck against the overwhelming expanse of the land. In silence they trudged back "home." Where were the parties and the singing at wheat-harvest time? Where was all the food and the sound of an accordion? Where were the potato-fires with fresh potatoes roasting in the embers? Whenever Hank thought back to those happy harvest days at home, he felt it must have been only a beautiful dream, a story from an unreal past. Here, to pocket one potato was called "sabotage."

In winter, besides lumbering, some worked in the potato cellar cutting seed potatoes; others loaded wheat. A wood-fired caterpillar tractor pulled a train of sleds loaded with wheat across the frozen tundra to Kustenai. Outside work would be suspended only if it was so cold that water thrown from a cup froze in the air or ice sealed the eyelids. During such temperature extremes the woods resounded with

"That's the way it was." – Hank

gunshot-like sounds of trees being split by the frost and the nights
were filled with an eerie brightness as any moisture in the air was crys-
tallized into a myriad of tiny light-intensifying and reflecting mirrors.
"Even when the sky was overcast, one could almost read a newspaper,"
Hank said.

On some days the foreman would let the workers ride to the work site on the wagon or sleigh carrying the work implements. It was considered a special privilege. Though none of the Russians in charge abused or mistreated the deportees in Hank's camp, they chose to remain aloof, their demeanor distant, trying to project an impersonal efficiency.

Like the exiles, they also worked under a cloud. They had to fulfill a quota and the threat of being accused of "sabotage" hung over them as well. To make exceptions, to show a human side, were signs of bourgeois individualism and were to be suppressed. The system to which they had to conform affected their behavior unconsciously, but relentlessly. It was the reason behind the drabness, the all-pervasive silence so characteristic of Stalinist societies. Be it in villages, towns, or cities, people hurried along the streets without eye contact and looked with suspicion upon a friendly greeting from an outsider. Those in the Soviet-occupied countries who had managed to preserve their emotional independence would later apply the pejorative term "Homo Sovieticus" to them.

The times when Hank experienced a spark of human emotion and kindness were indeed rare and fleeting. They usually came from outside his camp environment, while at play with Boris, a Russian boy who had befriended Hank, or the Kirghiz boys, or from Boris' mother. The dreary surroundings of the camp, the misery, and daily toil soon relegated even these small gestures of humanity to insignificance.

Next to food, wood was a daily necessity for the inmates of the camp—wood for heat, wood for cooking. Every day they had to range farther away from camp in search of it. Although they were allowed to gather fallen branches, they were forbidden to fell trees.

Near their quarters, just at the beginning of the woods, stood a large birch tree. One wintry night Hank and his grandmother cut it down and heaped snow over the trunk and the severed branches to hide their "sabotage." How his grandmother had gotten hold of a two-handed saw and an ax remained a mystery to Hank. When the foreman asked who had cut down the tree, nobody spoke up, though most in the camp knew. Fortunately, the foreman did not pursue the matter. Had he perhaps realized their desperate need and satisfied his rule-abiding conscience with a perfunctory inquiry? Without blinking an eye Hank's grandmother asked for and was given permission to salvage the branches. And while she gathered them, Hank cut and chopped more wood from the tree.

School was held in a converted church located in the Russian village. It was the only brick building besides the machine shed. Education was important to the Soviets, but to be a teacher one had to be an ardent communist. "Get to them, while they are young," was the saying. Enough children lived in the settlement to fill grades one through six. All deportee children under 12 years of age had to attend classes as well. They were put into the grade they had left when they were taken. Hank was the oldest boy in his class and the only child in school from their camp. Since he spoke Ukrainian, he easily understood the teacher's Russian.

For Hank, however, school lasted only three days. On his first day in school, true to the communist line, his teacher said: "The Soviet Union is the only country where the workers and peasants are free. It is the only country of freedom!" Hank raised his hand and asked: "If this country is so free, why am I here?" The next day the teacher lectured on the descent of man and told them that man is related to monkeys. Hank again raised his hand, but this time he was ignored. He stood up anyway and, giving words to his thoughts, burst out: "Maybe you are, but I am not!"

It was time for recess, and as Hank stormed out of the room some of the Russian boys came after him swinging sticks. Hank, in turn, grabbed a broken brick from the ground near his feet and threw it at the nearest boy. It hit the boy in the head, he fell and had to stay in the hospital for several days. This ended Hank's school days. The teacher told his mother he was not to return to school; he was put to work in the woods with the adults instead.

Hank detested everything about the Soviets: their uniforms, their emblems, and their slogans. He detested the Soviet state, all its representatives, and everything they stood for.

"At times my hatred of anything Soviet was more intense than my worry about the fate of my father," he said.

That hatred, born on the railroad siding in Krasne on the day of his captivity, festered inside him and emboldened him. "My hatred was stronger than any fear," he said later. "Once you develop such a hatred, you stay that way. I was like a wounded animal; I lashed out where I could. After my mother died, I could have killed."

Yet, thanks to his parents' example and teachings, he was able to distinguish between the Russian people and their ideologies and institutions. This allowed him, for instance, to form a friendship with Boris, a Russian boy about his age.

Hank's friendship with Boris grew out of the relationship their mothers had formed and which was perhaps the most fortunate event of their exile. Boris' mother had met Hank's mother soon after their arrival, and the two women developed a rapport that soon ripened into a friendship with unmeasurable consequences.

Hank was almost eleven years old when he was deported and soon outgrew the clothes he had brought along. Meanwhile, they also had become so threadbare that they readily tore while he worked among the brush and branches.

Footwear was especially critical. Not only did his shoes pinch him severely, but they were also leaking at the seams and their soles were almost worn through. His mother feared that, come winter, he could lose some toes or even a foot from frostbite. By that time, however, his and his mother's relationship with Boris' family had become well established. Many of Boris' discarded clothes fit Hank and they were given freely. Boris' outgrown "*valenki*" (pressed felt boots) saved his feet.

Boris' father was the chief NKVD officer of the settlement and the local commissar. Outwardly he was also a professed communist. Due to his position he had a larger and more comfortable house than any of the other Russians. The living room was always immaculate, and Boris, as the only child, had a room of his own. They also kept a cow in a small shed near the house.

Boris' father remained aloof in regard to the women's relationship and their children's friendship. Boris' mother therefore, despite her husband's position, could at times help Hank's family with a few kopecks or clothing from her own meager stores; at other times with a pitcher of skim milk, a few eggs, or, though rarely, that most precious commodity of all, a piece of soap. In return Hank's mother would help her around the house.

Boris and a friend of his kept apart from the other Russian boys in the village. Although both had witnessed his outburst in school, they befriended Hank nonetheless—or perhaps because of it.

"They never talked or bragged about communism, and we came to respect each other," Hank said of them. As Hank's friendship with Boris deepened, the other Russian boys left Hank in peace.

Hank and Boris got together about once a week. Every so often Hank visited Boris at home. They sat in his room and talked, played checkers, or looked at books. Boris' mother always had a slice of bread and a glass of milk for Hank. Sometimes Boris came to the camp to see Hank. They played in the barns or the grain bin, walked about, or went swimming together. Hank shared with Boris what he knew of plants, wild fruits, and mushrooms. One day Boris asked Hank to teach him Polish.

"I'll teach you Polish, if you teach me Russian geography," Hank answered his request.

He was eager to learn all about the country. Although he was only 12 years old at that time, he was planning to escape. Only his loyalty and attachment to his family restrained him from making this a reality.

"Should anything ever happen to them, I am going to leave," he had decided. "Boris can teach me where the towns are and which rivers I'd have to cross. I can survive off the land. I know which berries and what roots are good to eat, which mushrooms I can pick, and how to catch crayfish. Grandfather showed me." He did not look upon this as an idle dream since he had already put into practice so many things he knew about nature. It was his favorite subject at school and the reason he had brought his treasured nature book with him. Now he could also use it for the Polish lessons requested by Boris. Yet—and this was perhaps the true measure of the depth of their friendship—when Hank finally left he gave Boris his nature book to keep.

About 50 Kirghiz lived in a dozen or more sod houses across the road from the Polish camp. They, like the Poles, had been forcefully exiled from their homeland and were therefore sympathetic to the Polish group. "Had it not been for their help, we might not have survived," Hank said in acknowledgment. Despite their own poverty they often shared with the Poles their horse meat, their beef, and their Koumiss.

The colonization of the Kirghiz lands with Russian settlers had begun under the tsar, but the Kirghiz settlement of *Swinsowchos 641* dated back to one of Stalin's early efforts at deportation and Russian colonization. Though the Kirghiz Soviet Socialist Republic was not formally established until 1936, during the early years of the Soviet takeover the nomadic Moslem Kirghiz responded with guerrilla warfare to Stalin's attempts to settle them and take away their herds. They also fought against the continued colonization of their lands by Russians and Ukrainians. Eventually, their resistance was broken, and many were deported to the far ends of the Soviet empire.

Though the Kirghiz now lived in permanent sod houses, they were still nomads at heart. They evaded the Soviets through their network of settlements, stabling their horses in one village, getting their Koumiss from another. As Mohammedans they abhorred alcohol and pork. To call them "swine" was the ultimate insult—and here they were in *Swinsowchos 641*!

Their houses, dug halfway into the ground, had walls of layered sod and were plastered smooth inside with clay. Upright timbers partitioned a space the size of a large living room while also supporting the roof. Their only source of daylight was one or two windows usually covered with transparent animal bladders instead of glass. Their roof consisted of timbers covered with branches and straw and finished off with a layer of soil and sod. Every roof had a trap door, because in winter the heavy snows buried their low entryways. A stove made from stones and clay with a metal top for cooking provided heat and was their only source of light after dark. Wooden bowls of various sizes served for eating and for preparing food. The houses were bare except for a low stool, their only furniture, on which stood their most precious possession, a brass samovar. It had an insert into which they would put glowing charcoal or burning sticks to heat the water. They made tea in cups, but drank it from saucers, holding a sugar cube in their mouths. They slept on straw and sat, usually with their legs crossed, either on bare ground or on hides or blankets. Their clothes hung from wooden pegs pushed into the walls. Except for hot summer days, they commonly wore parkas and quilted trousers. They chewed a gum from birch sap which was boiled and rolled into balls about one inch in diameter. It tasted bitter at first, but became sweet as one continued to chew.

The local Russians discriminated greatly against the Kirghiz, just as Hank had seen among some Polish people toward the Ukrainians back home. But he also saw how willingly the Kirghiz helped his people, and how important their help was for his family's survival. "How could I look down on them; they were the ones helping us," he said.

Hank's outburst in school had impressed not only Boris and his friend but also some of the Kirghiz boys. They adopted him as their own and did what they could to protect him from any threat or injury from the boys in the Russian village. Taking their clue from the attitude of the adult Russians toward the Kirghiz, the children of the Russian and the Kirghiz community constantly fought with each other. Tempers always ran high, and Hank was soon drawn into their feud.

Spoiling for another fight, the Kirghiz boys asked Hank to stand in a path and taunt a group of Russian boys while they hid in the brush nearby. The Russian boys promptly answered Hank's jeers by coming after him, only to be rushed by the Kirghiz boys. Gleefully Hank watched the Russian boys run off with bloody noses and black eyes.

With Boris for a friend, Hank came to know more about the life of the local Russian population. Most were descendants of past exiles sent to Siberia by the tsars, but if any of them felt sympathy for the plight of the Polish deportees they were reluctant to show it. Many were afraid of others as possible informers. Besides, they also lived at the end of "nowhere," and most were too poor themselves to be of any help. They had learned to make do with little and no longer lived with the specter of starvation hanging over their heads. Hank watched a Russian cobbler at work. Instead of leather for the soles, he used pieces of a tire and shaved the profile down. For the thin leather needed between the sole and the foot he substituted birch bark. He boiled resin into pitch to seal the shoes.

May Day and the anniversary of the October Revolution were the most important holidays for the Soviets, but in this Russian village little was celebrated.

In several Russian homes Hank saw a towel or sheet hanging in the corner of the living room hiding a picture or statue of Christ, the Virgin Mary, or some other religious icon. Later, in Kustenai, Hank would see more of the suppressed religious spirit of the local population surface. Even at Boris', officially a communist family that prominently displayed a picture of Stalin in their house, a covered icon hung in the living room.

Easter, their first away from home, had passed quite unnoticed by the deportees, buried as they were in deep snow. The icy wind had blown away the dates of Lent, Good Friday, and every other religious holiday that they had known. Later in the year, as they became familiar with their daily routine, they began to reorient themselves. The work-schedule and the bulletins posted at the commissary helped to fix the dates; so did the occasional newspaper. What difference did it make, however, to know what day was Christmas? They were neither permitted nor did they feel like celebrating. Rather, many mourned for the loved ones they had lost or left behind.

On Christmas morning Hank's grandmother said: "Today is Christmas." In the evening they sat together not having even a candle to burn. Hank read aloud from a prayer book. How could they sing the traditional Christmas songs when hunger gnawed? Christmas, more than any other day of the year, had become for them a day of sadness, of longing for their home so far away. And so they sat in silence.

During their transport when someone had intoned a prayer the others soon had joined in. In camp, however, to pray in public was forbidden, as were any other organized religious expressions or activities. Once they had fallen into their daily routine and established their own spaces, religious thoughts, practices, and prayers became a personal matter. Those whose faith sprang from the "Christ within" as Dietrich Bonhoeffer put it, found reassurance and comfort therein.

Hank's mother and grandmother never wavered in their faith. Every morning and evening they knelt in prayer. Hank's grandmother led them in saying the rosary, and they always made the sign of the cross before eating. Hank, too, kept his conviction that God would protect him and would eventually lead him out of Russia—someday, somehow. He vowed to go again on a pilgrimage to the shrine at Malinte, not if, but when God would deliver him from the Soviets and see him safely home again.

On their weekly day of rest and on an occasional long summer evening Hank's undaunted spirit surfaced. Despite his hardships he found time to play with the Kirghiz boys or visit Boris. The road from their camp passed the pigsty and from there continued to another village. About five blocks down that road was a swampy pond where Hank, the Russian, and Kirghiz boys went to swim. In winter the Kirghiz boys skated there on homemade skates. They tied a bowed root under their shoes and strung a wire along it for an edge.

At times Hank played with other boys in the large grain bin. They climbed an outside ladder to the top, slid across the rafters, jumped onto the piles of wheat, and slid down with the flow of the loose grain. This is where the wheat came from he gave to his grandmother. Being a boy at play allowed him to get away with many things impossible for an adult.

A horse stable was near a bend in the road. Close by, pairs of Russian and Kirghiz men stood in a saw pit and sawed logs into thick planks by hand. Once, Hank was in the woods gathering strawberries when the horses came back from the pasture. They were small and scrawny. Hank jumped on the last one trotting past. Startled, it took off in a gallop passing all the others. Riding bareback, in desperation Hank grabbed its mane and managed to hold on for a while. His sore seat reminded him of this misadventure for days.

During their first summer in Siberia, in 1940, Hank's mother fell ill. She was taken to the hospital in Kustenai with a high fever. One night while she was still in the hospital, Hank dreamt that he heard her cry out and awoke with an overpowering urge to see her. With a bottle of water and a piece of bread in his pocket, he went to Boris' before dawn and knocked on his window. Boris was familiar with Kustenai; one of his aunts lived there. He agreed to show Hank the way. His mother gave them a bottle of milk and extra bread for their journey.

Every day large truck-trailers with wood-burning generators hauled wheat to Kustenai. Boris and Hank waited at a curve for one to slow down and jumped on its bed. They arrived in Kustenai late in the afternoon and spent the night at Boris' aunt. In the morning Boris showed Hank the way to the hospital. Once there, his requests for directions were so often ignored that it took Hank half the day to find the "experimental station" in back of the main hospital. He climbed the steps, knocked at the door, and after another long wait was finally able to ask to see his mother.

"Your mother died this morning. Send someone to get her body," a voice told him abruptly through the half-opened door. Then the door slammed in his face. When Hank returned to camp, his grandmother was at Boris' inquiring about him.

"I don't remember how I got back. I found my grandmother doing something in the cow shed. I went in and told her. I could not cry," he said.

Within a couple of days his grandmother went to Kustenai to claim her daughter's body and bury her. Someone had made a cross from iron pieces for her grave. Hank stayed in camp with his sister.

"I had to split her nightgown in order to bury her in it. She was all cut up, in pieces, the arms, the legs, the head," his grandmother told him afterwards.

A few weeks later an elderly physician visited Hank's grandmother and the children in camp. He spoke quietly and asked that they not mention his visit. He explained that he did not know the nature of Hank's mother's illness. "She had a fever and was taken to the experimental unit for treatment," he said. "They injected her with a new kind of medication after which she went into convulsions and died. The students did a dissection to find out what happened." He did not know the results of the autopsy.

Hank was never able to visit his mother's grave in Kustenai while at camp, nor later, when he was there with the other orphans. He was neither given the time nor the chance to do so. Years later, when Hank needed a birth certificate, the Catholic parish office in Kutkorzu in Poland complied with his request. The entry in back of his mother's, his sister's, and his own name stated: "*wywiezione na Sybir*" (exiled to

Siberia). Following his mother's entry was noted: "died June 29, 1940, in Kustozyn (Kustenai).

Death was no stranger to the deportees. It arrived early on their trek; it remained with them in their camp. Hank had become aware of it from the beginning of their journey regardless of how much the adults tried to shield him. When the train stopped, he had seen the soldiers remove the dead from their car and fling them into the snow by the tracks. Burials had been impossible in the frozen ground. Then the train had moved on, carrying with it the laments, the tears, and the sadness of the survivors. With every new death Hank's worry about the fate of his father deepened, and now that unknown fate was compounded by his mother's death. Hank felt a profound sense of loss.

Not long before their train arrived at Kustenai, another infant had died. Its mother rolled the tiny corpse into a cloth and kept it near her hoping to find a few rough boards for a makeshift casket in which to bury her child. Someone sprayed a sweet-smelling perfume on the bundle to control the odor. Its smell combined with the odor of decaying flesh nauseated Hank intensely. Even now, decades later, the fragrance of a sweet perfume makes Hank recall the entire scene and reexperience the profound aversion and nausea he felt then.

After their arrival at camp, they could at least bury their dead. The Russian cemetery filled with Polish names on wooden crosses showing the years of birth and death of the deceased. Relatives decorated the graves with transplanted wildflowers and made wreaths and bouquets from blossoms and colorful branches. Though Hank heard the adults speak of their loss, in camp he never witnessed the actual process of dying and did not attended any burials.

Of the 78 people from Krasne who had been packed into a freight car on February 10, 1940, only 18 survived to the end of the war. This included Hank, his sister, and Hank's grandmother. Hank's sister, seven years old at the time they left the camp for the orphanage, was the youngest surviving child of that group. His grandmother remained in the camp until the war ended.

Shortly before Hank left the camp for the orphanage in Kustenai, he stood in the daily bread line alongside a counter containing a sparse assortment of items for sale, most of them of poor quality. That day

115

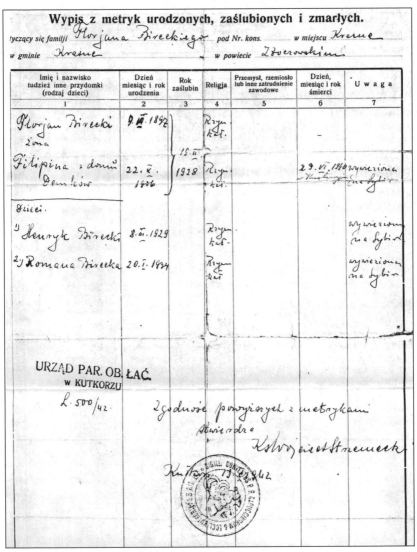

Wypis z metryk urodzonych, zaślubionych i zmarłych.

tyczący się familji Florjana Bireckiego *pod Nr. kons.* *w miejscu* Krasne

w gminie Krasne *w powiecie* Zborowskim

Imię i nazwisko tudzież inne przydomki (rodzaj dzieci)	Dzień miesiąc i rok urodzenia	Rok zaślubin	Religja	Przemysł, rzemiosło lub inne zatrudnienie zawodowe	Dzień, miesiąc i rok śmierci	U w a g a
1	2	3	4	5	6	7
Florjan Birecki żona	9.IV.1892		Rzym. kat.		–	
Filipina z domu Demków	22.X. 1896	15.II. 1928	Rzym. kat.		29.VI.1940 wywieziona na Sybir	wywieziona na Sybir
Dzieci:						
1) Henryk Birecki	8.III.1929		Rzym. kat.			wywieziona na Sybir
2) Romana Birecka	20.I.1934		Rzym. kat.			wywieziona na Sybir

URZĄD PAR. OB. ŁAĆ.
w KUTKORZU

L. 500/42.

Zgodność powyższych z metrykami
stwierdza

Ks. Wojciech Strzemecki

Kutkorz 13.VI.1942

A copy of the parish record of Hank's family.

the others in line crowded Hank so much that his small frame was lifted up against the edge of the counter displacing its glass cover. Seeing an open box of pocketknives, he quickly grabbed a handful and pushed them into the front of his shirt. But his conscience bothered him; he knew that he had stolen and that this was against the commandments. He gave all of the knives away to his Kirghiz friends. "But

I did not take the knives for myself and this is a Soviet store," he rationalized. "It was just another chance to get back at the Soviets, that's all." The theft of the knives was investigated and Hank was found out. Fortunately by that time he had already left the camp.

Hank had never considered it "stealing" when he filled his pockets with wheat or when his grandmother hid potatoes under her skirt. Neither did he regret cutting down the birch tree during the night. These things were done for survival and God, Hank was sure, understood and forgave.

On June 22, 1941, the Germans attacked the Soviet Union. This brought more hardships. The rations were reduced, and the one free day per week was canceled. As the news of the defeats of the Red Army became known, Hank and the other Polish prisoners rejoiced in secret. Every Soviet setback strengthened their conviction that some day they would get out of Russia. They were unaware of the German plans for the permanent enslavement of the Polish people.

In the wake of the German invasion Polish-Soviet tensions eased somewhat, and a Polish-Soviet treaty was signed on July 30, 1941. One of its provisions called for an "amnesty to all Polish citizens at present deprived of their liberty within the territory of the USSR." This article was supplemented on January 3, 1942, by a Soviet agreement allowing orphaned Polish children to leave the Soviet Union.

In early spring 1942, the thaw in the Polish-Soviet relations finally penetrated the depths of the Siberian woods. An emissary of the Polish government-in-exile came to the old horse stable. He explained that the orphans and those children who did not want to stay with their families could leave the Soviet Union for somewhere in the West, some as yet undesignated territory, but under the control of the British or the Americans. "The Polish government has set up a gathering orphanage in Kustenai. The children are to go there first," he said.

A door had opened. It remained ajar for a time, until it shut again on April 25, 1943 and the cold of the Siberian winter returned as a "cold war" for nearly half a century. Hank did not understand the details, but the phrase "to be taken out of the Soviet Union," was enough for him.

"I am going," Hank told his grandmother as he prepared to leave

Hank's grandmother after her return to Poland from Siberia.

with the emissary on one of the many trucks headed for Kustenai. His grandmother replied: "Yes, go and see what it is all about. You can always come back here."

"If everything is all right you can bring Romana," Hank said. He had made his decision already. He knew instinctively that this was perhaps their one and only chance to get out of that frozen wasteland.

Three days later, one of the Polish representatives traveling through the area brought Hank's grandmother to the Kustenai orphanage for a visit. Adamant in his conviction that his sister should be with him Hank painted an especially rosy picture of his new life. But his grandmother could see for herself that the children were much better off than in the camp. They were well cared for and had plenty to eat. She stayed a while, shared a sandwich with Hank, and talked to the Polish officials in an office downstairs. The next day, late in the afternoon, she brought his sister to join him.

"I can't stay," she said with tears in her eyes. "I'll have to leave right away to get back."

When his grandmother left to return to the camp, they all felt that this might be their final parting. "From now on my sister and I are the only ones left of the family," Hank said to himself.

One can only imagine the pain Hank's grandmother felt during this separation and on her way back to camp. Only the thought that the children were leaving the Soviet Union and were hopefully on their way toward a better future, may have somewhat eased her sorrow.

Hank heard nothing more about his grandmother's life in Siberia, but in his mind's eye he could see her solid frame among the dwindling number of Poles trying to survive at *Swinsowchos 641*, sharing her deep devotion and practical wisdom with them, and grinding wheat in the coffee mill to thicken a bowl of soup for herself and her compatriots. After the war Hank's grandmother neither wished nor could return to her former home in Zuratyn. The area had become a part of the Ukrainian Soviet Socialist Republic.

In the first week of November 1939 the inhabitants of Soviet-occupied Poland were given a chance to "elect" regional assemblies. Some of the candidates were actually Soviet citizens, there was no choice among them, and only a "yes" or "no" vote was possible. Neither were the ballots secret; voting had to be done in front of NKVD officers. Those voting "no" were soon afterwards arrested.

As their first action, these newly-"elected" assemblies petitioned to make the Soviet-occupied territory a part of the Soviet Union and its inhabitants Soviet citizens. The Supreme Soviet graciously accepted the "will of the people" and acted accordingly. This sham was finalized at the Yalta conference. At the end of the Second World War the

Hank's grandmother after the war with her great-grandnephew.

indigenous Polish people were given the option of renouncing this forced Soviet citizenship. If they did, however, they could no longer continue to live in the Soviet-annexed territories but had to settle within the new Polish borders which had been shifted west. Over one and a half million ethnic Poles native to the area were thereby removed from their ancestral homes and "repatriated" to the so-called recovered territories of the "new" Poland.

Like so many others Hank's grandmother opted for her Polish citizenship. She joined her son-in-law, Hank's father, who had survived the war and had been resettled in that area of western Poland formerly controlled by Germany. Among the belongings she brought back from Siberia was the brass coffee mill. In her new home she helped to take care of her son-in-law's younger sister who was pregnant at that time. Later, this woman in return attended to the needs of Hank's grandmother when she began to fail. Born in the 1880s, Hank's grandmother—a remarkable woman—died peacefully in the early 1960s.

9.

A Door Opens

Hank had traveled the route from *Swinsowchos 641* to Kustenai for the last time. The Polish representative brought Hank to the orphanage where someone took him upstairs to the dormitory, showed him his cot, and gave him a sandwich. It was late in the afternoon and time to eat. Hank was happy to see so many children who spoke his language, who shared his culture. He had missed speaking Polish to boys his own age and was anxious to talk to them, to find out if any of them came from his home region. Although a couple of boys came from Busk, just a few miles from home, none of them were from Krasne.

Later that evening Hank laid back on his cot. Ever since he had been taken he missed being alone, being just by himself. He often longed for the times at home when he could sit in the attic, a book or magazine in hand, and listen to the rain drum on the roof. The crowded dormitory made him feel more confined than ever but he was warm and his belly was full. He hoped that his sister would soon be sleeping next to him.

Professor Stanislaw Kot, Minister of the Interior of the Polish government-in-exile, had been named Polish ambassador to the Soviet
Union. In accord with the Polish-Soviet agreement of January 1942,
his embassy established two major orphanages and put them under the
control of the new Polish army. One of them was located at Guzar near
Samarkand in the eastern Uzbek SSR.; the other in the Azerbaijan
SSR. Eventually 139 gathering orphanages and nurseries were established.

To free the many Polish children from the labor camps and the
Soviet children's homes, the "*dye doms*" or "*dietdomy,*" Polish army
volunteers in civilian clothing traveled to the most remote corners of
the Soviet empire, often having to contend with the objections of the
local authorities and the obstacles they placed in their way.

The Polish government-in-exile in Britain was aware of the dire
conditions of its countrymen in the Soviet Union. One of its first aims
after the diplomatic relations with the Soviets had been established was
to arrange for immediate assistance to the civilian deportees. The
Soviets immediately rebuffed any appeals for help on their part. They
had made their attitude abundantly clear before by giving reduced
rations in the camps to children and to people unable to work: Only
those who worked were entitled to food. Many of the children, therefore, arrived at the Polish orphanages in the most pitiful condition,
undernourished, and with abysmal hygienic pathologies. Unable to
carry the entire burden itself the Polish government-in-exile appealed
for relief supplies abroad.

Many governments and civic organizations throughout the West
answered the Polish appeals: The American Government became one
of the largest contributors under the lend-lease program, Indian Rajas
organized a relief effort, and all Polish government workers in Britain
contributed two percent of their pay. It was, however, not until spring
of 1942 that the relief effort began to reach the areas in need.

The logistics of transporting the supplies were complex. Many had
to be shipped from overseas. If they survived U-boat attacks, they then
had to be transported by land in a roundabout way through Iran. The
Polish embassy established a distribution system with regional depots
overseen by its delegates. These, in turn, arranged to distribute the

supplies to the people through local "men of confidence" selected from among the deportees.

In Kustenai a three-story building was converted into a Polish center for the area. The Polish consulate occupied the first floor. The third floor was turned into one large dormitory: a collecting center for the Polish children arriving from the surrounding camps. Polish adults, freed by the amnesty, worked at the consulate and also cared for the children.

From the very beginning the Polish authorities tried to create for the children a feeling of "home," a semblance of community bound by a common culture, language, customs, and religion. With more food available they also began at first to halt, then gradually to reverse the physical consequences of the children's severe deprivations.

Fortunately for Hank and his sister the Kazakhstan Soviet Socialist Republic had been the first district organized by the Polish embassy, and the Polish relief efforts there had received active collaboration by the local authorities. (The orphanage in Kustenai had been among the first to be opened.) The Polish relief institutions in Kazakhstan were also the first to be closed-in July 1942, long before the January 15, 1943 Soviet decree to this effect.

By the time Hank and his sister came to Kustenai, the system of "gathering orphanages" had been well established, and the relief supplies were finally reaching their destinations. Fate had opened a door easing Hank's and his sister's conditions in Kustenai and on their further journey.

The "gathering orphanages" were the first step to rescue the Polish children from the claws of the Russian bear. Many stations still lay ahead of them, and all the children would wander for years before their desire for a new home would be fulfilled.

In Kustenai one large dormitory housed boys and girls together; only the older girls were quartered apart. The sleeping cots of the 200 or more children, from toddlers to Hank's age, took up every available space, even the halls and corridors. They had no place to play, and it was still cold outside. Standing or sitting wherever they found a space, they talked about where they came from, when they might leave and where to, about the adults in charge of them, and about the parents they had lost. Hank shared with them what he had seen of the war, and what he had found out while walking through town.

At mealtime the children stood in line, received their meals on a tray, then ate sitting on their cots or standing about. The food was provided by the Polish Red Cross; it varied little, but at least they could eat as much as they wanted. Given their craving for salt, British bouillon paste on bread was a favorite.

Hank's and his sister's stay in Kustenai lasted a few weeks. Although they were in dire need of clothes there were no new ones to be given out. At least they could wash regularly—even if only from barrels—and the lye soap was harsh, but they had enough to go around. They also had an outhouse.

Gradually the weather got warmer and the snow began to disappear from the yard. Last to melt was a large snow bank behind the building where the snow had slid off the roof and lay in a huge pile against the back wall. The children could now play in the fenced yard or even walk into town whose center was only a few blocks away. Each had been given a few kopecks spending money. Hank had enough to once or twice buy himself a Russian soft drink. It tasted faintly like root beer and was made from fermented and sweetened bread and water. When Hank walked through some of the Russian stores he was surprised at how little there was to buy. He saw a lot of toys for sale, but food was scarce. Moreover everything was expensive, even the *valenki*, the felt boots which were so essential in winter. Hank knew he could not have managed without them. He realized how fortunate he had been that Boris' outgrown shoes and clothes fit him, and he felt deeply grateful to Boris' parents for their help. He wanted to visit his mother's grave, but the cemetery was on the other side of town and he would not have known where to look. Besides, the Polish officials did not allow the children to go that far by themselves and there was nobody to take him there.

One Sunday a Polish priest celebrated Mass in the yard behind their building and everyone attended. Going to Mass and partaking of Communion for the first time since he was taken from home more than two years ago moved Hank deeply. Listening to the Polish priest reaffirm a faith which had been his since childhood was another link to home. Although it was a Roman Catholic service, many Russians also thronged the open gate and crowded into the yard until it was packed with people. The Russian police did not interfere.

The enforced idleness made Hank restless. He was anxious to explore, to investigate his surroundings. A ladder led to the attic tempting him to see what was up there. The ladder was hinged at the ceiling beneath a trap door and could be lowered by a rope. Hank imagined the arc the ladder would follow if he let it down from the ceiling and concluded that its end fitted between two cots. He pulled it down, climbed up, and pushed the trap door open. Leaning through the opening he looked around. The attic was spacious, but empty; a layer of sand filled the spaces between the joists. Hank pushed himself up. Above him stretched a metal roof just like at home.

The attic was lit by two windows, located on opposite sides. Carefully balancing on the narrow joists Hank made his way toward one of them, opened it, and climbed out onto the roof to have a look around. The building next door was one story lower and shared a common wall with the orphanage. Hank had noticed it before. A ten-foot wooden fence screened it from the road, and Soviet soldiers were often seen going in and out of the gate. Now, as he looked down on its flat roof, he saw disassembled machine guns lying in rows, their freshly-oiled steel glinting in the sunlight.

At the beginning of the war, the machine gun fire from the German airplanes had frightened Hank much more than rifle shots by its randomness. The bullets struck whatever got in their way: things, animals, people. He had never forgotten the dead horses in the field near his home, and the expression "a hail of bullets" in his imagination had turned into reality. Now he saw machine guns spread out before him—Soviet machine guns! Though taken apart, in pieces, they could be reassembled at a moment's notice and be ready to fire. Hank pictured a Russian soldier loading the belt and slamming the lock shut. The thought of metal striking metal brought him back to that day on the railroad siding in Krasne when the doors on their car were slammed shut, his mind hearing again the harsh sound of the lock falling into place. And he thought of that morning at the hospital in Kustenai when the door was slammed in his face with the words:

"Your mother died this morning." Hatred surged in him, hatred of anything Soviet.

Hank remembered the sand in the attic. Climbing back through the window he filled his pockets with it. "What if they catch me?" Crossed his mind; but also "I don't care." He returned to the edge of the roof and, with a sweeping motion like the sower seeding the soil, broadcast the sand over the field of gun parts. He heard a shout and saw a Russian soldier coming across the lower roof toward him. Instead of climbing back through the window, Hank ran along the roof to the back of the building. He slipped and tried to catch himself on the gutter, but it gave way and he fell three stories into what was left of the huge snow bank next to the building. Though he was nearly submerged, the snow had broken his fall. Unhurt, he scrambled out, entered the building through the back door, and quickly mingled with the children inside. His heart raced. It was a narrow escape.

A few days later, the children, including Hank and his sister, left for their next destination: the Polish orphanage and army camp at Guzar, near Samarkand in Uzbekistan, not far from the Caspian sea. It was to be their last camp in the Soviet Union.

10.

"These Children Have Suffered Enough!"

At the beginning of the Second World War the Polish government first fled to Romania, from there to France, and finally to England. The pressure of the German invasion and the initial disastrous setbacks of the Red Army prompted Stalin to establish diplomatic relations with this government and to agree to negotiations for the release of any imprisoned and deported Polish nationals. On July 30, 1941, the Polish commander-in-chief and premier of the Polish government-in-exile in London, General Wladyslaw Sikorski, and the Soviet ambassador, Ivan Maisky signed the Polish-Soviet treaty. This treaty restored diplomatic relations between the two countries and annulled the German-Soviet Non-Aggression pact of 1939. It also provided for a Polish army to be formed in the USSR and to be equipped and trained by the Soviets. On August 8, General Wladyslaw Anders was made commander-in-chief of these Polish forces. The treaty also offered an "amnesty" to Polish nationals detained in the Soviet Union whose only "crime" had been that they were Polish and belonged to the alleged anti-Soviet elements.

Hank, his sister, and his mother were three of these "criminals," condemned because the head of their household had been a "representative of the Polish government"—a policeman in a small village.

The Soviets, however, refused to return the Soviet-occupied Polish territories to Poland, to move their border back to where it lay before the war: the line established by the 1921 Treaty of Riga between Poland and the Soviet Union. To the disappointment and sorrow of the Polish people the Polish government-in-exile yielded to the pressure of the Western Allies and did not, and could not, pursue their rightful claim. The overriding concern at that time was the defeat of Germany and for that, the help of the Soviet Union was indispensable.

By October 1939 over 200,000 Polish soldiers from privates to generals had been captured by the Red Army. (About 70,000 of them were eventually evacuated from the Soviet Union.) After Stalin authorized the formation of the new Polish army, General Anders was able to mobilize two divisions by September 1941. Because only about 1,600 officers of the estimated 15,000 that were captured could be found, General Anders' command made an intense effort to locate the rest. Jozef Czapski, a Polish officer who along with 60 others had been miraculously removed from a camp where all others perished, became his delegate and personally met with the highest officials of the NKVD and the Gulag administration in his search for the missing Polish officers. His book, *The Inhuman Land*, describes how his inquiries met with evasive answers, insincere assurances, and plain stonewalling by the responsible Soviet officials. The answer to the fate of the missing Polish officers was finally given when in April 1943 German troops unearthed the remains of over 4,000 former Polish officers in the forest of Katyn. They had been executed by the Soviets in the spring of 1940. Among them was General Jozef Haller, the first choice to command the new Polish army. Eventually four different sites where Polish officers were executed en masse were identified. Katyn, however, stands as a symbol for all of them. Czapski reflects on his experiences as a prisoner of war under the Soviets and the fate of his comrades: "I thought back to 1939 and to all the ensuing period. I could see in it nothing but death, camps, and the progressive degradation of human life."

Prompted by General Sikorski, Winston Churchill, the British prime minister, was able to convince the Soviets to allow General Anders to move his newly formed Polish army out of the Soviet Union to the Middle East. In March 1942 the Soviets also agreed to let the families of the soldiers leave. A British-Polish commission was appointed which had to produce a list of Polish people over 16 years of age, including their names, ages, and sex, together with names of three persons who could vouch for their Polish origin. If all was in order, only then would the Polish civilians be released, and they numbered into the hundreds of thousands.

One day, in late spring 1942, Hank, his sister, and the other children of the temporary orphanage in Kustenai stepped out of the building, lined up in twos, and made the short walk from the orphanage to the train station. There they climbed again into freight cars. Only the Polish adults in charge went with them. There were no Soviet soldiers, no guards.

Hank carried his few belongings in a paper bag. He still had both his parents' photographs, torn from their railroad passes, and he still had the wristwatch his godfather had given him on his sixth name day, though it had stopped working quite some time ago. His sister stayed close at his side. Then, and throughout the rest of their journey, the Polish personnel who looked after the children made sure that Hank and his sister did not lose contact.

It was the beginning of a long trek. This time no Soviet guards slammed the doors shut. This time their cars had wooden bunks filled with straw. And this time the train stopped frequently for food and water at stations, not on remote sidings as it had done on their way to Siberia. There was nothing to hide. Their car also had a toilet in the corner with a curtain in front.

At the stops their caretakers distributed food from the supply car: sandwiches or canned food, enough to satisfy any hunger. The bread had been baked in Kustenai before they left. It was made from wheat or light rye flour, and therefore not as heavy and dark as before when they were prisoners. On it they put butter and honey or a meat spread similar to spam. Sometimes they ate pork and beans from a can. Each car carried a large container of drinking water which was refilled whenever the train stopped. At times they also had hot tea to drink. A man and a woman, both in Polish army uniform, rode in every car and watched over the children. Every morning and evening they led the children in prayer. They traveled for days and traversed most of the Soviet Union from north to south in this way.

Hank was elated. He relished his new freedom, his first step in a long journey. "I'm on my way out of Russia!" went through his mind again and again. In the all-pervasive mood of relief and joy even eating had lost its importance. Stopping often during the day, their train slowly made its way to Uzbekistan, to the Polish orphanage at Guzar in the Uzbek SSR.

As they proceeded further south, nature also smiled on the train filled with children: the sun shone. It became warm enough so that they could leave the car doors open and, with only a rope strung across, sit there letting their feet dangle in the balmy air. Jarred by the tracks the train swayed back and forth. A boy, about five or six years of age, suddenly fell off. Had he been careless, or was he ill? He was small and the rope stretched above his head. Fortunately the train also carried freight and therefore was not going very fast. Hank saw him fall and heard someone shout, then everybody in the car crowded at the open door and blocked his view. One of the Polish adults in their car jumped off after the boy. To everyone's surprise and relief, both rejoined their car at the next stop, unhurt, not even bruised, and with their clothes intact.

After leaving Kustenai and the flat country around it, they passed through the broad foothills of the southern Ural Mountains. Evergreen forests, meadows, and vast expanses of low-growing bush cherries Hank remembered so well from his days at *Swinsowchos 641* seemed to be the only vegetation for miles around. Eventually the land became flat again. For a long time they traveled through the rolling fields and undulating grasslands of the steppes, then through dusty and arid plains. Along the southern part of their route the land turned to desert, interrupted only by oases, where since ancient times a system of canals irrigated the parched country with the abundant water from the Pamir and Hindukush mountains. Where there was sufficient water, cotton fields stretched from horizon to horizon, dotted here and there by clumps of mulberry trees. Further on apricot orchards lined the tracks, and villages became more numerous. Their houses stood apart, each within its own orchard and garden, not clustered into the big kolkhozes (collective farms) that Hank had seen in the north. Everywhere apricots were spread out to dry on the flat roofs of the houses and on large sheets on the ground. As they approached their destination, they crossed many rivers which ran fast and high, and distant mountain ranges rose into view.

On their journey they passed the discarded trash left by the troop trains going west toward the front. At stops Hank became irate every time he read the labels of the empty food cans thrown away by the soldiers. Inevitably they were British or American made with labels in Cyrillic "made in the Soviet Union" pasted over them. He felt particularly bitter when he saw railroad cars still bearing the emblems of one of the Soviet-occupied countries, but now crudely painted over with USSR. Worst of all was if some cars carried the acronym PKP (Polish State Railways) with the white eagle beside it.

Eventually the train stopped at a small station. They disembarked and boarded open trucks for a short, dusty ride to their next waystation, the Polish army orphanage at Guzar.

This orphanage had one permanent building which housed the offices, the kitchen, the mess hall. Due to the children's deprivations in the past and the ever present illnesses, it also had to serve as a morgue. To have a morgue remained a sad, but essential part of all the camps in the Soviet Union, as well as later in the first camps in Iran. Women in Polish army uniforms cooked the food and looked after the children. The orphanage was near a small river, separated by a gravel road. On the other side of the orphanage a rough-sawn picket fence marked the boundary of an apricot orchard, a boundary the children were forbidden to cross. Hank made contact with one of the orchard workers, an older man, through that picket fence and traded his worn out wristwatch for a bag of apricots for his sister.

By this time most of the children's clothes were not only thoroughly worn out but also outgrown. The women care-takers, using the same gray fabric, soon outfitted the children with uniform, but new, shorts and shirts.

The children slept in tents, six to a tent. Fifty tents or more stood near the main building. They were round and tall enough for Hank to stand up in the center. A drainage ditch surrounded every tent on the outside. A central trench inside the tents left a raised platform of earth on either side that was covered with blankets for the children to sleep on. The staff attended closely to their bodily hygiene. Their hair was kept short, and they washed every day with lye soap in the nearby river.

Every so often a priest visited the orphanage to celebrate Mass, and one of the female care-takers gave the children religious instructions. Hank and his sister prayed on their own. Easter again passed without notice. There had been so many changes in their lives since leaving their detention camps in Siberia. They did, however, celebrate Polish Constitution Day on May 3 flying their red and white flags and listening to a speech. The speech saddened Hank deeply for it made him realize again that Poland was not free. He longed for home, a home lost more and more in the mists of time and distance. He thought about his mother, now dead, and he missed his father. His concern for the fate of his grandmother, whom he left but a short while ago, was particularly intense.

The children had to help with the chores of the orphanage, mainly gathering firewood and getting water for the kitchen from the river. One day they went together to a small forest of thorny trees for firewood. It was quite a distance from the orphanage and the trip took nearly all day. Hank tried to be clever by intentionally lagging behind. He reasoned that by being at the end of the group he would be the first to return and therefore would have to carry his share of the wood a shorter distance. While the others had already stopped in a clearing for a rest and some sandwiches, Hank was still walking down the path. He happened to look back and saw a big yellow snake raise itself on the path behind him. He had heard about snakes in school at home, but so far he had never seen any. This was his first encounter. Without any further thought Hank grabbed the snake just beneath its head. His grip forced the snake to wrap its body around his arm in a tight coil, its tail reaching to Hank's neck and flailing against his cheek. Try as he may, he could not uncoil the snake's body from his arm, and none of the others offered to help him. They were evidently afraid and only kept saying: "Uncoil it. Uncoil it." Hank's arm began to get numb and he had to hit the snake's head several times against his knee until he killed it. But even then nobody helped him, not even the adults, and he had to unwind the snake from his arm by himself.

If their chores were finished the children were allowed to do as they pleased. Hank used his free time to walk about, to talk with other boys, or to play at the nearby river. Freed of the daily worries over work and food, and full of hopes for their future, Hank and the others found joy in being just children at play once more.

The river, their favorite place, was only about 20 feet at its widest. It came from the mountains and ran cold and swift. Because of the strong current Hank had to enter it well upstream if he wanted to reach the shore opposite from where he was standing. After a rain the river swelled rapidly, often overflowing its banks, and many uprooted trees floated by with the current. Hank soon made getting wood for the kitchen from the river his "specialty." He would swim out to one of the trees with a rope, tie it to one of the larger branches, and then have other boys pull the tree on shore. Though Hank had become a strong swimmer, he still had to use care. The trees tumbled in the rushing water, and he had to avoid being dragged under.

The river banks were rather steep—sixteen to eighteen feet in some places—and of densely packed sand. Imbedded in the sand were many small black particles which lined up in the force field of one of the boys' magnets. Standing on a narrow ledge running along the bank, just wide enough only for young, agile feet, the boys dug caves into the firm sand with sharpened sticks. They were their "getaways," their places of temporary solitude. After years of being crowded together Hank relished this feeling of privacy.

One sunny day Hank and several other boys climbed one of the higher banks on the river. At its foot swirled a whirlpool. On a dare, though Hank was afraid, but felt he could not back out, he closed his eyes and leaped into the water. The whirling water took him down until he felt the river bottom, then shot him out into quiet water some distance away. He surfaced beneath a clump of brush downstream. He remained hidden for a while on purpose, then quietly climbed out and sneaked up behind the other boys. They were staring intently into the river. One of them said: "He's gone." When he showed himself they were startled and relieved. After he told them how it felt to be sucked down and taken around and around by the whirlpool, adding: "Just let yourself go. It'll take you down and then shoot you out to the side," they all soon followed his example.

One afternoon, an incident occurred in front of Hank's tent. It involved a small boy, five or six years old, Hank knew from the orphanage in Kustenai. Having been previously in a Soviet orphanage the boy had learned to swear in Russian without knowing the full meaning of the words he used. As he was swearing away at one of the woman helpers in the camp, she became so angry that she took off her uniform belt and began beating him with its heavy metal buckle. Hank was sure the boy did not know what he was saying, and the unrestrained furor of the woman incensed him. As she swung the belt again, he grabbed it from behind. The woman lost her balance, fell into the mud, and badly soiled her uniform. Hank was afraid she would turn on him next and ran off to hide in one of the caves at the river.

He missed the evening inspection which was conducted by a Polish general, and his absence was noted. A camp cook reported the incident. One of Hank's friends knew where he was hiding and was sent to tell him that he would not be punished. Hank was relieved. He returned to camp, told what had happened, and made the boy show the bruises on his body. At that point the general became furious and, facing the woman, shouted: "These children have suffered enough!" She was transferred elsewhere the same evening. Hank felt vindicated, but the incident stayed on his mind. He feared something like this could happen to his sister. "Are they treating you all right?" became one of his first questions from then on whenever they met. Many years later when Hank was telling this story, he pointed to a photograph of boys in their *junak* (young men's labor brigade) uniforms and explained: "This is like the belt she was using; see how heavy a buckle that is."

Hank did not stay long in the orphanage. Not long after his arrival, he was transferred to the *Junak* camp.

In March 1942, when the Polish civilians were allowed to leave the Soviet Union, the Soviets tried to hold back all children between the ages of 12 and 16 claiming that they were Soviet citizens and "too old" for an orphanage. Consequently many Polish children were left behind after the fall of that year when the Soviets withdrew their permission for the exodus. They had deported an estimated 200,000 children from Poland; only about 7,000 of them eventually reached the West through Iran.

To protect as many Polish children as possible from being held back by the Soviets, the Polish army formed the *junackie brygady* (youth brigade), a paramilitary organization under its control. Boys and girls in the threatened age group as well as those who could not prove their Polish origin were put into uniforms provided by the British and called *junacy* (cadets).

Hank had just turned thirteen and was in the age group at risk. As a *junak* member, however, he was eligible to be released from the Soviet Union. This dressing of children in uniforms provided by one ally and making them members of the army of a second one in order to keep them out of the clutches of the third, is but one example of the strange and often seemingly absurd moves in this grand chess game between East and West, made all the more bizarre as all three— the British, the Poles, and the Soviets—were fighting the same foe at that time.

The *Junak* camp was not far from the orphanage. Its tents, similar to those of the orphanage, stood on a flat expanse of land surrounded by cultivated fields. Some distance away was a small grove of brush and stunted trees. Irrigation ditches, about two feet across, one foot deep, and spaced about an acre apart, traversed the fields at regular intervals. They fed off the nearby river and therefore always carried fresh flowing water. The *junak* members washed themselves and did their laundry in them. Hank was issued an adult-size British uniform that was much too large: long pants which he had to tie around his ankles, a shirt, and a garrison cap. The shoes were also too big and very heavy. Every morning he and his comrades lined up for inspection. They raised the flag, sang the Polish anthem, and had roll call. Then they marched off to breakfast, usually oatmeal, prepared at a field kitchen and dispensed into their mess kits. Sometimes they trained with army rifles. They learned how to break them down and to clean them but were never given ammunition or allowed to shoot. In the evening they had roll call again. At night the *junacy* took turns as guards.

One rainy night Hank was on guard duty, and one of their instructors, a man in his sixties, had gone for an evening walk but failed to return. Hank was sent to search for him in the pouring rain. His poncho, too large as was everything else he had been issued, dragged on the ground. He found the man in a clump of trees not far from the camp. Obviously too ill and too weak to get up by himself, he only mumbled: "Just let me die here." Hank was eventually able to get him up on his feet and back to camp. He had to support most of the man's weight as he sloshed through the mud in his outsized boots while gathering his poncho to keep it from getting caught under his feet and making him stumble.

Despite their more peaceful surroundings, improved sanitation, and better and more plentiful food, death and sickness continued to intrude upon their lives. Hank saw one boy about his own age suddenly reel backward and fall into the latrine which was nothing more than a trench with a pole across to sit on. Had he been not feeling well? Weakened from illness? By the time the boy was pulled out he was already dead. Several of the men took his body to an irrigation ditch and washed it in the running water. The sad irony of this boy's death disturbed Hank very much. "To die like that," he reflected, "after all he had come through!" Although since the time Hank had been deported, now more than two years ago, he had witnessed death many times, any death still touched him deeply, he felt diminished thereby. The repeated tragedies had not blunted his feelings, and neither he nor anyone else around him took refuge from their pain in jokes or glib remarks.

One death during his time in the *Junak* camp affected Hank deeply: the death of his childhood friend from Krasne, Joseph, the son of the former police sergeant. Back home they had played together, and their parents had been friends. Joseph, like Hank, had been deported to Siberia with his mother; his father had been among those killed in the massacre in the city hall of Sassow, though neither the boys nor Joseph's mother knew this at the time. One morning at roll call Hank had heard Joseph's name with the customary response "Present." Hank was overjoyed to have found a childhood friend. In tears they embraced each other and talked about their journeys from Poland to this remote place, about the camps in which they had stayed, but most of all about their homes and Krasne and about those times so irretrievably lost when they swam together near the railroad bridge or paddled kayaks on the lake. It was a sad reunion, much more than just two friends meeting again after a time of separation; they were each other's link to home, childhood, and a common past. Joseph's mother was also in the camp area, and the boys made plans to see her. Hank was looking forward to this visit very much because she had been his mother's closest friend and was always kind to him. If he was searching for a mother surrogate, he was not doing it consciously. "I was a *junacy*," he said later, "and once I became a *junacy*, I was going to stay one. That was the way I felt." Yet, his beloved grandmother had stayed behind in Siberia, and who else was there? As Anna Freud had observed about children of war who had lost their mothers: "If not their mother, then a familiar person as mother substitute."

Whatever dreams Hank may have had, whatever unconscious longing had possessed him, whatever hopes—they were shattered as abruptly as they had come. Barely a week after their reunion, Joseph became ill with dysentery. Hank saw him being taken to the hospital. After a few days, when Hank inquired about his friend at the dispensary, he was told: "He won't come back to camp. He died in the hospital." Joseph was an only child, and Hank never did meet his mother.

The death of his childhood friend strengthened Hank's prior decision to adopt the middle name "Joseph" at his upcoming confirmation. He had selected this name out of admiration for Jesus' father, and now this same name would also commemorate his friend who died so suddenly and so far from home. Hank was looking forward to his confirmation for another reason: he had never met a bishop before, and only a bishop could perform this ceremony.

On confirmation day the *junak* members went by truck to one of the camps of the new Polish army. An altar had been erected in the center of a large field. The *junak* candidates for confirmation drew up in formation in front of the altar. Behind them stood masses of Polish soldiers. The bishop, Field Bishop Joseph Gawlina, had come from England to visit the Polish troops. He conducted the special confirmation ceremony dressed in the uniform of the Polish army. To bless every single candidate individually would have taken too long and so, by compromise, he asked them as a group to say their chosen names out loud. Hank firmly said: "Joseph". At the end of the ceremony all sang the Polish national anthem, "*Jeszcze Polska nie zginela*" (Poland has not perished yet).

Not long after his confirmation Hank fell ill. Later he called it a "sleeping sickness" for a reason: One morning at roll call he collapsed, fast asleep. He kept on falling asleep and was sent to the first-aid station. There, falling asleep again, he fell off the plank he was sitting on and was taken to the hospital. Hank never knew how long he was asleep, nor how long he was in the hospital; he had lost all sense of time. Afterwards he said, "In the hospital the nurses kept waking me up; it made me so angry. All I wanted was to sleep. It felt so good." Later the nurses explained to him that he would have died had they not awakened him on a regular schedule.

After he had recovered sufficiently, and was sent back to the orphanage he found out that his *junak* unit had already left their camp. Unfortunately the effects of this illness lingered for years and may have contributed to a tremor of his hands which Hank developed in his late twenties and which eventually disabled him for his work in America.

After his discharge from the hospital, another opportunity presented itself to Hank to reestablish a tie to his home and family. In Guzar the "Command Post of the Center Organization of the Polish Army in the Soviet Union" had been established and attracted thousands of refugees seeking its protection.

By chance Hank met an uncle on his father's side who had also been deported along with his wife and his two sons. Hank pleaded with him to accept his sister and him into their family, and the Polish authorities even offered his uncle a stipend for foster care, but the man told Hank: "No. We have been through too much already. I cannot take on another responsibility." Perhaps it was the words he chose, or perhaps Hank had put his hopes too high, but in any case, Hank felt shattered. "I wanted so much to have a family, and now I lost it again," he said. His uncle's refusal filled him with a lasting bitterness. "We— my sister and I—are now truly alone," he said to himself.

After his return to the orphanage, his stay was short. Soon the children climbed into another train for the long ride to Krasnovodsk, a port on the Caspian Sea. There they boarded one of the transport vessels set aside to take the Polish refugees to Iran, and Hank was to experience his first ship voyage.

On their way to the ship they passed crowds of their countrymen who were also waiting to board. Many of them had spent days without food or water in the dust and intense heat on the pier, in the streets, or at the railroad station of Krasnovodsk, having given their last Rubles or traded in their last valuables just to stay alive. And they lived with the constant fear that their papers would not pass inspection by the NKVD when they tried to board, that they would be turned back in sight of deliverance.

When they finally were allowed to board, they had to leave behind even the few things they still had managed to preserve from home. The ship had no space to spare, and the pier was littered with their discarded belongings.

On board the children were put into the dusty hold with some adults to supervise them. All others—over a thousand of them crowded the ship—were required to stay on deck. The seas were high, and for most of the 250 miles the ship with its human cargo heaved severely in the high waves. Wave after wave washed overboard. One woman was swept off the deck, but due to the rough sea nobody could help her. A few days later, her body washed ashore on the beach at Pahlevi. Many were seasick. There was no way to get to a toilet, and they had to vomit where they sat or stood. Some suffered in silence, others moaned or cried, and still others shrieked in fear with each toss of the ship. Those in the hold bore its dust and the stench of the vomit; those on deck shivered, drenched by the waves. All were frightened, especially after night fell.

The SS *Zdanov* filled with refugees.

Eventually this journey also came to an end. At daybreak, those on deck saw high distant mountains rise out of the mist. They were the Elburz Mountains of Iran, they were told, though they still called the country "Persia" among themselves. The children had to stay in the hold until the ship moored at Pahlevi, Iran. On shore, rows of white tents stretched along the sandy beach: their homes for the next few days. From there they were to be taken inland to new camps and to the new life all of them hoped for.

After the ship docked some of the passengers fell on their knees and kissed the rough planks of the pier. Others waved their arms and hands shouting "freedom, freedom!" Most, however, were too sick from the voyage to react. Their energy spent by their hazardous travels and the unaccustomed heat, their bodies sapped by illness and challenged by the rich food now so abundantly available—all took their toll. Many of them had no more strength left and with the release from their daily struggle for existence they were overcome and took their final breath on the beach at Pahlevi. Over 600 travelers were buried there.

Hank, his sister, and a shipload of Polish adults and children had

finally stepped through an open door. They had escaped the claws of the Russian bear and had done so in the nick of time. Soon the door slammed shut again, trapping those who had not yet been able to pass through it.

At the end of 1942, the NKVD closed all Polish consulates arresting the employees and confiscating any remaining Polish State property. On January 15, 1943, the Council of Peoples' Commissars of the Soviet Union decreed that all Polish relief institutions were to be brought under Soviet administration. One day later, on January 16, 1943, Stalin revoked the "amnesty of 1941" by decree and declared all Poles who previously lived in occupied Poland Soviet citizens. Many of them refused to exchange their Polish passports for Soviet ones. Those who persisted in their refusal were arrested. On January 31, 1943, the German surrender at Stalingrad turned the tide for the Red Army, further hardening the imperial aspirations of the Soviet Union.

Polish-Soviet relations continued to deteriorate, and on April 25, 1943, Stalin severed diplomatic relations with the Polish government-in-exile of General Sikorski using the Polish protests over Katyn as a pretext. The Allies continued to support the Soviet Union until the end of the war. In Poland the Polish Home Army had to stand on its own in its resistance to Germany, hampered, not helped, by the Soviets and their partisans.

In all about 115,000 persons—43,000 Polish civilians (among them 7,000 Polish children) and over 70,000 Polish troops passed through Iran in 1942.

11.

Strange Lands, Strange Customs

⌒

After the fall of France, and until the entry of the United States into the Second World War, Britain had been the lone sentinel of freedom for the Western World. Together with France it had stood by its treaty obligations to Poland guaranteeing the inviolability of its borders. Both Britain and France declared war on Nazi Germany on September 3, 1939. Counting on their indecision, Hitler had rebuffed their ultimatums for immediate German withdrawal from Poland. Had they aggressively pursued the war at that time, history may well have been changed for the better and millions of deaths might have been avoided. London eventually became the seat of the Polish government-in-exile.

After the British government succeeded in persuading the Soviets to allow the newly-formed Polish army to be transferred to the West, and to liberate its Polish civilian deportees, thousands of exiles streamed through the Russian port of Krasnovodsk and voyaged across the sometimes raging Caspian Sea to the beach near Pahlevi in

Iran, their first steppingstone toward a humane existence and ultimate freedom. Some still dreamt of returning to Poland after the war, others hoped to find a new home somewhere else, but all wanted to be free of Soviet oppression.

The dispersal and isolation of the camps throughout the vast Soviet Union delayed the notification of the Polish exiles in many instances. Some became aware of the "amnesty" as early as August 1941, others did not find out about it until spring of 1942. Unlike the Polish orphans, such as Hank and his sister, the adults and children with parents had to make their way on their own until they reached one of the Polish army centers in the southern part of the Soviet Union. For many of them this journey brought new and unforeseen dangers as they traveled by rafts and barges and waited for days at train stations in freezing cold or stifling heat. Many perished on the way south, falling victim to typhus, cholera, or just sheer exhaustion. The local people were either suspicious of them or too poor to help, and the Soviet authorities not only refused support, but often held them up and used them as unpaid laborers.

In her book *My Flight to Freedom* Anita Paschwa-Kozicka, then 12 years old, gives a moving account of her journey: of forced labor and starvation, sickness and death, dust and heat, and of her narrow escape from a kidnapped group of children during her journey south. Traveling on a home-made raft she, her sister, and her sister's child succeeded in reaching the southern part of the Soviet Union only to be rounded up along with others by Soviet authorities and taken to a kolkhoz for the cotton harvest. The living conditions there were even worse than those they had experienced before the "amnesty." After all the cotton had been harvested, they were left to fend for themselves. Meanwhile, Kozicka's eight year old niece was dying of typhoid fever. As they continued on their way, Red Army soldiers suddenly appeared and offered the older children a ride in their truck, but instead of taking them to their destination, they brought them to an out-of-the-way building and placed them under guard. Kozicka escaped during the night and, walking the entire day in the dust and the heat of the steppe without any food or water, managed to rejoin her sister and her group late the next evening.

Eventually she reached the Polish orphanage at Guzar.

Another girl, Stella Synowiec-Tobis, walked 100 kilometers with her mother and older sister, often through waist high snow, in order not to miss the last train south before more snow closed the line. On the train the two girls were separated from their mother. The train had stopped along the way and their mother had gone out in search of bread. It left unexpectedly before her return and they never saw their mother again. Both girls were also picked up to harvest cotton and had to work without pay, hardly any food, and having to exist in a miserable shelter. Fortunately they were found and taken to a Polish orphanage.

John Stanclik, now living in Schaumburg, Illinois, had been deported from Lwow to a region east of the Ural mountains. He also found his way south and worked as a secretary for the "Polish Delegation of Social Welfare" at Guzar in Uzbekistan. He distributed food, then, after their supplies ran out, traveled through that area to find Polish children and bring them to the orphanage. He said: "Many of the deportees stayed behind. They did not have the means to travel or were too old or too weak. Often mothers with small children begged me to take their children with me; they wished that at least their children should have a chance at a future."

Soldiers and civilians alike were channeled through Iran, their first way station on their journey to the West. The British had assumed the responsibility for their support but were so overwhelmed by the crowded transports that they had to hire Iranians as drivers, butchers, and bakers. The British set up the field kitchens and provided the flour and the animals; the Iranians helped to build the camps and prepare the food.

All the refugees, both military and civilians, went first to a "dirty" camp, and later, after sanitary procedures including delousing, to a "clean" one. Because the caretakers in Hank's orphanage in the southern Soviet Union had been particularly mindful of the children's hygiene, they passed rather quickly from the former camp to the latter, although their hair was cropped again. One woman refugee describes her arrival in Iran as follows:

"We had to strip, and our clothes were burned. Our hair was cut short, and after a shower they gave us a towel and new clothes: a blouse, shorts, and a pair of sandals."

Crowded together during their travels and in the camps many had been unable to bathe adequately. The abrupt change to a rich diet further challenged their bodies. Boils became one of their most common afflictions. The hot climate in the southern Soviet Union had brought flies and mosquitoes and with them malaria. Filth and pollution brought cholera and typhus. Lice spread typhoid fever. Deaths from these and other illness occurred daily.

Even in Iran sickness and death—a holdover from their time inside the Soviet Union—plagued the children, but with ever diminishing frequency and barbarity. At the same time came recovery from the years of deprivation, albeit slowly; like a wave, with ups and downs, but gradually losing its force and blending into smoother waters. Gone were the daily toil, the endless scrounging for the bare necessities of life, and, most importantly, the constant fear for one's existence that shadowed their lives in the Soviet Union. Though they had been under the control of the Polish army there, even children like Hank knew that the political wind could change at any moment. In Iran, the refugees were forbidden to leave camp or talk to outsiders about their experiences in the Soviet Union. They had heard about Soviet soldiers being in northern Iran. (The Soviets had occupied northern Iran in the summer of 1941.) But they knew that there were British soldiers there also and felt protected. Hank, for one, felt very reassured every time he saw one of the latter.

After a few days on the beach in Pahlevi one sunny morning Hank's group of children left in a convoy of trucks. Most of the drivers were Iranians, but there was at least one American among them. Thirty years later, in 1973, Hank met him by chance at a service station in northern Michigan. He was serving in the American Armed Forces and had been sent to Iran as an interpreter.

From their open trucks the clear atmosphere let the children see far into the distance. The road across the Elburz mountains was steep and treacherous; at times it was no better than a field path with ruts and rocks and tight switchbacks carved into the sides of the mountains. There were no guard rails and the mountains fell steeply into the valleys below, valleys so deep that the houses and farm animals appeared like toy miniatures. At one point of that treacherous road, the children watched in horror as one of the trucks slid over the edge and, turning end over end, fell to the valley below spilling its occupants into the void like dolls out of a box. Their screams hung over the valley as they rolled past but there was no place to stop and nothing could be done.

Later in the day they rode through Teheran and continued along a dusty highway south toward the historic city of Isfahan. The road wound again through a mountainous terrain, barren with nothing but desert and rock. In the evening, after a long day's drive, the convoy reached its destination: a camp next to the highway, not far from Isfahan, within the walls of an old fort and among ruins dating back to the time of the Medes.

Isfahan, the historic capital of Persia under many past dynasties, is now a major industrial city. It is also the site of ancient mosques and palaces and a center of Persian art. Already a settlement in the ancient kingdom of Media, it was recorded in the history as *Jabe*, and later as *Jay*, by Cyrus, Alexander, and Ptolemy. In the course of its long and turbulent history it saw Persian, Arab, Mongol, and Afghan rulers. During the Second World War it came to be referred to as "The City of Polish Children." From April 1942 to October 1945, some 3,000 Polish children filled its 21 orphanages, boarding schools, and camps. Supported by the British, the Polish government-in-exile did its utmost to bring about a semblance of Polish life in schools and churches, in Scouting, and even in play.

In Hank's camp several of the old buildings were still intact and were put to good use. They were stone buildings with arched entrances without doors and had windows with iron bars, not glass. Blankets were hung to cover the openings. One building served as an office, another as a first-aid station and also as a morgue. The children slept in tents, each holding about 20 boys or girls. The toilets were still poles across a ditch, but at least they were now enclosed.

Polish refugees, under the aegis of the British Red Cross, looked after the camp and were responsible for the welfare of the children. Their leader would remain with them throughout their stay in Iran and would accompany them to their camp in India and finally to their camp in Mexico. The day-to-day work was done by adult women refugees who volunteered their help. Still regimented, still far from being able to enjoy even the smallest luxuries of life, and still pawns in the power struggle between East and West, the children now nevertheless experienced the devotion, the care, and the good will of those whose charges they had become.

During his time in Iran, Hank, as always, stayed in close contact with his sister; the adults also made sure that the two were not separated. His sister slept only a few tents away, and he would often watch her play with other girls and stop to ask her how she was feeling and if she was being treated well. He remained very concerned about this; the picture of the "caretaker" beating that small boy in the Soviet Union remained vivid in his memory.

Ever since his arrival in the orphanage in Kustenai, for Hank hunger had become a thing of the past, although from then on their food consisted mostly of bread, potatoes, and cabbage, sometimes pea soup, and occasionally canned meat. Here in Iran, however, Hank, like the other children experienced a profound change both due to the improved diet and better sanitary conditions. Slowly their cheeks began to fill out, their muscles re-developed and with them their strength, the smaller children put on baby fat again, and the older girls resumed their menstrual periods.

In Iran the food was rich, so rich that some had difficulties getting used to it and often suffered from indigestion. There was much meat, mainly lamb, and sugar and milk were plentiful. The bread, baked from wheat flour, was white. They had sandwiches for breakfast and afternoon tea, soups and sandwiches for lunch and dinner, and lots of dried figs, dates, and pomegranates. They marched four times a day in formation to the field kitchen mess tent and ate at tables from mess kits freshly provided at every meal.

At first the children washed every morning in a spring-fed, cold creek near the camp. Later, a wash trough with spigots was installed, but the water was still cold. Winter was approaching and on some mornings the edge of the stream glistened with thin sheets of ice which quickly melted in the rising sun. Hank was glad that the days were warm; he did not miss the snow—he had had enough of it in

Siberia. Because of the cool mornings and evenings, sleeveless lamb-skin vests were handed out to the children. Hank's was black, and he would keep it for years. At night they covered themselves with camel-hair blankets. Hank still feels itchy when he thinks of their coarse texture, but also recalls with pleasure how warm they kept him.

When school started, the children were placed in the same grades they were in when they were taken from home. Hank resumed the fourth grade. School hours were short because of a lack of teachers. Still, besides the "three Rs," the children were taught history and biol-ogy. Since books and writing materials were also in short supply, many of the lessons relied on oral reports and recitations. For homework the children received printouts which they had to memorize and later recite in class. Once, the entire school went on an excursion to see *Shahr Rey*, the residence of the Shah of Iran and the trip took most of the day. Although they saw the extensive gardens only from the out-side, their magnificence left a lasting impression on their young minds.

The immediate surroundings of the camp, however, stimulated Hank's curiosity most. The sprawling fort with its walls, ruins, and tunnels begged for exploration. Whenever Hank could, he strolled about the old fort, crawled on his hands and knees through partly-col-lapsed tunnels, and looked into every nook and cranny. And he ate his fill of the green, ripe figs from the many fig trees in that area.

Within the walls of the fort a ravine with 30- to 40-foot banks enclosed a small palace. In front of it was a spring-fed pond sur-rounded by a large mosaic as ancient as the building itself. Goldfish swam therein.

A large hall formed the center of the palace. Mosaics of birds, flow-ers, and hunting scenes covered its walls, and the tile floor was set in a delicate floral design. Spaced every four to five feet apart, two- to three-foot high openings connected a low corridor to the hall along the entire circumference. It had a ledge to sit on. From it extended many partly caved-in side tunnels in a radial fashion. In some of these Hank found bones and rusty pieces of chain. Had they been dun-geons? He imagined a guard in medieval armor at one of the tunnel entrances, ready to beat down anyone trying to escape. He was con-cerned that one of the tunnels might collapse on him, but could not help admiring the intricate design of the mosaics which also here still covered parts of the ceilings and walls. Some of the tunnels disappeared in the walls of the old fortress, others led outside the palace walls. Most of the walls and the ceilings, however, had fallen in so much that it was impossible to trace them any distance. The nearest building was two blocks away. Had they connected that far? Hank followed one tunnel all the way to the far end of the ravine, a distance of about one and a half blocks from the palace. It ended at a tall, round tower, but Hank could not find an entrance to it.

One of Hank's teachers was an elderly lady who also accompanied them to India. She took a special interest in Hank, his progress, and his activities, and asked him to share with her in detail all his adventures. One day, he was so preoccupied with exploring an old tunnel that he was late for school. This particular teacher felt that she had to punish him somehow and made him learn a number of history dates as extra homework, but afterwards, he was asked to tell her about everything he had seen. Hank not only enjoyed talking about what he had found but also looked at his extra homework as a "bonus" in his quest for knowledge.

Sometimes alone, sometimes with a friend, Hank liked to visit the nearby part of town and its markets. The camp had a main gate and side gates, but the children were not permitted to wander off by themselves. Hank and his friend, however, found an opening in the wall through which they were able to squeeze through and make their way into town without being seen. Under the walls of the old fort and along the streets leading into town were many stands under awnings and inside tents. Most everything could be found for sale, and Hank was astonished not only by the abundance of dried figs but also by the huge swarms of flies everywhere.

In one tent several robed and turbaned men appeared to be buying and selling women. Standing next to the men, the women were heavily veiled and completely covered by long, black robes. Though the boys did not understand the language, the tone of the men's voices and their gestures seemed to indicate that they were haggling over the price. The boys were totally amazed—selling women? That, they had never seen before. One of the men eventually took a woman with him.

When he lifted her veil, Hank saw her greet the man with a wide and toothless smile. At other stands the customers and the vendors also struck Hank as if they were bargaining back and forth. This too was new to him, something he had not been accustomed to at home.

One man sold dromedaries. When Hank stepped up to pet a dromedary, the owner let him mount it and ride it for a while. Its peculiar gait made Hank seasick. Hank also saw a man whose hand had been cut off, but he did not understand the significance of it until somebody explained it to him later.

Like so many of the refugees, Hank too became seriously ill: he contracted malaria with jaundice. At the same time his reduced resistance brought on boils over most of his body, especially his arms and legs. A truck took him to the hospital in Teheran where he spent two weeks until he was well enough to return to the orphanage.

The hospital, a converted storage building or stable as Hank heard later, was a tall, old building with high windows and lacked electricity. It once served the Soviet troops in northern Iran, but now stood next to an overcrowded British hospital. Space was critical due to the number of patients. Hank was put into a great hall with over 200 of them. The cots, standard army issue, were narrow and stood close. There was just enough space for an egg crate sitting on end between them. Covered with a cloth it served as a bedside stand. The nursing shift ended at five o'clock in the afternoon, after which time only a minimal number of personnel looked after the needs of the patients. Anyone who died after five PM was left on his cot until the next morning.

One evening the man next to Hank died. Later during that night Hank was awakened by wailing cries and saw the sheet of the dead man move up and down. Hank was quite helpless because his arms and legs were heavily bandaged, and he had trouble moving about. Frightened, he turned for help to the patient on the other side of his cot, but he too had died. Unable to go back to sleep Hank spent a long night lying awake between these two corpses. When daylight came Hank finally solved the mystery: a roaming cat had kicked over the bedside crate and then had become entangled in the bed sheets of the "arm waving" dead man.

Christmas was coming, their first Christmas to be celebrated since they were taken from their homes almost three years ago. Hank looked forward to it with some feeling of joy and anticipation, but a deep gratitude for his delivery from the Soviet Union was still foremost in his thoughts. With the approach of Christmas he wished for a little snow, but just enough for the holidays. On Christmas Eve the children attended Mass and later walked among the tents singing Christmas carols. Three boys dressed as the three kings. They led two others who had covered themselves with a blanket pretending to be a camel. The first one held up a broom as its head. Paper ornaments made by the children and the staff decorated their Christmas tree.

During the latter part of 1942, as German troops were advancing toward Stalingrad and the Caucasus, the Shah of Iran wavered between favoring the Germans or the Western Allies. This troubling indecision prompted the Allies to get the Polish soldiers and refugees out of Iran.

From Iran the Polish troops went to the Mediterranean where they distinguished themselves in the campaign in Italy. The Polish civilians and orphans, on the other hand, were spread out among four continents for the remainder of the war. A large number went to camps in Africa. Another 22,000 were evacuated from Iran through camps near Karachi to various more permanent refuges in India, Australia, New Zealand, and to a haven in the New World called Colonia Santa Rosa in Mexico.

One day, early in 1943, the group of children to which Hank and his sister belonged boarded another train and later a convoy of trucks bound for the port of Ahwaz, near Basra, on the Persian Gulf. There they boarded a British vessel, the *City of London*, for Karachi. Their voyage through the Persian Gulf and the Arabian Sea lasted several days and was uneventful.

On their way to Ahwaz, Hank was surprised that the train would stop, no matter where, when it was time for the Mohammedans to pray. On these occasions, the faithful would step off the train, spread their rugs on the ground next to the tracks, recite their prescribed prayers, then climb back on the train, and resume their journey.

By the time Hank and the other children arrived in India, an earlier camp in the old Hindu quarter of town had been replaced by a tent camp in the desert and called "Country Club." After a brief stay there, they went on to camp Malir where they were quartered in military-style barracks for several months until their final transfer to Mexico. These camps were isolated and the surrounding country was barren with neither trees nor flowers to ease the eye.

At camp Country Club the children slept in large army tents each holding about 50 children. Two tents were for boys, three for girls, and the children were assigned to them by age groups. Khaki shorts, shirts, and pith helmets to ward off the tropical sun were issued to them soon after their arrival.

The solid barracks of camp Malir were only a few miles from camp Country Club, but it took another truck ride to get all the children there. Because of the heat, the barracks windows did not have glass, only screens. Mosquito netting was strung around the beds. For the first time the children's camps had not only wash basins, but also showers. Though the water was not heated, the hot climate kept it tepid. They also had separate toilets, but they were still located in out-houses.

Near the barracks of camp Malir was an airfield. It was not in use at that time, and many mock-up planes from wood and canvas stood in long rows. The surrounding country was a desolate, flat, and barren desert without any cultivated fields or any signs of water or water holes. Only rocks, gravel, cacti, and brush covered the terrain. At night hyenas barked close by, and monkeys screamed in the thorny bushes next to their barracks. Cinders covered the camp roads and bare areas to keep the dust down. Fierce dust storms appeared without warning, and the everlasting heat distressed everyone.

Neither of the camps were close to any village or settlement, but every so often a villager in his traditional garments appeared in their vicinity. Once, when Hank chanced upon a cemetery near the camp, he noticed that dishes of food and milk had been put by the grave sites. He also noted that the offerings were gone by the next morning.

Already during their stay in Iran, Boy and Girl Scout troops provided the children with organized activities. Though in India the intense heat forbade any field trips, they could get together as a troop to talk about scouting lore and to work on projects with their scout-masters. A few had uniforms; Hank had his Scout kerchief.

Besides scouting, the children played soccer and watched the weekly soccer games between the British and the local teams. Hank was impressed by the agility and spunk of the local players as they ran after the ball barefoot across the cinder field. Their British opponents were outfitted with soccer shoes and knee socks. Once a week they sat on the ground in front of an outdoor screen and watched a movie played for them by the British soldiers.

Although in Iran Hank had felt a profound sense of relief to be out of the Soviet Union, the Soviet troops stationed in northern Iran still had caused him unease. In India, any danger from the Soviets was fur-ther mitigated both by time and distance.

In Iran, the sights, sounds, and smells, though new, had stirred some associations, struck some familiar cords. This was due, perhaps, to Hank's close contact with the Kirghiz in Siberia and his time in Uzbekistan. Or perhaps the call to prayer by the imam from the minaret of the mosque reminded him of the ringing of the bell from the tower of the church back home. At their camp in Isfahan the ruins of the old fortress with their tunnels and ancient mosaics, even if partly destroyed, spoke of a history linked to the history of Europe. Though their wares were different, people at the markets bought and sold from makeshift tables under roofs of canvas just like it was done on market day at home. Besides, in Iran it had been winter, though with balmy days and no rain clouds to darken the sky, but still with nights cold enough for ice to form on the edges of the streams.

India, however, was very different. Much seemed strange to Hank and the contrasts startled him: the dark-skinned people, the women carrying baskets on their heads, and the white-washed houses, so bril-liantly white when the sun was high that Hank had to squint his eyes. It was another world. And it was hot! For the rest of his life Hank associated his stay in India with a blistering heat he had never known before; heat and dust—and also canned sardines for breakfast.

In Karachi they rode in British army trucks from the ship to Country Club camp. The drive was chaotic. The heat, the whirling clouds of dust, the milling crowds of people, and their trucks honking incessantly—that's what he remembered; that the town seemed endless, that none of the buildings seemed taller than two or three stories, and that every so often the convoy would stop to let a cow pass. At first Hank thought it strange for cows to have the right-of-way, but as he learned more about the reverence with which the Hindus regarded this animal, he came to think of the special reverence for bread he had been taught as a child back home in Poland.

Just as in Iran, their days in India centered around meal-times. Four times a day a suspended piece of railroad track was rung with an iron rod to announce them. The youngest in front, first the girls and then the boys formed two rows and marched side by side to the mess tent, or in camp Malir to a barrack. Canned sardines became a breakfast staple, day in and day out, and, in the tradition of the Royal British Navy, they had to eat a sweetened lime with every lunch. The afternoon snack consisted of bread with butter and lots of honey.

As school resumed, the mess tent or barracks doubled as a schoolroom and also as a church where Mass could be said whenever a priest came to visit the camp. Here too teachers and supplies were scarce, just as in Iran.

Once, the children went to a village some distance away. Its people revered crocodiles which they kept in a large pool sunk six to eight feet into the ground surrounded by a stone wall. Sheep and goats were fed to the crocodiles as a sacrifice. The water of the pool was muddy, and it churned violently every time a sheep or a goat was thrown in. Hank found it difficult to understand that the villagers were willing to raise animals for sacrifice when food seemed to be so scarce.

As in the other camps, here also, Hank managed to occupy his free time. He started to explore, formed friendships, and looked for prankish outlets for his boyish exuberance. In Country Club camp one night Hank rolled his lambskin vest into a tight ball, the dark fur to the outside, and tied a long string to it. One of his friends crawled through the tent of the older girls and passed the string beneath the canvas at the far end of the tent. Then the boys imitated the bark of hyenas while jerking the end of the string. With each pull a dark ball of fur, Hank's rolled-up vest, bounced ominously along the tent floor frightening the girls. They screamed and trying to rush out of the tent collapsed it on top of themselves. Hank and his friends, meanwhile, quickly ran to their own quarters and pretended to be asleep on their cots.

Many colorful birds fluttered among the bushes near their barracks. In relays of three or four the boys chased the birds from bush to bush until the heat and the lack of water tired them and they were easily caught. The boys tried to keep the captured birds under the mosquito netting of their beds, but were told to let them go. Once Hank caught a hedgehog which his teacher put into a box in her room. Overnight it delivered four babies, but they did not survive.

Hank watched the local men catch vultures. The men lay down on the ground and covered themselves with a red cloth. When a circling vulture, thinking it was a piece of meat, landed on it, the man beneath the cloth would grab the vulture by its legs while another man quickly stuffed it in a sack. Hank, of course, also tried to hunt vultures. He made himself a bow and a set of arrows tipped with metal from a soda can. Being too dull they simply bounced off the feathers of the first vulture he hit, and instead of flying away, the infuriated bird dove at Hank with wings outspread and hissing beak wide open. Hank ran away thoroughly frightened and never tried to hunt vultures again.

Their stay in India lasted several months. So far all their camps had been temporary stations on the way to a more permanent location. Even though the war was beginning to turn in favor of the Allies, the steps crucial to the defeat of Germany and Japan lay still in the future. The Polish refugees, it was decided, needed a safer place in which to stay for the remainder of the war. And so the children left their camp to board a coastal steamer, the *Cap Tourane*, for the voyage to Bombay. From there they were to be transported to America. American sailors manned the ship.

Hank felt good about going to America. In Hank's mind America was the place of ultimate security, half-way around the world from the Soviets, the farthest away from them one could get, and it was a big and powerful country. It was so big, he thought, that it could feed itself. To feed oneself, to be self-sufficient, was a concept familiar to Hank. His parents had had their garden, their cow, and their chickens. One grew what one needed. This idea of self-sufficiency, so widely understood and accepted by people of Hank's background, had been politicized by the German propaganda machine as the need for *Lebensraum* (literally "space to live," but meaning "sufficient space to supply one's needs"). The Nazis exploited this concept to justify to the German people the war and their planned eastward expansion (Heinrich Himmler's infamous *Generalplan Ost*).

The children's voyage to Bombay was smooth, the sea remained calm. On the way the sailors took the opportunity to impress the children with the fierceness of piranha fish by putting a piece of meat on a hook and hanging it overboard. Suddenly the water seemed to boil, and the hook came out clean.

On their arrival in Bombay the *Cap Tourane* docked next to a large ship with the Polish eagle on the funnel and the Polish flag flying from its stern. It was the famous *Batory*, a former Polish passenger liner which had escaped to England at the beginning of the war and was now used for troop transport. Seeing a Polish ship and their country-men, the children waved and shouted joyously to her sailors. Polish words and greetings flew back and forth as they wished each other good luck and bon voyage. Though the *Batory* was now under the British flag, she was for the children a visible and impressive tie to their country, a harbinger of good news, a reminder of home. Hank also heard that the Polish submarine *Wilk* (wolf) was lying in the harbor, but he did not see it.

The *Batory* was named in honor of Stefan Batory, admired as one of the most able kings of Poland who had successfully waged war on Moscow and Ivan the Terrible. After finishing her duties in the Indian ocean, she sailed the Mediterranean bringing Polish soldiers from Palestine to the battlegrounds of Italy. After the war she kept her name and continued as passenger liner and cruise ship under the flag of communist Poland until she was decommissioned in 1979.

It had been more than a year since Hank left *Swinsowchos 641*, a year of changes, filled with new impressions, at times overwhelmingly so. Yet in his quieter moments, at times of rest or during the night, Hank often thought of his home and hoped to eventually return there. This hope remained with him until the end of the war, as it did with most of the refugees, even in Mexico. With his thoughts of home came the thoughts of his parents. His mother was dead, that he knew only too well. But he strongly believed that his father was still alive, and that he would someday see him again. The fate of his grandmother worried him greatly. He felt that her chances of survival in Siberia—who knows for how long—under the conditions he knew so well, seemed much less likely.

12.

Twelve Thousand Miles Across the Sea

$$\sim$$

Ⅰn Bombay the children boarded an American navy vessel, the USS *Hermitage*, for the voyage to North America. Her keel had been laid in a Baltimore shipyard and she had served as an Italian passenger liner. Confiscated at the entry of the United States into the war, she was rapidly outfitted and put into service as a troop carrier for the United States Navy. She brought fresh troops to India and returned with the wounded to Australia and the United States. On board were over 700 wounded American soldiers.

This was her second voyage with Polish refugees from Bombay to Los Angeles. She took over 700 of them, including 400 Polish orphans and had carried as many Polish refugees to North America the first time. Later Hank liked to refer to her as "my *Santa Maria*."

"After all, she brought me to America," he said.

Her voyage via Australia and Bora Bora took six weeks. She stopped for a few days in Melbourne, Australia. From there she stayed well to the south in the Pacific, away from the fighting. She changed

The USS *Hermitage*.

course frequently in order to avoid Japanese submarines. The children had frequent life-boat drills, and it was forbidden to throw anything overboard for fear of leaving a trail of debris in her wake. All announcements were made in English, but the sailors made sure everyone knew what to do. On several occasions, when Japanese submarines had been reported in the area, the ship stopped and shut off her engines, and the children had to put on their life jackets. At one time the silhouette of another ship appeared on the horizon. When she did not answer the light signals of the *Hermitage*, all guns were trained in her direction and everybody had to don life jackets until she disappeared below the horizon.

The *Hermitage* carried two funnels, a large gun was mounted aft, smaller guns stood forward and on both sides of the ship. During the day the children roamed the decks; at night they slept in pull-down beds mounted to the walls in stacks of five or six. They were made of canvas tied with ropes to a metal frame and with enough slack to keep their occupants from rolling out even in heavy seas. The sea, however, remained calm during their entire voyage.

Hank often stood at the bow and watched the flying fish sail over the waves. He also saw a few whales. Learning to anticipate the rise and the fall of the ship in the ocean swells, he acquired "sea legs," and after their voyage it took him a while to get used to walking on land again. He studied the ship while strolling about the deck. The size of the barrel of the large gun greatly impressed him. "It's wide enough for me to crawl into it," he thought.

As on land so aboard ship the meals determined the schedule of the day. Weather permitting, school and other organized activities took place on deck. The children played games, had a poetry club, and the girls formed singing and dancing groups. During his free time, Hank wrote verses and thought about getting back home and seeing his father and his relatives again. He regretted that his grandmother could not share his new life.

The ship anchored briefly in a lagoon off Bora Bora. Mountains clad with lush green vegetation rose steeply against a cloudless blue sky, and the water was so clear that one could see far into its depth. To Hank, Bora Bora was one of the most beautiful sights he had ever seen, and its serene beauty temporarily assuaged all the sorrows of the past. Hank watched as the sailors and soldiers on board threw coins into the water and the natives dove for them. From high on board he could see the coins tilting from side to side as they slowly floated deeper.

Being away from home and perhaps thinking about their own families, many of the sailors on board lavished their affection on the Polish children at every opportunity. One of the sailors bought Hank a pocket knife from the ship's store; others bought tee shirts for the boys or sailor hats for the girls.

The ship carried wounded soldiers and those who died were buried at sea. Sown into canvas the body was placed on a plank and covered with the Stars and Stripes. The chaplain held a brief ceremony, then the plank was tilted, and the flag went flat. Death still depressed Hank, no matter how often he had encountered it before.

The voyage through the Indian Ocean and the South Pacific was safe and uneventful; the days with nothing but sky and sea. When seagulls appeared, the children were told that land was ahead and that soon they would be in America. One morning as they awoke, the engines had fallen silent. "We're in the States," somebody said. During the night of October 24, 1943, the *Hermitage* had entered Los Angeles

Harbor and docked at San Pedro. Still below deck, they were divided into groups. On the pier, busses, not open trucks, were waiting to take them to their first stop on the American continent, the United States Army camp Santa Anita.

The bus ride from the ship to camp Santa Anita was short and the children did not see much of the city. Upon their arrival they were taken first to the mess hall where they ate their biggest and, for many of them, the best meal yet on all their travels. A Polish speaking soldier translated the sign over the long counter: "Take what you want, but eat what you take." Hank took his tray and followed the others along the counter. He was overwhelmed by the choices put before him: two kinds of meat, potatoes, different vegetables, salad, and fresh fruits. The mountain of oranges and the buckets of ice cream impressed him the most. At home, before the war, he had occasionally bought ice cream from a street vendor with a pushcart who served it in a seashell-shaped waffle. Here the ice cream was spooned out for him into a bowl and he could have as much as he wanted. After their meal they were shown their quarters. "Quarantine," was the official reason for their stay in the wooden barracks with the comfortable cots.

Hank now felt more secure than ever before and he began to relax. Even on board ship with nothing but sea around them, the submarine warnings and lifeboat drills had made him apprehensive and anxious from time to time. But now all this was behind him. He was in "the States," on the other side of the world, as far from the Soviet Union as one could get, on firm land. And the sun shone warm, and there was so much to eat.

Polish refugee women acted as their den mothers. They alone told the children what to do and where to go. The soldiers gave no commands; instead, some of them from the nearby base climbed the wire mesh fence at the perimeter of the camp, their pockets filled with candy bars and "Hershey's" for the children. "It's no big deal to cross that fence," they said. The Red Cross gave out new clothes, but Hank held on to his lambskin vest from Iran. After a few days they went by bus to a railroad station. A train was waiting for them.

In the United States secrecy surrounded the Polish refugees. In order to maintain friendly relations with their Soviet ally, the United

States government suppressed all adverse statements against the Soviet Union for the duration of the war. By that time, of course, the massacre at Katyn had come to light and had become widely known, and a strong anti-Soviet feeling existed among Polish-Americans. And so the fate of the Polish people under the Soviets was kept from the American public. It would take years before Hank and the other refugees could speak out openly about their trials and tribulations. And even more time would pass before they could find their personal niches and carve out lives of their own.

For the time being, however, one more leg remained on their journey. They boarded passenger cars this time, not freight cars, but the train still was surrounded by guards. From Los Angeles the children were taken to Mexico, where under a tropical sky and in the shade of palms a Polish refuge had been established at Colonia Santa Rosa. There, the children were received into the arms of their own countrymen.

13.

Haven Under the Palms

A t the border to Mexico the children left one train and marched to another, past the American soldiers in their olive-drab uniforms and toward the Mexicans with their round visored caps with a broad red band. This, more than anything else signaled to the children that they were going from one country to another. Not only the uniforms, the train they boarded was also different: less luxurious and less comfortable. In the States they had sat on padded seats; now the benches were wood. It was hot, and the smell of the coal-burning engine filled the train. They rode south through nearly half of Mexico, through more desert with rocks and cactus. From their train they saw villages that reminded Hank of the Russian kolkhozes, dusty and drab, with dirt roads, and chickens and pigs on every corner. The air was hotter though, and the villages were much closer to the tracks than in Russia. In the distance bare mountains rose from the desert. Any water was confined to the valleys and nourished only narrow belts of green.

Almost a year and a half had passed since Hank had climbed on the bed of an open truck and ridden the road between *Swinsowchos 641* and Kustenai for the last time. Since then he had crossed fertile plains, deserts, mountain ranges with raging rivers, and even an ocean. Although this country stirred his interest anew, he was getting used to the many changes of scenery. The cacti in particular intrigued him. Later he would learn about their fruits, eat them fresh, and taste cactus leather and cactus jelly—and he would also learn to appreciate the sharpness of their spines and refrain from sitting down on them again.

The train arrived in the town of Leon in Mexico, their destination. Hank, the other children, and the adult refugees boarded waiting buses. After a short ride through a sun-drenched plain, a cluster of buildings rose in the hot sun before the weary travelers: "Colonia Santa Rosa, Leon/Guernaquarto." Spanish in style, its buildings were towered by a large four-story structure standing in their midst. Armed Mexican police guarded the entrance to the compound.

Eileen Egan, an American executive working with the Catholic Relief Services for years, accompanied the children on their trip to Mexico and worked with them at Colonia Santa Rosa. In her book *For Whom There Is No Room* she observes:

> During the trip I studied their faces, the faces of children who had gazed on the great nameless wastes of Siberia, of Asiatic Russia. They had been deported with their parents into a vast empty land. They had seen them break virgin earth—earth that had not been opened to the plow since time began. And they had looked down on the agonizing and dead bodies of their parents. These little faces showed no curiosity about the new surroundings. There was no visible reaction at all to the grotesque dead trees that curled and writhed over the swampland through which we rode, to the brilliant flowers that caught the sunlight, or to the pale green cactus that grew in clumps at the approach to the camp. They were reserved and still, these faces, and they wore the expression of old men. It was with old men's eyes, that they looked out on this strange new country, on the fourth continent they had touched on their journey.

Father Lucjan Krolikowski, a priest and teacher of Polish orphans in Africa, recalls in his book *Stolen Childhood, A Saga of Polish War Children*:

> They were different from children their own age living under normal conditions....They were always guarded, not ready to trust...in general they wanted to make up for their losses in learning and upbringing and...had idealistic attitudes toward life and a high degree of morality. They learned to fight adversity and developed a deep compassion for the handicapped and suffering....Twelve-year-old boys were expressing views of life on a level seldom achieved at that age.

Egan describes their new home as follows:

> The town of Leon, in the province of Guanajuato, an important commercial and industrial center, is situated in the fertile plain of central Mexico. A short bus ride into the country takes the traveler to an old hacienda, the Colonia Santa Rosa, named for Saint Rose of Lima, once self-sufficient with manor house, abundant stores for produce, its own granary and gristmill, and one-room homes for hundreds of workers. It has its own chapel.
>
> Spacious and secluded it was the perfect home for about fifteen hundred Polish children and adults yet to be kept away from the prying eyes of the world, particularly on the North American continent, lest their stories should upset the delicate balance between the Western Allies and Soviet Russia, so essential to bringing the war to a victorious end for the West.

The complex of buildings contained all the necessities of village life, from the blacksmith's forge to the butcher shop and the bakery. After their arrival, the first group of refugees had established a dispensary, a pharmacy, and a hospital. They repaired the rusty narrow-gauge rails which connected the estate with the town of Leon by a horse-drawn or sometimes mule-drawn trolley. A flat-bed trolley brought produce and supplies to the compound. The tall, four-storied building, called the *Moline* was renamed *Mlyn* (mill) by the Polish refugees. It had served as a mill and a granary in the past. A graveled walk in front of it wound through an ornate garden and between shrubs and flowers around a central date palm. Among the older buildings of the former hacienda, was a stone chapel. Its wall facing the cemetery was chipped by bullets from the executions during the Mexican revolution, a generation ago. Once Hank understood the history of the chipped stones, their sight disturbed him deeply and filled him with unease.

Mexico was one of the four countries that founded orphanages for Polish children liberated from the Soviet Union; the others were Africa, India, and New Zealand. On December 30, 1942, the Mexican president, General Avila Camacho, and the Polish premier, General Wladyslaw Sikorski, had signed an agreement to the effect that Mexico offered Colonia Santa Rosa as a temporary asylum for the Polish refugees "until the end of the war in Europe." It thus became a home away from home for the Polish refugees, a haven for them to reestablish their own culture in freedom from need and oppression. The government of the United States assumed the financial burden of its day-to-day operation. In addition, it received the liberal assistance from the National Polish War Relief, Polish civic groups—chiefly the Polish National Alliance of North America headquartered in Chicago —and the Catholic Church of the United States. Colonia Santa Rosa harbored Polish refugees for many years. The last children left for the United States in 1950. Some of the adult refugees followed the same route; others settled in Mexico. (In 1979 Polish-Mexicans formed an honor guard for the Pope at his visit to Mexico.)

The children's first dormitories occupied two of the older buildings not far from the *Młyn*. Later, the space between these two buildings was enclosed to make extra room for showers, wash basins, and toilets. The high ceilings of the rooms were supported by pillars; the windows high up in the walls afforded light but no view. Wooden cots stood in rows, a small bedside stand in between each of them. The children hung their clothes on pegs on the wall.

Within a year the children moved to a newly constructed building near the periphery of the compound. Its rooms were smaller, the floors tiled, and the windows were set so as to give a view of the surrounding countryside. A small altar stood at one end of every room. Like many other living quarters the new building was built around an enclosed patio with shrubs and trees.

Although separated during school and organized activities, Hank and his sister saw each other frequently. They exchanged a few words during their free time and at play, and Hank, the "older" brother, frequently expressed his concern for her well-being. A small store next to the *Młyn* sold candy, soft drinks, and some of the necessities of camp life. At times, their American visitors gave the children a little money as a gift. With his money Hank once bought his sister a jar of mustard; she craved it so much that she took a spoon and ate all of it at once.

New and unwelcome guests came with the tropical setting. Every morning Hank shook out his shoes. Scorpions loved hiding in them. One morning a scorpion stung Hank's finger when he reached under his pillow. His finger stayed swollen and blue for several days.

The children received new clothes for play and a school uniform, but Hank still hung on to his vest from Iran. As one of the older boys, he wore a gray suit with a white shirt and a tie to school; after school he changed into shorts. The girls had gray-and-white-striped dresses, or navy-blue skirts with white blouses. The refugee women at the Colonia sewed all of the clothes worn by the children.

As the refugees became more settled, the day-to-day life of Colonia Santa Rosa began to reflect their Polish culture. Mass was celebrated regularly. One of the priests had been a professor at the university of Lwow. Hank's *junak* records had been lost, and so he was confirmed again. Again he took "Joseph" for his middle name. The confirmation ceremony was conducted in the Basilica of Our Lady of Guadalupe in Mexico City, the holiest church in Mexico. The confirmants went there by bus. A group picture taken after the confirmation shows the Mexican bishop sitting in front center with the confirmants drawn up in formation, most of them in Scout uniforms. One Girl Scout (Anita Paschwa-Kozicka, the author of *My Flight to Freedom*) is holding a partly-unfurled Mexican flag. Hank, in scout uniform, is standing in the first row of the boys to the far left.

The children's daily life remained regimented. In the morning they awoke to the blow of a whistle. They washed and then marched by twos for breakfast, first to the kitchen to get their food and from there to the mess hall. The kitchen, the mess hall with long wooden benches

Confirmation in Mexico.

lining the tables, and the bakery were across from the *Młyn* in a former storehouse. The youngest girls went first, followed by the older
ones, and finally the boys. After breakfast, again by twos, they
marched to school. School lasted until noon; the classes were held in
the *Młyn*. They returned in formation to the mess hall for their noon
meal and then back to their dormitories for a half- to one-hour siesta.
The afternoon was free for the children in grade school, but they had
to be on time for supper. Mealtime was announced by ringing a suspended short piece of railroad track, just like in the camps in India.
At its sound the children lined up by twos. Hank remembered not
only its ringing but also its sharp edge after he hit his head on it one
dark evening.

The children's food was cooked and served by the women of the
camp: butter, honey, and bread for breakfast; a warm meal at noon;
and sandwiches in the evening. The noon meal had Polish sausage and
pierogi; mashed potatoes with chicken, beef, or pork; and bean soup,
sauerkraut soup, or *barszcz* (borsch) on its menu. Sometimes they had
pierozki (small pierogi filled with fruit and sprinkled with powdered
sugar) for desert. Their milk came fresh from the cows on the compound, and the bread too was baked at the Colonia. At times their fare
was augmented with locally grown fruit, and the children learned

about red bananas—smaller and thicker, but sweeter than the yellow ones. Honey had always been a staple of the Polish kitchen and for Hank another reminder of his childhood. At home honey had not only been used as sweetener. In the past, when a child was born, honey was saved in a keg and allowed to ferment for years to be served as mead at the child's wedding.

Free time for the children was not all play. They not only tended to their small garden plots which every one of them had as their personal responsibility, but also cared for their rabbits, fed them, and cleaned their cages. Hank fed his rabbits hay and the greens from his garden. Only then was there time for play.

Not far from the garden plots was a swimming pool which the refugees had repaired. The hot weather made it a favorite place for so many, children and adults alike, that all had to keep to a definite schedule to use it. Hank always anxiously awaited the time when it was his turn to go swimming.

Polish teachers from the camp and several Felician Sisters who had come from the United States taught school. The Sisters also supervised the children of the orphanage. A Mexican teacher taught Spanish.

Finally Hank's schooling was not going to be interrupted any longer. At the outbreak of the war, he was to have entered the fourth grade. Four years later, when he was 14, he finally completed it. At the time he left Colonia Santa Rosa for the United States in 1946, he had finished the sixth grade, the grade for graduation from school in Poland at that time and equivalent to the eighth grade in the United States.

Most of Hank's classmates continued on to high school, but even before he graduated from elementary school Hank had decided he wanted "to work with his hands." Vocational training was available because members of the Polish Alliance had donated the money for the various shops and the tools to equip them.

Hank took up silversmithing. This trade was taught by a Polish and a Mexican teacher. At first Hank was made to work with copper. Only after he had achieved enough proficiency and knew how to engrave and hammer this metal, was he allowed to work with silver. Eventually

Graduation class, Hank is standing second from the right.

he was able to spin a goblet on a lathe, to make letter openers and ash trays, and he also engraved a tea tray. Through this training Hank met some of the Polish visitors from the United States. They bought the silver work and sold it back home to raise extra money for the orphanage. Later, on his entry into the States, he found some of his work at the home of his first host. Silversmithing did not fulfill Hank sufficiently, however, as a career for the future. It did not answer his desire to do "real" work, such as factory work.

Colonia Santa Rosa was a close-knit community. Being refugees in a foreign land brought the members of the Polish group closer to each other and the teachers shared much of their spare time with their students. The Polish silversmith teacher built a kayak and allowed Hank to use it. His Spanish teacher was an amateur wrestler and often took some of his students with him to his meets. The wrestling matches were very rough, and at one of them the teacher was thrown out of the ring and broke his arm. He had to teach with his arm in a cast for several weeks.

Hank fondly remembers a particular Sunday afternoon when he and a number of others sat in the shade of a large tree near a water reservoir. A priest read to them from *Quo Vadis*, a Polish classic. He enunciated the words like an actor and used a different tone of voice for each character. This made the scenes come unforgettably alive for Hank. Once this priest fell ill and was confined to bed. He asked Hank to shave him and held out a straight razor. Hank was worried, he had never used a straight razor before, but he accomplished his task without an accident, though with much trepidation.

The camp administration, teachers, volunteers from among the refugees, and the visitors worked together to provide entertainment and outings for the children. They put on theater productions and folk dances and organized trips to interesting parts of Mexico. A bus was available for their excursions, and the recreation building had a stage and a game room. Chess was a favorite. Boys and girls enrolled in scouting.

One of the most active and helpful teachers was Father Jozef Jarzebowski, a priest from Chicago. Later, Father Jarzebowski continued to work in England with Polish people and their heritage until his death in 1964. He organized ball teams, taught, and helped wherever he could. Hank remembered his guidance well.

Their first outings did much to bring the children's lives back to normal. Not far from Colonia Santa Rosa, at Comanhijo, a resort had been built around several hot springs. Eileen Egan tells about one of the early excursions there: "They [the children] moved quietly and orderly. Their expressions were withdrawn and devoid of spontaneity. They looked at you with dull suspicion and smiled secretly to each other. At the hot springs they had their first hot bath for years and soon swam, laughed, and played with each other."

The trip to the hot springs was one of Hank's first excursions at Colonia Santa Rosa also. The smell of sulfur hung in the air and he was surprised how hot the water was as it came out of the ground, hot enough to boil an egg. A cemented trough distributed the hot water from the springs to several pools. Dividers in the trough allowed people to bathe in small groups or by themselves. After their swim the children had a picnic, and Hank ate his first red banana.

One of their bus trips took them to the top of Parykutin, a volcano, which was still active at that time. In an abandoned town nearby, Hank saw vestiges of the lava flow that had halted short of one of the ruined buildings and solidified. He also went to Mexico City, to Guadalajara, and to Lake Chapala.

On another of their outings they went to the summit of a high and steep mountain. A church was being built at the top, but only the foundations had been laid when they were there. The children took the bus part of the way up, then most of them finished the climb on foot along a steep and narrow trail; the others rode a donkey. Hank marveled at the amount of labor and effort that had to be spent carrying the building materials along that challenging path, the only one leading all the way to the top.

After Hank joined the Boy Scouts, he went on camp-outs, and marched as a scout in Mexican parades. The Polish Alliance had donated the tents and the scout uniforms. Once a high ranking Polish officer visited Colonia Santa Rosa. He shook Hank's hand and greeted him with "How are you?" in Polish.

When the children were free to play, feeling secure in their new home encouraged many, and Hank foremost among them, to leave the grounds and to explore their surroundings. The desert was full of gophers, and the boys liked to catch them. Crouching by a gopher hole, they poured water into it and caught the gopher in a pillow case or a sack as it came out. They kept one as a pet in a drainage channel they had closed off with flat stones and fed it kitchen scraps. It was still there when Hank left for the United States early in 1946.

Not all the holes in the desert, however, were homes to gophers as Hank and a friend of his found out. One day, as they poured water into what they thought was another gopher hole, a small black animal with a white stripe along its head and back emerged. "How cute! It looks like a kitten," Hank's friend said and put it into their bucket. As Hank continued his watch at the hole, a second animal, larger this time, with a dark head and a white stripe on the forehead appeared in the opening. Its snarling mouth and sharp yellow fangs looked frightening. He quickly threw a pillow case over the animal and pulled it out. Then something very strange and unexpected occurred: with the struggling animal in Hank's grasp the pillow case turned green, and Hank was enveloped in a penetrating acrid smell which stung his nose and eyes. He immediately let go of his catch, but his friend ran after the escaping animal and caught its full discharge in his face. His friend's eyes burned so much that he threw himself into the nearest ditch and rolled in the muddy water. Neither of the two had been told about skunks before and were totally ignorant of their powerful defense mechanism. Being peculiar to the Western Hemisphere, skunks were animals that Hank never learned about in his nature book from Poland. He now knew. Undismayed, however, the boys took their bucket with the baby skunk to show it off at school.

"Stay out! And put the animal back were you found it!" they were told emphatically when they tried to enter the classroom.

For the time being at least, Hank and his friend were made to live outside, and their meals were handed to them from a safe distance. Their clothes were burned, and they were given fresh ones together with some old blankets to sleep in. They had to shower several times a day, away from the others, and with every shower the skunk smell rose anew. It took three days for them to be finally readmitted to school and allowed to join their friends.

Rains were rare but heavy, and flash floods roared down the mountain slopes. A system of reservoirs prevented flooding and saved the precious water for a time of draught. At one time it rained so hard that the reservoirs overflowed and inundated the plain. In Colonia Santa Rosa water stood at the foot of the dormitory buildings, for Hank and a schoolmate the perfect occasion to use the teacher's kayak. While the two were paddling about, some older boys forced Hank and his friend out. They quickly overturned it, however, when they tried to hit a duck with the paddle and Hank and his friend had to swim out to bring the kayak back to shore.

Snakes were abundant in the desert. During the same flood Hank saw what appeared to him a tiny island with a clump of reeds. "A good place to swim to," he thought. As he came closer, he saw that his "tiny island" was nothing more than floating brush crawling with snakes which had sought a refuge there. Hank made a quick turnabout and swam away as fast as he could.

Shortly thereafter, another snake frightened Hank much more. Swimming about in one of the reservoirs he happened to look back and saw the sinuous curves of a huge snake moving rapidly toward him. Using all his strength he raced toward the nearest levee. He did not know if the snake was after him or if it had the same intention as he: to get to dry ground. He only knew that the snake was less than 50 yards behind him and gaining. As Hank raised his head he saw an old Mexican man standing on the levee. Silouhetted against the sky he looked down on Hank. A slender figure with a sombrero on his head and a serape slung across his shoulders, he appeared to be the veritable personification of the country. Coming closer Hank noticed the man's mustache, his gray beard, and the sandals on his feet. Leisurely the man raised an ancient muzzleloading rifle and pointed it in Hank's direction. "Is he aiming that gun at me?" flashed through Hank's mind. With a single shot the old man dispatched the snake. Hank climbed the levee and thanked him with the few words of Spanish he knew. With a combination of words and gestures the old man made Hank understand that he may use the gun, balls, and the powder horn for a day. Hank was excited with this prospect. Together with a friend he went to look for a suitable target in the desert. One of the slowly-circling buzzards seemed perfect. He loaded the gun as best he thought, aimed, and fired. Either Hank had not understood, or the old man had not told him how much powder to use. The recoil threw Hank off balance and forcibly sat him on a clump of cactus. The rest of the day his friend had to help remove cactus spines from Hank's buttocks. When Hank returned the gun the next day, the old man explained to him: "For a large load you put enough powder on the flat of your palm to cover the ball; for a small load you cup your hand."

About a mile from the Colonia, at the edge of the desert, Hank found a brick kiln. He wished he could see someone at work there. The ground was pure clay, with water nearby, and plenty of brush all around to feed a fire. The bricks had been cut by hand and stacked into a large pyramid. Inside the pyramid a fire had been started which had baked the inner bricks fully, half-baked the ones in between, and left the outside ones air-dried for use as adobe bricks.

Another time Hank came to an elevated plateau a couple of miles distant from Colonia Santa Rosa near the foot of the mountains. A steep climb through brush and boulders brought him on top. He made his way past rocks and through dense brush growing in the cracks and crevices to where the plateau gently fell off toward a verdant meadow. A clear mountain stream ran through the meadow and left it by a deeply cut, rock-strewn gorge. The soft grass of the meadow felt good under his feet, and it was refreshing to splash in the stream. Hank greatly enjoyed the beauty and serenity of the scenery. The verdant grass and the gurgling stream presented such a contrast to the desert which surrounded him everywhere else. He did not mind that the stream was full of leeches. It was exciting to climb over the rocks past the sheer walls of the gorge. On its far end, high up on a precipice, he saw the nest of an eagle. Hank told the nun in charge about his find and one Sunday after Mass led her and a number of the older children to the stream for a picnic of fresh bread, butter, and honey.

Though Hank never felt restricted in his movements, he heard that in the beginning passes had been required to leave Colonia Santa Rosa on longer trips. At the time of his arrival Mexican police still stood at the entrance, but soon they were withdrawn, and the Polish refugees were free to move as they pleased. Eventually some of them even found work in town.

Hank and his friends often went into Leon on the horse-drawn trolley, though they first had to ask one of the supervising nuns for permission to do so. One day a friend of his came back from town with an exciting story. He and two other boys had been in the market square when they heard the people shout and saw them run away. They soon found out the reason: Mexican soldiers had surrounded the crowd and singled out young men as recruits for the Mexican army. His friend, being quick on his feet, got away. The other two, however, were not so lucky. One had trouble with his feet and could not run well; the other was a deaf-mute. Both were caught in the roundup, and it took the Polish embassy two days to get them released.

Hank had been at Colonia Santa Rosa almost two years at that time. Despite being among his own, despite his increasing freedom and acclimation to his surroundings, Hank and the other refugees regarded it as a temporary home only and hoped to eventually be able to get back to Poland. Preoccupied before by the ever changing impressions of the journey, his thoughts now more often returned to his father, his grandmother, and their fate. Though conscious of the persistent threat to their well-being, Hank never lost hope for their survival and their eventual reunion.

Like the others, Hank understood that they were to stay in Mexico only until the end of the war in Europe. After the war was over, their plans for returning to Poland changed, however, when they found out that the Soviets were in control of all of Eastern Europe, including Poland. The inhabitants of Colonia Santa Rosa therefore turned their thoughts to finding a new home in the Western World, somewhere, but certainly free of Soviet control. The postwar communist Polish government sent a representative to Mexico to urge them all, especially the orphaned children, to return to their home country. Hank does not recall anyone from Colonia Santa Rosa who opted for a return to Poland.

At the conference in Yalta, Stalin had insisted on repatriation of all displaced persons to their country of origin. Initially the Western Allies had not only consented to this, but in the immediate postwar period had even forced some forced-laborers, POWs, and others who had made their way to the West to return to Soviet-occupied countries against their will. Instances of forced repatriation occurred particularly in the United States-occupied sector of Germany. Some of those affected committed suicide rather than facing the certainty of arrest, deportation, and even execution by the Soviets. Father Krolikowski in his book *Stolen Childhood* gives a stirring account of the rapid decisions, ingenuity, and even subterfuge needed to keep his charges out of the hands of the Polish communist officials.

By the time the Poles at Colonia Santa Rosa had decided not to return to Poland, the Western Allies had fortunately reversed their previous position and vehemently opposed forced repatriation in the United Nations deliberations regarding this matter. The refugees were advised they could be repatriated only if they so wished. The Mexican government, moreover, readily offered permanent residence to any of the Polish refugees should they want to remain in Mexico.

Hank, too, did not want to live under Soviet rule, he hoped to go to the United States instead. He had seen very little of it on his bus ride from the ship to camp Santa Anita or on the train from there to the Mexican border. But the little he had seen—the camp, the food, but especially the demeanor and disposition of the American soldiers and the Polish-Americans on their visits—had left him with the impression that north of the Mexican border lay a familiar country whose people were similar in their ways to those of the country of his birth and where life seemed to follow the comforting patterns of his happy childhood. For Hank the United States represented order and solidity. He wanted to live in the country that was called "the land of freedom."

In Mexico Hank still felt like an outsider and knew that he would always feel that way. It did not matter how cordially any individual Mexican had received him or how kind the old man with the gun had been and how willing to share, for Hank, much remained foreign in Mexico: the desert with its heat, the people's customs, their dress, and their complexion. They also seemed to be so passionate in all they did. Everything was full of noise: their music and the dancing in the parks, the fire crackers, and the shooting off of guns on holidays. And in a park in Leon he had heard the word "gringo" uttered behind his back. Yes, he was a "gringo" as far as the Mexicans were concerned, and he felt that he always would be one.

There was something else that made Hank apprehensive about Mexico, something that rekindled a feeling of insecurity, that insecurity that had crept into his life with the first bombs on that sunny day in September 1939 and that had left him only after their ship docked in the United States. As passionately as the Mexicans celebrated, so also did they pursue their politics. At one of their elections there had even been riots and shooting. He also recalled the way the army had picked up its recruits and how roughly the soldiers had treated the people. The very thought of Mexican soldiers made him feel powerless, and the bullet holes in the walls of the old church were vivid reminders of a violent time, a time not that long ago—when his father would have been his age.

Father Krolikowski wrote about a similar attitude in the Polish orphans in Africa: "[T]hey were desperately afraid of war and developed the habit of praying for peace." Hank, too, yearned for peace.

Yes, at present everything seemed peaceful, but would it last? Not long ago a girl was shot through the head as she sat reading under a tree on a Sunday afternoon. Perhaps it was just an accident, a stray bullet from somebody hunting or playing around or celebrating, but she was dead.

Death had accompanied Hank through all the camps and it was still there, even in Colonia Santa Rosa. It came to some as the result of a lingering illness dating back to their years as prisoners, but to others it came anew and unexpected: like that girl shot under the tree, or the boy who died from gangrene after his leg had been caught under the trolley. He was an only child and had come to Santa Rosa with his mother. As the years passed and Hank became older, he began to accept death as a part of life. Though far from being callous, he was no longer stirred to the depth of his soul by it—except when he thought about his mother and his grandfather. Their deaths would always remain a profound personal loss for him.

One day at assembly, representatives from the Polish Alliance of Chicago accompanied the nuns. They announced: "Ten boys from this camp will go to the United States. They will first go to Chicago and from there to a college in Pennsylvania." The names were read; Hank's was among them. "Your sister will be joining you later," he was told. With the help of the Polish Alliance the orphaned children were brought to the United States. Hank was among the first to have his dream fulfilled.

14.

In the Land of the Free

Ten Polish teenagers and their adult guides left Colonia Santa Rosa in central Mexico in March 1946. The camp bus took them to the railroad station. In Laredo, Texas, they changed trains and continued to Chicago. They entered the United States on March 3, five days before Hank's seventeenth birthday, not as "refugees," but as "students" with a student visa.

Hank wore his suit and tie. He had been given a small suitcase for his few belongings: some underwear, an extra pair of stockings and his Persian lambskin vest. He kept that suitcase and the vest until some time after he had joined the military.

Hank kept his parents' pictures from their railroad passes on his person at all times. He had always guarded them closely. They were the only link to his family until, in 1963, his father sent him the coffee mill his grandmother had brought back with her from Siberia. He watched over the photographs of his parents even more after he found out that the Soviets had usually confiscated all documents and pictures of the

Hank prior to leaving Mexico for Chicago. 1946.

deportees. Perhaps they had overlooked their orders back then, perhaps he had just been fortunate that they had not searched him being only a child.

Hank boarded the train with a great sense of relief and anticipation. He was finally going to the United States. The parting with his sister was brief since neither of the two were given to grand shows of affection, and besides, they both knew it would only be a matter of time before she would join him. Meanwhile they would keep in touch by frequent letters. Both were waiting to hear if the nuns in charge of the orphanage had been successful in locating any of their surviving relatives. So far, however, no answers had been received. Hank and his sister remained in doubt about the fate of their father and did not think their grandmother had survived.

When the ten boys arrived in Chicago it was cold and snow lay on the ground. The abrupt change in climate made them shiver. A small crowd of people in heavy overcoats was waiting for them on the platform. One of them, a representative of the Polish Alliance, directed the boys to their host families. Hank and two other boys became the guests of the president of the Polish Alliance, Charles Rozmarek.

Charles Rozmarek was at that time a leading spokesman of the Polish-American community. Very early during the war, he had foreseen the ultimate Soviet domination of postwar Poland and what would happen to the Poles under a Stalinist regime. His warnings, however, had been ignored both by the Roosevelt and the Truman administrations. The wholesale arrest of the members of the underground Polish Home Army by the Soviets beginning in 1944, and the entire sequence of atrocities perpetuated by them against the Polish nation in the postwar years vindicated Rozmarek's dire predictions. Only later, with the realization of the Cold War did the Truman administration appreciate the dangers of communism and with it Mr. Rozmarek's position.

At the station the three boys were ushered into a waiting car. Hank found it impossible to lean back in the comfortable seat; he was too excited. The tall buildings and the overhead trains of this big city, the second largest city in the United States, filled him with awe. He had never seen streets so crowded with cars, with trams and buses, and with people. It truly was a "new world" for Hank. At their host's house two girls in their teens welcomed them warmly and everyone spoke Polish. Hank was to encounter the younger of the two girls again later at the college in Cambridge Springs, where she attended a summer camp in Polish culture.

Hank and his friends were overwhelmed by their new impressions: the weather, the huge city, the big and comfortable home, and especially the warm reception they received. After a formal dinner in the large dining room, they fell into bed exhausted. As Hank pulled up the covers he realized that this was the first time since the Soviets had pounded on their door back home in Krasne more than six years ago that he was going to sleep in a real bed in a private bedroom, of a private home. But he was almost too exhausted to care.

Hank and his friends stayed in Chicago for three days, days filled with excitement. They had so many new things to see and do. One evening all ten boys were taken to dinner in an exclusive restaurant. The food was Polish, so was the decor, and everyone around them spoke Polish. Had they come to a part of Poland they had never heard of before? Untouched by the war? No, they knew only too well that they were in the USA.

At his host's house Hank, to his surprise, saw a letter opener that he himself had made and a tea tray that he had engraved at Colonia Santa Rosa. Though he had seen the American visitors purchase silver work from the vocational students at the Colonia, he had never expected to find his work again. His hosts found it difficult to reconcile their young guest with the artisan who had crafted the pieces until Hank showed them where his engraving knife had slipped on the letter opener.

One experience in Chicago had a lasting effect on Hank. One day after their arrival, he and the other boys were asked to speak before a large assembly of Polish-Americans on what happened to them and how they came to the United States.

Hank told them how he and his family were taken from home, about the Red Army soldiers pounding at the door, about having to pack within a half-hour's time, and about their transport in freight cars after waiting on a railroad siding for three days without any food or water. He spoke about the young woman passing her infant through the bars, the shouts and the shot, and how every day during their transport the Soviet soldiers removed the dead bodies from the cars and just dumped them by the side of the tracks; about their stay in Siberia, how they existed in the run-down horse barn, and their daily struggle to survive. Near tears he mentioned the death of his mother, and that he was never able to see her grave, that his grandmother had to go and bury her, and her words afterwards: "I had to split her nightgown in order to bury her in it. She was all in pieces, the arms, the legs, the head."

When he came off stage, he overheard a comment that "those

things could not have happened," and that "the boy does not know what he is talking about." Hank's respect for his elders prevented him from replying; instead, with hurt feelings, he withdrew and for years afterwards he would not speak about those times. What had happened to Hank as a young boy was, in early 1946, still beyond the imagination of many people this side of the Atlantic. Revelations such as Hank's often came as too much of a shock.

Among the population of the United States the Soviet actions in regard to the Polish people were virtually unknown in spite of the fact that the Polish government-in-exile had informed the American authorities about them. Moreover, after they arrived in Iran, most members of the Polish army formed in the Soviet Union had filled out detailed questionnaires about their homes, their conditions as prisoners of war under the Soviets, and the people they had met in the camps. The adult Polish civilians, too, had been debriefed in Iran about the circumstances of their deportation and their experiences under the Soviets, and older school children had been asked to write essays about them. Later, these testimonies were stored at the Hoover Institution on War Revolution and Peace in California and in many other archives in the United States and Europe. Meanwhile, the Germans told the world about the massacre of the Polish officers at Katyn.

Despite the silence on the part of the American government, however, news of these events had filtered through: Many of the refugees were friends or relatives of Polish-Americans, on board the USS *Hermitage* about one sailor in ten understood Polish, and several Polish-American organizations had protested to President Roosevelt. The Western Allies, however, continued to support Stalin to avoid any rift with the Soviet Union until the Allied victory.

But there may also have been other reasons for the official silence. Old prejudices often take long to die out, and the people from the Slavic countries had been their object since the turn of the century when, in the words of Dinesh D'Sonza (1995) "millions of Eastern and Central European immigrants faced an opposition far greater than found by many non-white immigrants today." This happened in America a mere generation prior to the 1940s, and "scientific racism" and the eugenic movement had been successfully challenged only a decade earlier.

Perhaps also, in the 1940s and even subsequently, the sheer numbers, the depth of the suffering, and the utter degradation of human lives were realities which a civilized mind simply could not comprehend. This may explain why even some of those whose positions gave them firsthand information were unable to truly empathize, to fully bridge the gulf between registering a fact in their consciousness and then making the emotional connection. Comparable experiences were lacking in the United States at that time. This may have also been a factor influencing the Western allies at the conference in Yalta where they so readily conceded to Stalin's demand for repatriation of all refugees after the war, even to the extent of forcing people to return to their country of origin against their wishes.

In any case, much needless suffering and death could have been avoided in the postwar years had the victorious Allies taken the Soviet policies regarding their own citizens and the citizens of the countries under their control into account at Yalta.

Hank's stay in Chicago was short. Within a couple of days, all ten boys went by train to the Polish Alliance college in Cambridge Springs, Pennsylvania. They lived in a dormitory and were looked after by its supervisors and the older students. To prepare them for life in the United States they were taught English, American history, and government. As they were yet under age, the dean of the college acted as their guardian. "He was a very kind man and we could talk to him about anything that troubled us," Hank said of him.

While some of the boys continued on to high school, Hank helped with the work around campus. One of his jobs involved assisting the butcher in the large kitchen. He soon established himself as an accomplished meat cutter and when the butcher left, Hank took over his job. Daily life on campus emphasized Polish folk culture, and Hank took a summer class in Polish culture, customs, and dance. At the end of the session he received a certificate that read: "Instructor in Polish Folk Dance."

Not long after his arrival in Cambridge Springs, Hank received news about his father that filled him with profound joy. A letter from

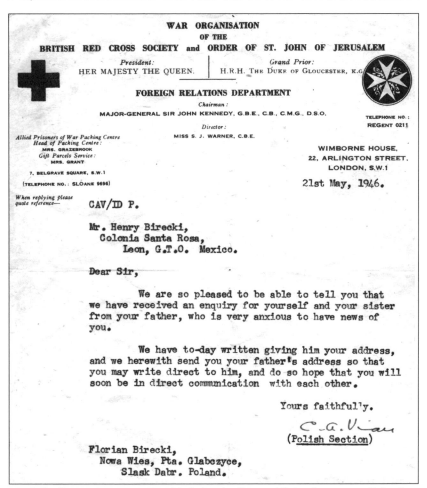

Hank finally receives news that his father is alive and living in western Poland.

The War Organization of the British Red Cross Society and Order of St. John of Jerusalem, dated May 21, 1946, informed him that his father was alive and gave his address in western Poland. Later, that same year, this was verified by a notification from the Polish Red Cross of the Middle East. Meanwhile Hank's father was also advised that his children were safe in Mexico. In the first letter from his father Hank found out that his grandmother had also survived. Years would go by, however, before Hank and his father would see each other again. "It

In late 1946 Hank received this notification from the Polish Red Cross of the Middle East. (Front)

was just as well that I was already in the States when I found out where my father was," Hank said. "Had I still been in Mexico I might have chosen to return to Poland."

While Hank was at Cambridge Springs, most of the other orphaned children were brought from Mexico and placed in orphanages in the United States. After he found out that his sister was sent to an orphanage in Buffalo, New York, Hank went by bus to visit her. "I had no trouble finding the place. The dean had given me instructions, and at that time you always found somebody in Buffalo who spoke Polish," he said.

Years later when Hank's father came to America, he also had no trouble finding a Polish-speaking cab driver to take him to his daughter's house. He did not know that she and her husband had gone to the airport to pick him up. They were looking for him there in vain. When they finally came home, he was waiting for them at their door.

When Hank saw his sister at the orphanage—she was then about twelve years old—she was still very shy and withdrawn. Fortunately, a

Druk B

Ref. *C.P. BIRECKI HENRYK/16*
I. BIRECKA ROMANA/16
W odpowiedzi prosimy powolac
sie na powyzsze haslo.

dn. .... VIII 19......
dotyczy .... pisma z
.... 2. IV. 1948

Centrala Poszukiwan P.C.K. na Sr. Wsch. uprzejmie zawiadamia, ze
p. *BIRECKI FLORIAN*
adres *NOWA WIES, P-ta GŁABCZYCE ŚLASK DABR*
poszukuje *BIRECKIEGO HENRYKA (SYNA), BIRECKIEJ ROMANY (corki)*
prosimy o ~~bezposrednie skomunikowanie sie z poszukujacym oraz~~ zawiadomienie nas,
czy poszukiwanie to dotyczy Pana

Przewidujac mozliwosc powstania trudnosci finansowych, przy ktorych Centrala
Poszukiwan moze byc zmuszona do ograniczenia swojej dzialalnosci, pozwalamy sobie
zwrocic sie z prosba o nadeslanie pod naszym adresem dobrowolnej ofiary (Postal
Order).

Centrala Poszukiwan. PCK. na Sr. wsch.

In late 1946 Hank received this notification from the Polish Red Cross of the Middle East. (Back)

Polish couple whose own children were already grown took her into their home as a foster child. Under their loving care she bloomed into a charming and lively girl. She stayed with them until she married. Hank and his sister had always spoken Polish to each other until then, but after she married and as her husband spoke only English, they gradually switched into English too.

At Cambridge Springs Hank discovered one classic aspect of American life: football. The Pittsburgh Steelers had their summer camp there, and Hank became personally acquainted with several of the team members. One of them once threw a long pass to Hank with an unfortunate result: two stubbed fingers on Hank's left hand and fractured end joints. Later, when Hank spent a military furlough in Chicago and the Steelers happened to be in town he visited the team. To his surprise, some of them not only recognized him but also arranged for a box seat at the fifty-yard line for him.

After living at Cambridge Springs for more than a year, Hank felt the need to be on his own. He realized that he had to break away from the Polish environment if he really wanted to learn English and make his own way. He also wanted to earn more money. He described his transition to independence as follows:

> My Polish acquaintances helped me to find a job with the Motorola corporation in Chicago, and I took a part-time job with a photographer on top of it. He taught me how to tint black and white photographs. A Polish couple rented me a room. It was near the EL, the elevated train. The windows rattled whenever a train passed, day and night. I never really got used to the noise, the commotion, and the din of the traffic in the big city. Any chance I had I took a book and found a quiet spot in one of the parks.

But he was satisfied, he was finally independent.

Winston Churchill gave his famous speech in Fulton, Missouri, on March 5, 1946. He spoke of the "Iron Curtain" which had descended "from the Baltic to the Adriatic Sea." In 1947 President Truman referred to the "Cold War" when the communist menace threatened to rear its head not only abroad, but also at home in the United States. Although Hank had begun to merge himself into life in the United States, his hatred of Soviet communism had stayed with him.

On April 28, 1948, just after he turned 19, Hank filed his declaration of intent for American citizenship; three months later, on July 15, he enlisted in the United States Armed Forces.

"I would do anything to get back at the communists. What once happened to me should never happen to others, not if I can help it," he said. "When I enlisted, they gave me an IQ test and sent me to the Army Air Corps."

After boot camp he applied for training as a radio mechanic but was sent to school for engine mechanics instead. By the time he left the service he had become a member of the newly formed United States Air Force and had switched his uniform from olive-brown to Air-Force blue.

Although his English improved over time Hank spoke with a heavy accent. On one occasion what some would have taken as an insult Hank accepted with pride:

In July 1948, at the age of 19, Hank enlisted in the United States Armed Forces.

In boot camp my buddies helped me learn English, they never made fun of me. After boot camp I was sent to engine school in Texas. It was tough, it was an eighteen-week course, and you could not miss even one day. I had to learn everything: armaments, sheet metal, engines. On weekends I took my books to a motel room and studied sitting by the pool. One evening we went to a bar. Some Texans made fun of my pronunciation and called me a 'damn Yankee'. My friends wanted to fight them, but I told them 'No! I was paid a compliment.' I was proud to be taken for an American.

In the service his immigrant status led to encounters with the FBI:

After I finished my training I was sent to Elgin field in Florida, the proving grounds. I was not yet a citizen and therefore had a problem with my security clearance. The FBI was always trying to check on me; they finally caught up with me after I had been working at the proving grounds for three months already. I was not supposed to be around experimental air craft; we had F-80s and T-33s, all new jets at that time, but my squadron commander cleared me. The FBI even looked up my sister. 'What kind of trouble are you in?' she wrote to me after they had come to her inquiring about me. I had kept in touch with some of my friends who came with me to the States, but when the FBI started checking on me I did not keep contact with them any longer. I did not want to get them involved. Soon they, too, joined the army, and we drifted apart.

President Truman came to Elgin Field to conduct an inspection and to witness a demonstration of new weaponry. Hank had just finished readying a fighter plane and was leaning against the wing waiting for the pilot. He suddenly saw the president striding toward the plane, as always, ahead of his Secret Service detail. Hank snapped to attention and Truman greeted him with his usual "How're you doing, soldier?"

"The Secret Service men rushed up to me. They frisked me and told me I had no business being there, that it was a restricted area," Hank said.

"Leave that soldier alone; he is just doing his damn job!" the president shouted at them and walked off.

From Florida Hank was transferred to Clark Air Force Base in the Philippines and told of his stay there as follows:

Every so often I flew with a pilot in a training fighter. Once we turned upside down, and I could look right down into the crater of Mount Pinatubo. That's the volcano which erupted not long ago and destroyed the base. I liked to meet people of different backgrounds and cultures. In the Philippines I lived off base with a Filipino family for several months, and on a furlough to Japan I became friends with a Japanese family who invited me into their home.

Every year in the service brought an advancement in rank for Hank; after five years he received an honorable discharge as staff sergeant. "I got a stripe every year," he said with pride. Soon after his discharge and still in uniform, on August 13, 1953, Hank appeared before a judge of the United States District Court, Western Division, of the State of New York to be sworn in as a citizen. He explained the nature of that ceremony as he, probably, alone experienced it:

> We applicants sat in the jury box. I was still in uniform. When the judge came in, he turned to the bailiff and said, "Get that soldier out of there, I don't need any coaching!" The bailiff explained that I was one of the applicants. The judge then pointed to me and said, "Look at this man. Even before he got his citizenship he chose to serve his new country." He never asked me any questions, though I had studied hard.

After his discharge Hank first lived in Buffalo, New York, near his sister and her husband. He worked on the railroad and for an electric company. From there he moved to Dayton, Ohio, and, after working in construction and with a cabinet maker, eventually found civil-service employment as an aircraft mechanic at the Wright Patterson Air Force base. He wanted to go to college to study mechanical drawing. Though he passed the entrance examination and had gotten the Veterans Administration's approval for his tuition, he had not graduated from high school.

Hank's formal education consisted of a total of six grades spread over ten years between Poland and Mexico. Nevertheless, he obtained his G.E.D. (General Education Diploma, a high school equivalent) after cramming for only two weeks working the afternoon shift on the base and going for his classes in the mornings.

"Wherever I worked I tried to learn something," Hank said about his various jobs. "The electric company in Buffalo was owned by a German. He showed me how to fix lamps and appliances and also let me work in his photography dark room. I learned a lot about building and woodworking on my first jobs in Dayton, and I have my certificate in heli-arc and gas welding."

In Dayton he rented a room from a co-worker and soon became

part of his family. He shared his free time with them and went along on their hunting and fishing trips, and through them he met Mary Lou, his future wife. He told how their happy and lasting union came to pass:

> "Every May we went to northern Michigan to pick mushrooms—morels. On one of those trips I met Mary Lou's father. I knew him before I met her. We stayed at his cabin, which was right next door to where we live now. My landlord was Mary Lou's godfather; he introduced me to her." Hank and Mary Lou were married on June 14, 1969.

Eventually, after a fifteen-year career as aircraft mechanic, Hank was forced to take a disability retirement. Over the years he had developed a worsening tremor, a shakiness of his hands, and a medical examiner eventually disqualified him for the precision work required of engine mechanics, Hank's protestations notwithstanding. His tremor may well have been a legacy from his time in Siberia, or, more likely the southern Soviet Union where he had been ill with what he called a "sleeping sickness," probably an inflammation of the brain, an encephalitis, due to an infection, such as typhus.

After Hank retired, his wide and varied mechanical knowledge continued to serve him well. He knew why he always "wanted to work with his hands." He not only enjoyed it, he had an aptitude for it.

"We moved to northern Michigan a couple of years after I retired. We loved the woods and the hills," Hank said. There, he applied himself to lapidary work, cutting and polishing stones and, drawing on his training as silversmith, fashioning belt buckles, rings, and broaches. True to the tradition of his family, he gardened and readily helped with any building or repair work needed at his own or his friends' homes. Following his heart surgery, however, he had to limit his physical activity. Also, his tremor had increased to such an extent that he finally had to part with his lapidary equipment. It did not take long, however, for him to find a new outlet for his creativity, and with the help of a computer he now designs pamphlets, announcements, and invitations for his friends and for his wife's church functions.

Hank and Mary Lou were married on June 14, 1969.

Mary Lou and Hank celebrate their 25th wedding anniversary.

During these years Hank had a joyful reunion with his father. He was also able to fulfill his vow to make a pilgrimage in gratitude for his delivery from the Soviet Union. Though the road he had traveled as a child with his parents to the shrine at Malinte was barred for him, he fulfilled his pledge at St. Anne de Beaupres in Quebec, Canada instead.

15.

Florian, Hank's Father

I met Florian Birecki, Hank's father, in 1984. He was 86 years old at that time and had come to the United States to spend his remaining days with his children. It would be not quite two years. His second wife had died not long before.

When the Soviets invaded Poland, Hank's father had gone into hiding. Warned in time of his pending arrest, he quickly shed his uniform and hid in the woods around Sassow. He lived that way for the entire 21 months of the Soviet occupation, helped only by his Polish relatives and some of the farmers who had remained in the area. After the German advance through this region, in June 1941, he felt it safe to emerge, only to be put into a German labor battalion and taken to work in Italy.

"They were sending people home who were too sick to work, so I ate lye soap until I got diarrhea, " he told Hank at their reunion. He made his way from Italy back to Poland on freight trains.

Florian, Hank's father, in 1948.

He told neither Hank nor his sister how he lived off the land in the depth of the woods. He had had his close calls, though. For example, one day a Soviet guard poked his bayonet through the hay of a wagon where he was concealed. Thank God a plow had been placed across the hay on top of him.

After the war he married the daughter of one of the families that helped him during his time in the forest. Together with her and her family he was resettled in western Poland, the former German area. Like so many others, they too had opted to retain their Polish citizenship in 1945 and therefore were forced to leave their family farm in that part of Poland annexed by the Soviet Union. One of Florian's sisters and, after her return from Siberia, Hank's grandmother joined him at his new home.

Hank's father was already living in western Poland when the Red Cross brought Hank the news that he had survived, but it took almost two additional decades for them to be reunited. In 1963 he was allowed to come for a three-week visit to the home of his daughter, Hank's sister, in Buffalo. He had to come alone; his wife had not been allowed to leave Poland at the same time as her husband, a policy standard throughout the Warsaw-pact countries to make sure the person going abroad would return. He arrived the day of Hank's birthday. When, early the next morning, Hank came from Dayton where he was working at that time, his father was still asleep. Hank recalled their reunion:

> When I arrived Dad was still sleeping. I woke him up. He looked up and said "By God, it is you!" Later that morning he pulled out a bottle of Vodka from his coat pocket, poured two glasses and said: "I guess you're old enough to have a drink with your dad." The vodka was the sharpest I ever drank; it had such a bite that it made me cough and my eyes were full of tears. It must have been pure alcohol.

Three weeks were a short time to talk about everything that had happened to them in over 20 years. As they spoke about Krasne and Hank's boyhood, Hank reminded his father of the time when he told the other policemen about the big explosion in a field and the boys he had seen running away from it. "You didn't know then that I was one of them, did you?" Hank asked him. And they both had a good laugh about it.

Twenty-one years passed before Hank saw his father again, in 1984—and this time he came to stay. Shortly after he arrived, Hank brought him to my office for an examination and served as his translator. I was struck by the beauty of Florian Birecki's voice. I had never heard Polish spoken in quite that way before. Sonorously intoned, his words first seemed to bounce between his cheeks and his tongue and then roll off his lips like a smooth round ball. I was also deeply moved

Father, Son Reunited After Separation In Poland In 1939

It takes a long time for a father and son to make up for a 29-year separation.

For Henry Birecki of 2332 Mechanicsburg rd. and his father Forian Birecki of Nowa Wies, Poland, there will only be three months, according to the terms of the latter's visa.

There won't be many reminiscences.

Henry Birecki was nine when he last saw his father. His childhood memories since then are of death in the cold Siberian winter and of orphanages in three countries.

The younger Mr. Birecki last saw his father in 1939.

That was the year Russia invaded Poland. Forian Birecki had been a policeman since 1900. One of the first things the new government did was release prisoners. The ex-policeman Birecki had to hide. He lived 22 months on the open land.

The next move of the new regime was to move many thousands of Poles into Russia where they worked in labor camps. Among those in the forced exodus were Henry, his five-year-old sister, Ronna, now of Buffalo, N. Y., his mother and grandmother.

His mother and grandmother died in Siberia.

Meanwhile, back in Poland Forian Birecki came out of hiding. The Russians were no longer as preoccupied with Poland's policemen as they were with the invading Germans.

Henry was taken to Polish orphanages in Tehran, Iran, India, and then Mexico. He entered the United States in 1946, sponsored by the Polish Alliance Club in Chicago, Ill.

As soon as he came of age he joined the U. S. Air Force where he spent five years.

In answer to those surprised at the number of countries in which he has lived, he answers, "But, that is what a displaced person is. He has no place."

The closest thing he has had to a permanent home has been for the past 12 years with Mr. and Mrs. Andrew Salts of 2332 Mechanicsburg rd.

The 39-year-old bachelor with blond, going-grey hair is "part of the family," according to Mrs. Salts. He works at Wright-Patterson Air Force Base and returns each evening to his adopted parents. Lately he has kept busy taking his father around to meet his friends.

A recent trip to downtown Springfield included a visit to the eye doctor and a clothing store. "He gained so much weight during his first week here that his pants are too small," said Henry Birecki.

The senior Birecki requested a special trip to a local airline office and to the office of Congressman Clarence J. Brown, Jr., who helped make arrangements for the trip. The two offices received his thanks.

The older man is impressed by the clean, wide streets, the lighting, the many clean and well-furnished homes, but most of all he said, according to his son's translation, he was taken by the kindness of the people.

The chance to see his children, however, far surpasses the marvels of America. "I have one month for each 10 years I didn't see them," he says.

Forian Birecki arrived in Buffalo March 8, on his son's birthday. Henry Birecki arrived at his sister's home in the early morning hours.

Henry Birecki, left, of 2332 Mechanicsburg rd., and his father, Forian Birecki, last saw each other when Henry Birecki was nine years old. They have recently been reunited for three months, the term of Forian Birecki's visa from Poland.

This article on Hank and his father's reunion appeared in a Buffalo newspaper in 1963.

Florian, Hank's father, came to the United States in 1984 to live with Hank and Mary Lou.

Hank enjoys a trip to Mackinaw Island with his father. (1985)

by the profound warmth and kindness which emanated from his blue eyes.

When I examined Hank's father, I found only a few minor abnormalities not unusual for a man in his ninth decade and was impressed by his overall fitness. In fact the day prior to my examination he had spent two hours cutting the long grass in Hank's apple orchard with a scythe without needing to rest.

I saw him again in my office three months later. He had lost his appetite for several weeks, had developed a fever a few days before his appointment, and was perceptibly jaundiced. Within a few days I had to perform exploratory surgery, but I only was able to give him some temporary relief from the effects of his inoperable cancer. He recovered from the surgery without complications and lived another 18 months in the affection lavished upon him by his son and daughter-in-law and with the support of a local hospice organization. He died peacefully on September 23, 1986. Two days later he was buried in the cemetery of a small community called Bliss, located in northern Michigan not far from Hank's home. He told Hank before he died: "To be buried among these woods and these hills makes me feel that I am at home. This country is so much like the one I grew up in."

Hank's father never failed to express his gratitude to all those who had helped him to rejoin his children. Deeply devout, he reserved his most profound thanks, however, for the one he looked upon as his guardian, the Blessed Virgin Mary. It was she, he remembered, who stood at the foot of his bed in Poland and told him: "You will be reunited with your children in the United States of America," and he had seen her visibly manifested in the many women who had been so helpful to him during his long life, particularly with the steps needed to come to America. Her image now graces his tombstone.

16.

"I'm an American"

I was once more on my way to talk to Hank. Over two years had passed since I first asked him if I could write his story, more than two years of often weekly get-togethers with searching questions on my part and increasingly detailed and specific answers on his, of library visits, and of lengthy telephone conversations. Had I come to the end of his story? Was there nothing else worthwhile to relate? Not by far! To close Hank's story at this time is an arbitrary selection of a point in the road at which to stop and look back.

To write Hank's story I not only had to familiarize myself with the stories of others who had shared his fate, but also had to immerse myself into the history of that time. A writer is said to learn as much from writing a book, as the reader from reading it. I question this statement; the writer always learns more. I have learned much, not only about the historical events herein contained. I also came to scrutinize my own life, particularly my youth. I found new insights, and gained a fresh perspective on life.

I thought that I knew about the suffering, the systematic degradation, and the willful destruction of lives during the Second World War. I had seen the pictures of the German concentration camps, the emaciated survivors, the corpses covered with nothing but skin and bones, piled up like so many cords of wood. I had visited the concentration camp Buchenwald more than once and in the hours I spent among its exhibits, photographs, and testimonials I became aware that even children had been among its inmates. And I had taken the time to read the personal stories in the holocaust museums that I have visited during the course of my life, and I said ENOUGH!

But the more I learned about Poland and its people during the Second World War, the more I realized that they had suffered under the Soviets just as much. Corpses of imprisoned Poles marked the death marches under the Soviets in front of the advancing German troops in 1941; corpses of inmates were left in the concentration camps by the Germans fleeing before the Red Army in 1945. Both the Germans and the Soviets attempted to destroy any Polish leadership, as for instance the executions of the professors of the university of Lwow by the Germans, or the murder of thousands of Polish officers in the woods of Katyn. Thousands were worked to death in the stone quarries of the German concentration camps, just as in the forests and the mines of the Gulag. In the mines of Kolima, seven out of ten Polish prisoners of war perished during the winter of 1940/41.

Thousands upon thousands of Polish families had been dumped into the steppes of Kazakhstan, the Siberian forests, and the Arctic tundra to labor like slaves with abysmal shelters and a starvation diet, often leading to a slow, but certain death.

The civilized world has a term for such premeditated extermination of one specific ethnic group: genocide. To this end the nationalist frenzies and ethnic hatreds in Poland had been systematically exploited both by the Soviets and the Germans.

Reading about the terror unleashed against the Poles by Ukrainian-nationalist groups forced me to think: "What if...?" The Jewish families deported by the Soviets at least had a chance for survival, however slim; those not deported were soon exterminated by the Germans. We can only speculate as to what might have happened to Hank, his sister, and his mother under the Germans had they not been deported to Siberia. Would they have been taken to Germany for forced labor? Would the children have been kidnapped and brought up as Germans? Would they have seen the Ukrainian members of their own extended family turn against them and make them their victims? After all, Hank's mother, though born into a Ukrainian family, had married a Pole—and a Polish policeman at that—and she was also a convert to Roman Catholicism. For many Ukrainian nationalists this was a deadly combination. Tadeusz Piotrowski in his book *Genocide and Rescue in Wolyn* recounts many instances of this sort with fatal results.

Among Hank's Ukrainian relatives one of his mother's cousins had been active in the Ukrainian-nationalist cause. Before the war he was close to Hank's family. He helped Hank's father set up his orchard, and Hank's father managed to have him released after he had been arrested during a demonstration. Hank fondly remembers the slice of homemade bread with butter and honey that he received at his house when he stopped by after crossing the swinging footbridge on his way to his grandmother's. But it had been he who had put Hank's family on the list to be deported! After the war he profusely apologized for this to Hank's father, and we will never know what pressures had been put upon him to do this or how severely he had been coerced. Instant retribution followed everyone who refused to cooperate. Hank's cousin, his mother's sister's son, for example, was poisoned by his own wife because, although he was Ukrainian, he had had strong pro-Polish sympathies.

These thoughts occupied my mind as I was driving toward Hank's house along my favorite stretch of the road, a few miles of dirt that wove its way through stands of maple and aspen, their branches forming live Gothic arches high over the road. More than two years ago when I first spoke to Hank about writing his life experiences it had been spring. Now it was fall, and the northern Michigan woods were ablaze with color. Today's display was set against a cloudless azure sky. I paused at a small stream and gazed at its graveled run before it disappeared in a dark stand of cedars.

It occurred to me that one can never give full justice to everything that happened or moved a person during a lifetime. In telling Hank's story I could but present the events most significant to him and interpret them in relation to the history of the time. Yet equally important is what lies between the lines, the unsaid which stirs our imagination.

Looking back, I was fortunate. Compared to Hank's, my life was straightforward, its obstacles minor. With very few exceptions, I always felt in control. Hank, on the other hand, was always under someone else's rule from the age of ten until he left the dormitory at Cambridge Springs. And during the first part of that lost youth, that rule was like a fist of steel.

My schooling was not disrupted as his had been, and I could struggle through my adolescence limited only by the restrictions imposed on daily life by the war. At the time I joined the medical service of the German navy in July 1944, I was ready and anxious to leave home, to step out into the world. Hank was not allowed to go through this period of life at his own pace. Perhaps this is the greatest injustice done to all children torn from their homes by the Soviets, the Nazis, and any other such faction. More than hunger, cold, physical deprivations and all the rest, it was this abrupt dislocation from childhood, a dislocation that stole their innocence and turned them into adults overnight, that was so tragic.

Hank's external environment too, had been the opposite of mine. From a childhood free of need, his life was degraded to the bare minimum of existence and a daily struggle for survival. After his liberation, despite providing adequate shelter, food, and clothing the camps were still devoid of even the smallest amenities of life. Even privacy was at a premium.

Hank also was faced with a technological progress unimaginable at the time of his childhood for which the rural life by the light of the kerosene lamp, his sporadic schooling, and the physically demanding, but primitive labor as a boy did not prepare him adequately. Yet he mastered the exacting and mentally taxing work with precious metals, jet engines, and lastly computers which only attests to his adaptability, his determination, and his intelligence. His life is exemplary of the millions who came to our shores from comparable backgrounds and circumstances whose steadfastness, hard work, and talents have contributed to weave the fabric of this nation.

I continued on my way, wondering what Hank now thought about his past, and how he had been able to adjust to the American way of life. By this time we both had lived and worked in this country for over forty years, had our own families, and felt thoroughly at ease with daily life in America. I wanted to know how he, like myself, had become an American.

Hank was waiting for me, and we retired to a comfortable nook in one of his work trailers. Mary Lou was cleaning house and we would be in the way.

"As I look back, everything went so smooth after I came to this country," he began. "These people from Chicago, the Polish Alliance, they were the ones who helped me the most." Hank always stressed how grateful he felt to the members of the Polish Alliance for bringing him into this country. "And in the service; I was not yet a citizen and should not have had security clearance, but they let me work on experimental airplanes, the newest. I had applied for training as a radio mechanic, but they trained me to service aircraft. That helped me later. I had a good job in the Civil Service."

From the time he had come to the orphanage in Kustenai Hank's life had run smoother than that of many of his compatriots.

"These girls, Anita [Kozicka] and Stella [Tobis], went through just as much hardship after the amnesty as they did during their deportation, until they finally got to Persia," he said. (Both had been with Hank at the orphanage in Colonia Santa Rosa.) "Even in Siberia to know Boris and his family and the Kirghiz boys, that all helped."

When I asked him: "Looking back, how do you now feel about your life, the past?" Hank spontaneously brought out the positive events in his life. This impressed me, and I told him so. This trait in Hank reminded me of his grandmother; her ability to cope with any situation and her resiliency in adversity. "I could not have lived had I concentrated on the sad things," he concluded.

How did Hank find his way amid the diversity of American life? Because of its isolation and the many common experiences of its residents, the Polish community at Colonia Santa Rosa had been exceptionally cohesive.

"To be able to speak English was the most important thing for me," he said, and added that he had realized this rather early. He knew he had to leave the predominantly Polish environment at Cambridge Springs and meet people of other backgrounds. He also wanted to be on his own. He therefore moved to Chicago to find factory work. All of this helped him to master the English language, but the close, continuous and varied relationships in the military were the most effective.

After his discharge from the service, he lived and worked among people with diverse ethnic and national backgrounds. He formed friendships outside the Polish community and eventually married an American girl. Like Mary Lou's family, most of his personal friends had been in America for generations. "I'm some of everything," Mary Lou liked to say. "You want it, you got it."

Racial segregation was still the law in the southern States when Hank was stationed in Texas and Florida. I asked him: "Discrimination, racial discrimination toward blacks in particular, how did you feel about this after you came to this country? Did it affect you? Influence your attitude? You were stationed for a while in the South, in Florida."

"I always accept people for who they are," he replied. "Ever since I was taken I met so many people of different nationalities, different religions: the Russians, the Kirghiz, in Iran, the old man with the rifle in Mexico. If you only saw how they tried to help, how can you make distinctions? The ones who helped me most in Siberia were the Kirghiz, and the Russians treated them like dirt. Sure, some have a different culture, but that's something you learn."

Culture is something one learns. What a simple and straightforward way of looking and dealing with the problems generated by ethnic diversity; five words, both to give definition and point toward the answer.

"Yes, I know about discrimination," he continued. "I was the one discriminated against. In Mexico I was a 'gringo.' When I was working I often heard the word 'Polack.' I always made a joke of it. If someone said something about 'that Polack over there' I laughed and told him: 'You know, I'm a Polack too.'"

I had just returned from a visit to Latvia where I had been involved in a hospice project. What I had heard and seen there intruded on my thoughts about Hank; there were many similarities. Its topography called to my mind what he had told me of his home: A rolling country with broad and silent rivers, with sections of woods and fields, with lakes and marshes—the northern part of the great plain stretching from the Baltic sea to the Carpathian Mountains. And lives of the people seemed to run in parallel. I recognized a continuum in the paintings by Fluek of the country life of a Jewish farm family in Poland and the paintings of Latvian country scenes at the Museum of Art in Riga.

Its people had also shared a common fate with the Poles. To control Latvia and the other Baltic states had been the aim of Russian imperialism for centuries, and, as in Poland, the Soviet invasion in 1939 had brought on subsequent waves of arrests and deportations. Later, the Nazis exploited the anti-Russian and anti-Communist sentiments of the people, and forced labor and concentration camps awaited all dissenters. After the war many people from the Baltic countries, like the people from Poland, found a new home in the United States. Rather than falling under the rule of the Soviets again, they had left their homes and possessions to the advancing Red Army.

Many elderly people who had left Latvia as children or young people were now returning to spend the last years of their lives "at home." On my retirement I, too, had been asked if I planned to return to Germany. Posing the same question to Hank, I was not surprised by his answer:

> My home is here. I'm an American. I have no desire to go back to Krasne, not even for a visit. There is nothing left there for me. I know no one; I would be like a stranger. I don't care to go to Poland either; I would feel as an outsider. The only place I might like to see would be our camp in Siberia. Maybe one or two of the Kirghiz boys are still around. They should be old men by now, but still, they might remember me. No, I don't want to go to a place which was taken away from me. If I go anywhere, I'll go to a place I left on my own accord, like that camp. But [and this he emphasized] I belong here, in this country.

His words touched me. I became acutely aware of a pain which still lingered, the pain of the loss of his childhood and all the relationships it entailed.

I was also taken by, and perhaps a little envious of, the clarity and the self-assuredness contained in his statement: " I am an American....I belong here, in this country." His words expressed what I felt, and what I often struggled to define more precisely and convincingly. I also think of myself as an "American," but no definition of that term had ever satisfied me; they all seemed rather stereotyped. But I knew what I felt most intensely and quite consciously on October 2, 1990, my sixty-fourth birthday and the last day of the divided Germany.

I had flown to Berlin. To be present at the German reunification was to me an historical occasion, one that I had not expected to witness in my lifetime. The festivities began with a joint concert of the bands of the four occupying nations: United States, Great Britain, France, and the Soviet Union. I listened to their music in the *Lustgarten*, a tree-lined square in front of the Berlin Dom and the great museums, and also the eastern end of the famous street Unter den Linden. When the concert was over and the American band was packing up its instruments, I felt the urge to ask if someone came from Michigan, from "home."

Yes, I was moved when at midnight the unification of the East and West was announced. I wished them well—"them," not "us"—I wished them progress within a united Europe whatever the economic consequences of that may be. I look to a united Europe as the only way to quell the age-old struggle for nationalist dominance which has caused so much suffering and destruction, has eaten the fruit of so much labor, and has dragged the world twice into hell itself. Europe's peace is our peace. But my thoughts, then or on any of my other visits to Germany, were filled with a profound, yet detached, interest. It is not my passport which makes me an American. I also know where I belong: in the country called the United States of America, my home. This is what makes me an American.

How did Hank and I become integrated into American society? Danute Mostwin researched the process and concluded that youth,

help from American institutions, knowledge of English, and job satisfaction were the crucial factors. All this applied to both Hank and me.

When we came to the U.S., Hank was 16; I was 26. We both had
help from American institutions: Hank from the Polish Alliance; I as a
"young colleague," from medical organizations and individual
American physicians.

Hank soon realized the importance of speaking English and set out
to acquire it. He was fortunate to find helpful comrades in the military
service. I also had the benefit of the American military in my pursuit
of English, though less directly than Hank. I worked part of my way
through medical school in Germany as a night orderly in the American
Air Force hospital in Wiesbaden—the same hospital which many years
later would receive the hostages freed from Iran. My work there
enabled me to put my high-school English to practical use, and I
arrived in this country with enough speaking experience to get
through the round of everyday life and to interact with my patients
and colleagues. Hank's and my own early incomplete knowledge of
English had its humorous side: Because he spoke in "broken" English,
he was labeled a "damn Yankee" in a bar in Texas; on one cold and
rainy April day in New York when I tried to order a hot toddy, not
knowing if any alcoholic beverages were served in that particular
restaurant, I asked the waitress, "Have you alcoholics here?"

"Probably," she replied, "but one can't always tell."

Eventually our English became good enough: for Hank to read the
rather complex technical manuals of jet engine repair and to prepare
for his high school equivalency examination in record time; for me to
author several medical scientific papers.

Job satisfaction and economic stability came to both our lives. Early
in my professional career I was advised: "If you give good service, you
never have to worry about income." I took this advice and can now
personally attest to its validity. Hank also found challenging and secure
work. His years of military and civil service gave him financial stability
in his retirement, and he was able to use his abilities and experiences
to supplement his pension.

Personal relationships outside our respective nationalities furthered
our integration. Both Hank and I developed friendships without any

cultural or ethnic preferences, and we both married women whose families had lived in this country for generations.

Yet, our complete integration took time, and it was not until 1962, almost ten years after my arrival in this country, that I felt I "belonged."

"It did not take me that long," Hank said. "I felt that way already in the service. It was not the military ceremony and the trimmings, but there was a patriotism in me. I had sworn my oath of allegiance to this country, and when the Korean War broke out I wanted to fight the communists—any communists, even if it meant fighting Poland." Hank's words betrayed the depth of his feelings, a passion born out of the personal suffering that I had been spared.

We both now belong, and not just because our every-day language has become English or because of how and where we live. We belong through our social life and, in particular, our political philosophy. We both feel the need to be politically aware and to participate, and we both cherish our American freedom—a freedom not of license, but a freedom that permits us to follow our inclinations and pursue our interests with the least restrictions. That freedom allowed us to become who we are and made us at the same time both socially and personally responsible. If one defines happiness as the maximum realization of one's potential, then both of us have found this happiness in America.

Yet, looking back on all he and I talked about, do I fully understand what motivated Hank during his life, how he coped with his experiences? Yes, I am sure I would recognize his home, go to the swimming hole beneath the railroad bridge, and find my way to his grandmother's house in Zuratyn. I feel I have walked with him to the camp commissary and waited in line with him for his daily rations. I also know that I crawled with him on my hands and knees through the tunnels of the old fort in Isfahan. But will I ever fully *understand* how Hank felt when he saw his home for the last time? Did I truly shiver with him in the cold and share his gnawing hunger? Did I feel *his* surge of hatred when he saw the Soviet machine guns on that roof in Kustenai and thought of the death of his mother? I know of the situations and have heard his descriptions of his feelings at those times, but am I *truly* able to identify with what he said and, more important, that which remained unsaid?

Ralph Waldo Emerson once said that to imagine oneself in another person's place requires "the blending of experience with the present action of the mind." Well put, but I never had to stand in Hank's shoes, never faced Soviet soldiers with fixed bayonets ordering me: "Pack your things. You have half an hour." I never had a door slammed in my face with the words: "Your mother died this morning"—or had to hear my grandmother's description of her butchered remains. But I have listened and tried to understand. And what I have learned is this: If we desire that such horrors as befell Hank and millions like him become remote history, our empathy must motivate our thoughts and actions toward that end, must make the sanctity and inviolability of every human being a daily part of our consciousness.

Hank and I finished our talk and the day was getting on. Frost was in the forecast, and I lent Hank a hand bringing in the last of the tomatoes from his garden. He made some tea. Mary Lou had just baked a fresh batch of cookies.

Appendix

Instructions of the Soviet Deputy Commissar
for Public Security, Serov

I.-INSTRUCTIONS

*Regarding the Procedure for carrying out the Deportation of
Anti-Soviet Elements from Lithuania, Latvia and Estonia*

STRICTLY SECRET

(Translated In London from the original Russian Text)

1. GENERAL SITUATION

The deportation of anti-Soviet elements from the Baltic Republics is a task of great political importance. Its successful execution depends upon the extent to which the district operative "troikas" and operative headquarters are capable of carefully working out a plan for implementing the operations and for anticipating everything indispensable. Moreover, care must be taken that the operations are carried out without disturbance and panic, so as not to permit any demonstrations and other troubles not only on the part of those to be deported, but also on the part of a certain section of the surrounding population hostile to the Soviet administration.

Instructions as to the procedure for conducting the operations are given below. They should be adhered to, but in individual cases the collaborators engaged in carrying out the operations shall take into account the special character of the concrete conditions of such operations and, in order correctly to appraise the situation, may and must adopt other decisions directed to the same end, viz., to fulfill the task entrusted to them without noise and panic.

2. PROCEDURE OF INSTRUCTING

The instructing of operative groups by the district "troikas" [a body consisting of three members] shall be done as speedily as possible on the day before the beginning of the operations, taking into consideration the time necessary for traveling to the scene of operations.

The district "troika" shall previously prepare the necessary transport for conveyance of the operative groups in the village to the scene of operations. On the question of allocating the necessary number of motor-cars and wagons for transport, the district "troikas" shall consult the leaders of the Soviet party organized on the spot.

Premises for the issue of instructions must be carefully prepared in advance, and their capacity, exits and entrances and the possibility of intrusion by strangers must be considered.

Whilst instructions are being issued the building must be securely guarded by operative workers.

Should anybody from among those participating in the operations fail to appear for instructions, the district "troika" shall at once take steps to replace the absentee from a reserve which shall be provided in advance.

Through police officers the "troika" shall notify those assembled of the Government's decision to deport a prescribed contingent of anti-Soviet elements from the territory of the said republic or region. Moreover, they shall briefly explain what the deportees represent.

The special attention of the (local) Soviet party workers gathered for instructions shall be drawn to the fact that the deportees are enemies of the Soviet people [author's emphasis] and that, therefore, the possibility of an armed attack on the part of the deportees cannot be excluded.

3. PROCEDURE FOR ACQUISITION OF DOCUMENTS

After the general instruction of the operative groups, documents regarding the deportees should be issued to such groups. The deportees' personal files must be previously collected and distributed among the operative groups, by communes and villages, so that when they are being given out there shall be no delays.

After receipt of the personal files, the senior member of the operative group shall acquaint himself with the personal affairs of the families which he will have to deport. He shall, moreover, ascertain the composition of the family, the supply of essential forms for completion regarding the deportee, the supply of transport for conveyance of the deportee, and he shall receive exhaustive answers to questions not clear to him.

Simultaneously with the issuing of documents, the district "troika" shall explain to each senior member of the operative group where the families to be deported are situated and shall describe the route to be followed to the place of deportation. The roads to be taken by the operative personnel with the deported families to the railway station for entrainment must also be indicated. It is also essential to indicate where reserve military groups are stationed, should it become necessary to call them out during trouble of any kind.

The possession and state of arms and ammunition of the entire operative personnel shall be checked. Weapons must be in complete battle readiness and magazine loaded, but the cartridge shall not be slipped into the rifle breach. Weapons shall be used only in the last resort, when the operative group is attacked or threatened with attack or when resistance is offered.

4. PROCEDURE FOR CARRYING OUT DEPORTATIONS

If the deportation of several families is being carried out in a settled locality, one of the operative workers shall be appointed senior as regards deportation in that village, and under his direction the operative personnel shall proceed to the villages in question.

On arrival in the villages, the operative groups shall get in touch (observing the necessary secrecy) with the local authorities: the chairman, secretary or members of the village Soviets, and shall ascertain from them the exact dwelling place of the families to be deported. After this the operative groups, together with the representatives of the local authorities, who shall be appointed to make an inventory of property, shall proceed to the dwellings of the families to be deported.

Operations shall be begun at daybreak. Upon entering the home of the person to be deported, the senior member of the operative group shall assemble the entire family of the deportee into one room, taking all necessary precautionary measures against any possible trouble.

After the members of the family have been checked in conformity with the list, the location of those absent and the number of sick persons shall be ascertained, after which they shall be called upon to give up their weapons. Irrespective of whether or not any weapons are delivered, the deportee shall be personally searched and then the entire premises shall be searched in order to discover hidden weapons.

During the search of the premises one of the members of the operative group shall be appointed to keep watch over the deportees.

Should the search disclose hidden weapons in small quantities, these shall be collected by the operative groups and distributed among them. If many weapons are discovered, they shall be piled into the wagon or motor-car which has brought the operative group, after any ammunition in them has been removed. Ammunition shall be packed and loaded together with rifles.

If necessary, a convoy for transporting the weapons shall be mobilized with an adequate guard.

In the event of the discovery of weapons, counter-revolutionary pamphlets, literature, foreign currency, large quantities of valuables, etc., a brief report of search shall be drawn up on the spot, wherein the hidden weapons or counter-revolutionary literature shall be indicated. If there is any armed resistance, the question of the necessity of arresting the parties showing such armed resistance and of sending them to the district branch of the People's Commissariat of Public Security shall be decided by the district "troikas."

A report shall be drawn up regarding those deportees in hiding or sick ones, and this report shall be signed by the representative of the Soviet party organization. After completion of the search the deportees shall be notified that by a Government decision they will be deported to other regions of the Union. The deportees shall be permitted to take with them household necessities not exceeding 100 kilograms in weight:

1. Suit.
2. Shoes.
3. Underwear.
4. Bedding.
5. Dishes.
6. Glassware.
7. Kitchen utensils.
8. Food—an estimated month's supply.
9. Money in their possession.
10. Trunk or box in which to pack articles.
    It is not recommended that large articles be taken.

If the contingent is deported from rural districts, they shall be allowed to take with them small agricultural stocks—axes, saws and other articles, which shall be tied together and packed separately from the other articles, so that when boarding the deportation train they may be loaded into special goods wagons.

In order not to mix them with articles belonging to others, the Christian name, patronymic and surname of the deportee and name of the village shall be written on the packed property.

When loading these articles into the carts, measures shall be taken so that the deportee cannot make use of them for purposes of resistance while the column is moving along the highway.

Simultaneously with the task of loading by the operative groups, the representatives of the Soviet party organizations present at the time shall prepare an inventory of the property and of the manner of its protection in conformity with the instructions received by them.

If the deportee possesses his own means of transport, his property shall be loaded into the vehicle and together with his family shall be sent to the designated place of entrainment.

If the deportees are without any means of transport, carts shall be mobilized in the village by the local authorities, as instructed by the senior member of the operative group.

All persons entering the home of the deportee during the execution of the operations or found there at the moment of these operations must be detained until the conclusion of the operations, and their relationship to the deportee shall be ascertained. This is done in order to disclose persons hiding from the police, gendarmes and other persons.

After verification of the identity of the detained persons and establishment of the fact that they are persons in whom the contingent is not interested, they shall be liberated.

If the inhabitants of the village begin to gather around the deportee's home while operations are in progress, they shall be called upon to disperse to their own homes, and crowds shall not be permitted to form.

If the deportee refuses to open the door of his home, notwithstanding that he is aware that the members of the People's Commissariat of Public Security have arrived, the door must be broken down. In individual cases neighboring operative groups carrying out operations in that locality shall be called upon to help.

The delivery of the deportees from the village to the meeting place at the railway station must be effected during daylight; care, moreover, should be taken that the assembling of every family shall not last more than two hours. In all cases throughout the operations firm and decisive action shall be taken, without the slightest excitement, noise and panic.

It is categorically forbidden to take any articles away from the deportees except weapons, counter-revolutionary literature and foreign currency, as also to make use of the food of the deportees.

All participants in the operations must be warned that they will be held legally accountable for attempts to appropriate individual articles belonging to the deportees.

5. PROCEDURE FOR SEPARATION OF DEPORTEE'S FAMILY FROM HEAD OF THE FAMILY

In view of the fact that a large number of deportees must be arrested and distributed in special camps and that their families must proceed to special settlements in distant regions, it is essential that the operation of removal of both the members of the deportee's family and its head should be carried out simultaneously, without notifying them of the separation confronting them. After the domiciliary search has been carried out and the appropriate identification documents have been drawn up in the deportee's home, the operative worker shall complete the documents for the head of the family and deposit them in the latter's personal file, but the documents drawn up for members of his family shall be deposited in the personal file of the deportee's family.

The convoy of the entire family to the station shall, however, be effected in one vehicle and only at the station of departure shall the head of the family be placed separately from his family in a car specially intended for heads of families.

During the assembling (of the family) in the home of the deportee the head of the family shall be warned that personal male effects must be packed in a separate suitcase, as a sanitary inspection of the deported men will be made separately from the women and children. At the stations of entrainment heads of families subject to arrest shall be loaded into cars specially allotted for them, which shall be indicated by operative workers appointed for that purpose.

6. PROCEDURE FOR CONVOYING THE DEPORTEES

The assistants conveying the column of deportees in horse-carts are strictly forbidden to sit in the said carts. The assistants must follow alongside and behind the column of deportees. The senior assistant of the convoy shall from time to time go the rounds of the entire column to check the correctness of movement.

When the column of deportees is passing through inhabited places or when encountering passersby, the convoy must be controlled with particular care; those in charge must see that no attempts are made to escape, and no conversation of any kind shall be permitted between the deportees and passersby.

7. PROCEDURE FOR ENTRAINMENT

At each point of entrainment a member of the operative "troika" and a person specially appointed for that purpose shall be responsible for entrainment.

On the day of entrainment the chief of the entrainment point, together with the chief of the deportation train and of the conveying military forces of the People's Commissariat of Internal Affairs, shall examine the railway cars provided in order to see that they are supplied with everything necessary, and the chief of the entrainment point shall agree with the chief of the deportation train on the procedure to be observed by the latter in accepting delivery of the deportees.

Red Army men of the conveying forces of the People's Commissariat of Internal Affairs shall surround the entrainment station.

The senior member of the operative group shall deliver to the chief of the deportation train one copy of the nominal roll of the deportees in each railway-car. The chief of the deportation train shall, in conformity with this list, call out the name of each deportee, shall carefully check every name and assign the deportee's place in the railway-car.

The deportees' effects shall be loaded into the car, together with the deportees, with the exception of the small agricultural inventory, which shall be loaded in a separate car.

The deportees shall be loaded into railway-cars by families; it is not permitted to break up a family (with the exception of heads of families subject to arrest). An estimate of twenty-five persons to a car should be observed.

After the railway-car has been filled with the necessary number of families, it shall be locked.

After the people have been taken over and placed in the deportation train, the chief of the train shall bear responsibility for all persons handed over to him and for their delivery to their destination.

After handing over the deportees the senior member of the operative group shall draw up a report on the operation carried out by him and shall address it to the chief of the district operative "troika." The report shall briefly indicate the name of the deportee, whether any weapons and counter-revolutionary literature have been discovered, and also how the operation was carried out. After having placed the deportees on the deportation train and having submitted reports of the results of the operations thus discharged, the members of the operative group shall be considered free and shall act in accordance with the instructions of the chief of the district branch of the People's Commissariat of Public Security.

DEPUTY PEOPLE'S COMMISSAR OF PUBLIC SECURITY OF THE USSR

Commissar of Public Security of the Third Rank.

(Signed) SEROV.

Original Reference:

US Congress. House. Report of the Select Committee to Investigate Communist Aggression and the Forced Incorporation of the Baltic States into the USSR. Third Interim Report, pp. 464-68. Washington: G.P.O., 1954. (original, US House of Representatives, files of Baltic Committee, Exhibit 16-H of 12.X.53.)

Note: The procedure of the deportations from Poland followed essentially the same rules. How they were applied in individual cases depended on the personal attitudes of the members of the troika; in instances liberally, particularly if the people to be deported had the presence of mind to dispense vodka, in other instances extremely harshly and without any regard for the conditions of their victims.

Sources and Suggested Readings

The books by Jerzy Gorski (1989), Esther Hautzig (1968), Apolonja Kojder (1995), John Kramek (1990), Zdzislawa Kawecka (1989), Eugene Lachocki (1996), Anita Paschwa-Kozicka (1996), Barbara Porajska (1988), Stella H. Synowiec-Tobis (1998), and Eugenia Wasilewska (1970) are first-person biographies of Polish youths (ten to sixteen years of age) deported by the Soviets together with their families under the same administrative procedure as Hank because of their alleged anti-Soviet attitudes.

Rachel Rachlin and Israel Rachlin (1982) refer to a Jewish family from Lithuania, not to Poles, but otherwise document the same experience.

B. Plezere-Eglite (1996) covers the same subject matter, "administrative deportation," as the above mentioned books, but of a Latvian—not a Polish—child, though of comparable age to Hank. Its particular value lies in the drawings by a ten-year-old child depicting the various steps of the deportation process.

Yehuda Nir's (1989) story of a Jewish boy in German-occupied Poland as a first-person biography is related to *Exiled to Siberia* because of the comparable age and similar personal attitudes of its protagonist.

None of the books referred to above discuss the underlying social, political and historical events and relationships of that time comprehensively. Several books are exceptions to the foregoing: Anna and Norbert Kant (1991) were deported as adults and describe their experiences as trustees for the Polish government in the Soviet Union and their life there after the revocation of the "amnesty." Andrzej and

Karolina Jus (1991) were a professional Polish-Jewish couple who describe their life in Poland during the war, first under the Soviets, then under the Germans, and eventually in postwar communist Poland. Jan S. Kowal (1992) was in high school when he was deported. He writes about his life in a city (Tarnopol) in prewar Poland, comments on the Polish class system, and gives examples of discrimination against Ukrainians. *Vengeance of the Swallows* by Tadeusz Piotrowski (1995) combines a first-person biography with the related political and historical circumstances, but the author and his family were deported to Germany, not the Soviet Union. His *Poland's Holocaust* (1998) contains a chapter on the Soviet terror in Eastern Poland as well as a chapter on the Nazi terror, but the remaining chapters deal with collaboration. His most recent work, *Genocide and Rescue in Wolyn* (2000), deals only with Polish-Ukrainian relations under the German occupation.

The Dark Side of the Moon is unique both in its content and time of publication (1946). Begun in 1943, its author, Zoe Zajdlerowa, had access to the official records of the Polish government-in-exile. She, however, wished to remain anonymous, perhaps out of a need to protect relatives in communist Poland. With a comment by Helena Sikorska, widow of General Wladyslaw Sikorski, and a preface by T. S. Eliot, the book covers the essentials of the history of Polish-Soviet relations until shortly after the end of the Second World War, including the formation and installation of the communist Lublin Government. It also depicts in moving language the trials faced by those Poles imprisoned, those condemned to a camp in the Gulag, as well as those simply deported. The political currents underlying the Soviet actions toward Poland as well as the formation of the Polish army under General Anders and of the Polish-Soviet Berling Army are also described. The book thereby gives a comprehensive overview of the fate of Poland from 1939 to 1945.

Books and articles written by Irena Beaupres-Stankiewicz et. al. (1989), Robert Conquest (1960), Jan T. Gross (1988), Peter Irons (1973), Richard Lukas (1982 and 1986), Robert Kesting (1991), Witold Majewski (1943), Rachel Toor (1981), Zbigniew Siemaszko (1991), Keith Sword (several 1994), and Elzbieta Wrobel and Janusz

Wrobel (1992) are primarily historical texts with brief narrative summaries of individual experiences as illustrative examples.

Irena Grudzinska-Gross and Jan T. Gross (1981) devote their book to the fate of Polish children during the deportation by the Soviets. They present 120 narratives without going into their individual pre-deportation childhood or their post-deportation experiences. Their main emphasis is on the children's deportation and survival until their liberation through the "amnesty." These short narratives were selected from among the thousands deposited in the Hoover archives.

Richard Lukas (1989) discusses Polish-Jewish relations in German-occupied Poland editing over 50 personal accounts. Some of these contain only brief comments on the Soviet deportations. His 1994 work deals with the fate of Polish and Jewish children under the German occupation.

Eileen Egan (1995) as well as Lucjan Krolikowski (1983) focus mainly on the post-deportation experiences of Polish orphans. They include illustrative narratives and psychological observations.

The book *The Rape of Poland* by Stanislaw Mikolajczyk (1948), the successor to General Sikorski, is a first-person narrative with extensive reflections on the history of the time. It is primarily concerned with the attempts to establish a democratic government in Poland after the conclusion of the war.

Joseph Czapski (1951) reports on the historical background of the Polish army in the Soviet Union in 1941–42 and on his experiences, especially his unsuccessful efforts to locate over 15,000 missing Polish officers, later found murdered by the Soviets.

Books more marginally related to the subject include those referring to: Polish customs and Polish-Americans (Sula Benet, 1951; Toby Knobel Fluek, 1990; H. C. Lopata, 1975; Rachel Toor, 1981); humanitarian and spiritual considerations (W. H. Auden, 1945; Dietrich Bonhoeffer, 1953); the general psychology of children (Bert Beverly, 1941; Robert Coles, 1964 and 1986); and refugee children (Fredrick L. Ahear, Jr. et al. 1991). The psychology of children in war is addressed by Anna Freud and Dorothy Burlingham (1943) and in more detail by Dorothy Macardle (1951). Kiryl Sosnowski (1983) addresses in particular the fate of children in Poland under Nazi occupation, but also makes extensive references to children of other ethnic groups, including German children growing up under the Nazi regime. Kati David (1989) narrates experiences of children from various countries, including Poland, during the Second World War. Factors influencing the integration of Polish immigrants are addressed by Danuta Mostwin (1971).

The writings by Gordon A. Craig (1955), Dinesh D'Sonza (1995), Leo Deutsch (1905), Abel Herzberg (1950, 1976), George Mosse (1964), Aleksandr Solzhenitsyn (1973), and Elie Wiesel (1988) contribute to the understanding of racism, the Soviet and Nazi relationships to each other, and to Tsarist and German imperial policies as well as the backgrounds and manifestations of both Nazism and Stalinism. In *Prince Roman* (1911) Joseph Conrad returns to the history of his native country and of his family.

Books:

Ahearn, Fredrick L., Jr., and Jean L. Athey, eds. 1991. *Refugee Children; Theory, Research, and Services.* Baltimore: Johns Hopkins University Press.

Anonymous. [Zoe Zajdlerowa] 1946. Preface by T. S. Eliot. *The Dark Side of the Moon.* New York: Charles Scribner's Sons. Originally published in London in 1946.

Auden, W. H. 1945. Commentary in *The Collected Poetry of W. H Auden.* New York: Random House.*

Beaupre-Stankiewicz, Irena, Danuta Waszczuk-Kamieniecka, and Jadwiga Lewicka-Howells, eds. 3d ed. 1989. *Isfahan: City of Polish Children.* Hove, Sussex UK: Association of Former Pupils of Polish Schools, Isfahan and Lebanon.

Benet, Sula. 1951. *Song, Dance, and Customs of Peasant Poland.* London, U.K.: Dennis Dobson Ltd.

Beverly, Bert I. 1941. *In Defense of Children.* New York: The John Day Co.

Bonhoeffer, Dietrich. 1953. *Letters and Papers from Prison.* London, Glasgow: Collins Clear-Type Press.

Coles, Robert. 1964. *Children of Crisis.* Vol.1 and 2. 1967. Boston: Little, Brown & Co.

_____.1986. *The Moral Life of Children.* Boston: Houghton Mifflin.

Conrad, Joseph. 1911. *Prince Roman* in *The Portable Conrad.* 1975. New York: The Viking Press.

Conquest, Robert. 1960. *The Soviet Deportation of Nationalities.* New York: St.Martin's Press.

Craig, Gordon A. 1955. *The Politics of the Prussian Army, 1640-1945.* New York: Oxford University Press.

Czapski, Joseph. Translated from the French by Gerard Hopkins. 1951. *The Inhuman Land.* London, U.K.: Chatto & Windus.

David, Kati. 1989. *A Child's War: World War II through the Eyes of Children.* New York: Four Walls Eight Windows.

Deutsch, Leo. 1905. *Sixteen Years in Siberia.* London, U.K.: John Murray.

D'Sonza, Dinesh. 1995. *The End of Racism: Principles for a Multiracial Society.* New York: The Free Press.*

Egan, Eileen. 1995. *For Whom There is No Room.* New York: Paulist Press.*

Freud, Anna, and Dorothy T. Burlingham. 1943. *War and Children.* New York: Medical War Books.

Fluek, Toby Knobel. 1990. *Memories of My Life in a Polish Village, 1930-1949.* New York: Alfred A. Knopf.

Gorski, Jerzy W. 1989. *Głodne stepy* [Hungry Steppes]. London, U.K.: Polish Cultural Foundation Ltd.

Gross, Jan T. 1988. *Revolution from Abroad: The Soviet Conquest of Poland's Western Ukraine and Western Belorussia.* Princeton: Princeton University Press.*

Grudzinska-Gross, Irena, and Jan Tomasz Gross, eds. 1981. *War through Children's Eyes: The Soviet Occupation of Poland and the Deportations, 1939-41.* Stanford, CA: Hoover Institution Press. *

Hautzig, Esther. 1968. *The Endless Steppe: A Girl in Exile.* New York: Thomas Y. Crowell Co.

Jus, Andrzej and Karolina. 1991. *Our Journey in the Valley of Tears.* Toronto: University of Toronto Press.

Kant, Anna, and Norbert Kant. 1991. *Extermination: Killing Poles in Stalin's Empire*. London, U.K.: Unicorn Publ.

Kawecka, Zdzislawa Krystina. 1989, 2d. ed. *Journey Without a Ticket: To England through Siberia*. Nottingham, U.K.: Z. K. Kawecka.

Kojder, Apolonja Maria, and Barbara Glogowska. 1995. *Marynia, Don't Cry: Memoir of Two Polish-Canadian Families*. Toronto: Multicultural History Society of Ontario.

Kowal, Jan S. 1992. *My First Survival or My Life in Poland and in the USSR*. Ann Arbor, MI: n.p.

Kramek, John S. 1990. *Refugee's Trails*. St. Clair Shores, MI: Refugee's Trails Fund, Inc.

Krolikowski, Lucjan. 1983. *Stolen Childhood: A Saga of Polish War Children*. Buffalo, NY: Franciscan Fathers Minor Conventuals, St. Anthony of Padua, Province USA. Printed John Deyell Co., Canada.*

Lachocki, Eugene. 1996. *No Return*. New Smyrna Beach, FL: Luthers.

Lukas, Richard C. 1982. *Bitter Legacy: Polish-American Relations in the Wake of World War II*. Lexington, KY: University Press of Kentucky.

___.1994. *Did the Children Cry? Hitler's War Against the Jewish and Polish Children, 1939-1945*. New York: Hippocrene Books.

___.1986. *The Forgotten Holocaust: The Poles under German Occupation, 1939-1945*. Lexington, KY: University Press of Kentucky.

___.1989. *Out of the Inferno: Poles Remember the Holocaust*. Lexington, KY: University Press of Kentucky.

Macardle, Dorothy. 1951. *Children of Europe-A Study of the Children of Liberated Countries: Their Wartime Experiences, Their Reactions and Their Needs, with a Note on Germany*. London, U.K.: Victor Gollancz LTD

Majewski, Witold. 1943. *Polish Children Suffer*. Foreword by Helena Sikorska. Canfield Gardens, U.K.: F. P. Agency Ltd.

Mikolajczyk, Stanislaw. 1948. *The Rape of Poland: Pattern of Soviet Aggression*. New York: McGraw-Hill Book Co. Inc.

Mosse, George L. 1964. *The Crisis of German Ideology: Intellectual Origins of the Third Reich*. New York: Grosset & Dunlap.

Mostwin, Danuta. 1971. *The Transplanted Family: A Study of Social Adjustment of the Polish Immigrant Family to the United States After the Second World War*. New York: Arno Press Inc.

Nir, Yehuda. 1989. *The Lost Childhood: A Memoir*. New York: Harcourt Brace Jovanovich Publishers.

Paschwa-Kozicka, Anita. 1996. *My Flight to Freedom: An Autobiography*. Chicago: Panorama Publishing Co.*

Piotrowski, Tadeusz. 2000. *Genocide and Rescue in Wolyn: Recollections of the Ukrainian Nationalist Ethnic Cleansing Campaign Against the Poles During World War II*. Jefferson, NC: McFarland.

___.1998. *Poland's Holocaust: Ethnic Strife, Collaboration with Occupying Forces and Genocide in the Second Republic, 1918-1947*. Jefferson, NC: McFarland.*

___.1995. *Vengeance of the Swallows: Memoir of a Polish Family's Ordeal under Soviet Aggression, Ukrainian Ethnic Cleansing and Nazi Enslavement, and Their Emigration to America*. Jefferson, NC: McFarland.*

Plezere-Eglite, B. 1996. *Through the Eyes of a Child: Drawings of Eleven-Year Old Nita Mailed from Siberian Exile to Latvia, 25.03.1949-56*. Riga, Latvia: "Latvia During 50 Years of Occupation" Museum Foundation, in Cooperation with the National Oral History Project, Institute of Philosophy and Sociology, Latvian Academy of Sciences.

Porajska, Barbara. 1988. *From the Steppes to the Savannah*. Port Erin, Isle of Man, U.K.: Ham Publ. Co. Ltd.

Rachlin, Rachel, and Israel Rachlin. 1982. *Sixteen Years in Siberia: Memoirs of Rachel and Israel Rachlin*. Translated from Danish by Brigitte M. de Weille. Tuscaloosa: University Alabama Press.

Solzhenitsyn, Aleksandr I. 1973. *The Gulag Archipelago*. New York: Harper & Roe.

Sosnowski, Kiryl. 1983. *The Tragedy of Children under Nazi Rule*. New York: Howart Fertig. Originally published in Polish in Poznan, 1962.

Sword, Keith. 1994. *Deportation and Exile: Poles in the Soviet Union, 1939-48*. New York: St. Martin's Press. *

___,ed. 1994. *The Soviet Takeover of the Polish Eastern Provinces, 1939-41*. New York: St.Martin's Press.

Synowiec-Tobis, Stella H. 1998. *The Fulfillment of Visionary Return*. Northbrook, IL: Artpol Printing.

Toor, Rachel. 1981. *The Polish Americans*. New York: Chelsea House Publishers.

Wasilewska, Eugenia. 1970. *The Silver Madonna*. New York: The John Day Co.

Wiesel, Elie. 1988. *Night Trilogy: The Accident*. New York: The Noonday Press. Edition du Seuil, 1961.*

Wrobel, Elzbieta, and Janusz Wrobel. 1992. *Rozproszeni Po Swiecie*. [Scattered Throughout the World]. Chicago, IL: Panorama.

Articles:

Herzberg, Abel. "The Not-Persecuted." *Jewish Frontier*. 17 (1950): 33-35. ___.1976. "Schurkenrol in Tragedie niet voor Leiders Joodse Raad." *Nieuw Israelitisch Weekblad*. "Dec.17, 1976."

Irons, Peter H. "The Test is Poland: Polish Americans and the Origins of the Cold War." *Polish American Studies* 30 (1973): 51-59.

Kesting, Robert W. "American Support of Polish Refugees and their Santa Rosa Camp." *Polish American Studies* 48 (1991): 79-86.

Lopata, H.C. "A Life Record of an Immigrant." *Society* 13 (1975): 64-74.

*The author's/publisher's permission to use the quoted material is hereby gratefully acknowledged.

Index

SAN 253-2042

CRESCENT LAKE PUBLISHING
404 N. Ball Street
Cheboygan, MI 49721
Tel. & Fax: 231-627-9748   E-mail: creslkpub@straitsarea.com

ORDER FORM

Please send me _____ copies of *Exiled to Siberia*
$27.95 (U.S.) or $41.00 (CAN)
Michigan residents add $1.68 per book (6% Michigan sales tax) plus shipping
(see below).

Ship to different address

Name _____   Name _____

Street _____   Street _____

City_____   City_____

State/Zip_____   State/Zip _____

Telephone_____

Payment:

❑ Check or money order payable to Crescent Lake Publishing enclosed

❑ VISA*   ❑ MasterCard*

Card Number:_____/_____/_____/_____

Name on card: _____Exp. Date:_____/____

*Will be billed through "DH Design" Indian River, MI at time of delivery.

Shipping (4th-class book rate) per address in U.S.: $3.50

Multiple order discount, priority, and international mail
available. Please inquire.

Fr
Colon

Hank

U.S.S.R.

Tobolsk

Krasnovodsk

Kustenai

Pahlevi

Samarkand

Teheran

Guzar

IRAN

CHINA

Karachi

INDIA

Isfahan

Indian
Ocean

AUS

Bombay

Melbour